The Religious Factor in
the 1960 Presidential Election

ALSO BY ALBERT J. MENENDEZ

The Geography of Presidential Elections in the United States, 1868–2004 (McFarland, 2005; paperback 2009)

The Religious Factor in the 1960 Presidential Election

*An Analysis of the Kennedy Victory
Over Anti-Catholic Prejudice*

ALBERT J. MENENDEZ

McFarland & Company, Inc., Publishers
Jefferson, North Carolina, and London

LIBRARY OF CONGRESS CATALOGUING-IN-PUBLICATION DATA

Menendez, Albert J.
 The religious factor in the 1960 Presidential election : an analysis of the Kennedy victory over anti–Catholic prejudice / Albert J. Menendez.
   p.   cm.
 Includes bibliographical references and index.

 ISBN 978-0-7864-6037-3
 softcover : 50# alkaline paper ∞

 1. Presidents — United States — Election —1960. 2. Kennedy, John F. (John Fitzgerald), 1917–1963. 3. United States — Politics and government —1961–1963. 4. Religion and politics — United States — History — 20th century. 5. Anti-Catholicism — United States — History — 20th century. 6. Kennedy, John F. (John Fitzgerald), 1917–1963 — Religion. I. Title.
 E837.7.M46 2011
 973.922092 — dc22   2011006120

BRITISH LIBRARY CATALOGUING DATA ARE AVAILABLE

© 2011 Albert J. Menendez. All rights reserved

No part of this book may be reproduced or transmitted in any form or by any means, electronic or mechanical, including photocopying or recording, or by any information storage and retrieval system, without permission in writing from the publisher.

Front cover: *insets* John F. Kennedy (Associated Press), Richard M. Nixon (National Archives); background © 2011 Shutterstock

Manufactured in the United States of America

McFarland & Company, Inc., Publishers
 Box 611, Jefferson, North Carolina 28640
 www.mcfarlandpub.com

For Shirley

Table of Contents

Acknowledgments ix
Preface 1

1. Before Kennedy 5
2. The Kennedy Campaign and the Issue of Religion 21
3. The Propaganda War: An Analysis 44
4. The National Vote 82
5. The Election by Region 97
6. Pennsylvania and Wisconsin Case Studies 187
7. Epilogue and Summing Up 211

Appendix: Two Kennedy Campaign Addresses on the Issue of Religion 227
Chapter Notes 239
Bibliography 247
Index 255

Acknowledgments

I am grateful for the valuable assistance provided by Maryrose Grossman, Audiovisual Archives, John Fitzgerald Kennedy Library, Columbia Point, Boston, Massachusetts.

I also appreciate the assistance provided by the following individuals: Bill Sumners, director of the Southern Baptist Historical Library and Archives; Scott S. Taylor, manuscripts processor, Lauinger Library at Georgetown University; David Hagen, Georgetown University Library photographer; and Jeff Bridgers, Prints and Photographs Division, Library of Congress.

Preface

Numerous political books and memoirs in recent years have promoted the idea that John F. Kennedy used his religion shamelessly to win votes in 1960 or that religious opposition to his election was not as bad as previously reported. A recent example of this type of defamation is by Professor Gastón Espinosa, who wrote as follows:

> [Kennedy] deftly used Richard Nixon's widespread mainline and Evangelical Protestant support against him by raising the shrill banner of religious intolerance to silence Nixon and stop his advisers from bringing religion into the campaign. Kennedy won the election by a razor thin margin, some say only because Nixon made the mistake of conceding the election too quickly to spare the nation the indignity of a contested presidential race. Regardless, Kennedy used Protestantism in a backhanded way not only to silence Nixon but also to push for the separation of church and state to prove his commitment to the secular Constitution rather than Rome or the papacy — a perennial Protestant fear.[1]

Julie Nixon Eisenhower's biography of her mother promoted this line. Several Catholic Republicans have concurred. Others, like evangelical guru Charles Colson of Watergate fame, continued to charge, as he did during Nixon's 1994 funeral, that Kennedy stole the election and that Colson's hero Nixon really won. A number of propagandists parrot this line, though they can't decide whether JFK stole the election in Chicago, Texas (thanks to LBJ) or, as Colson charged, in Essex County, New Jersey. Scholars, historians, newspaper columnists, and others have searched for evidence of this alleged fraud but have found the charges to be baseless.

Even during the 1960 campaign, two-time losing Republican presidential candidate Thomas E. Dewey "accused Robert Kennedy of injecting religion as a campaign issue."[2] James Michener answered Dewey and other Republican critics: "It was intellectual effrontery of the worst sort to suggest

1

that a man who stood to lose the Presidency of the United States because of his religion had somehow introduced the religious issue."[3]

The Religious Factor in the 1960 Presidential Election looks carefully at the vote and the campaign of 1960. Before the colors fade and the historical record is lost forever, I discuss both in this presentation, an accurate one based on available evidence from all 3,000 U.S. counties and from precincts wherever available, especially in Pennsylvania, Wisconsin, Iowa, Minnesota, New Jersey, and the six New England states.

Kennedy's narrow victory did not come primarily from greatly increased Protestant tolerance. He received about the same overall Protestant vote as Adlai Stevenson had four years before and a lower white Protestant vote. He won because of strong Catholic support (and because Catholics were a larger share of the electorate than in 1928 when Al Smith was crushed) and because of Jewish and African American support. I agree with historian Allan J. Lichtman, who wrote: "Kennedy did not win because Protestants became reconciled to a Catholic president. He won because blacks had become Democrats since 1928 and white Protestants were a smaller share of the electorate."[4] There were no exit polls in 1960, so we must rely on a wide array of hard-to-find, actual data from the vote, as well as two reliable postelection polls conducted by the Gallup organization and the University of Michigan to explore the voting patterns.

The first chapter briefly surveys the history of religious influences on presidential elections from 1800 to 1960. Since Catholicism was a recurrent issue, most attention is devoted to the "Catholic issue" in presidential politics. A section on the Al Smith campaign of 1928 concludes that religion was the overriding factor in his defeat.

Chapter 2 retells the dramatic events of Senator Kennedy's campaign, concentrating on how he handled the religious issue and attempted to defuse it. Considerable attention is given to the last-ditch smear campaign from religious extremists who nearly succeeded in defeating a well-qualified candidate because of his religious affiliation. Contemporary newspaper and magazine accounts are buttressed by retrospective historical analyses.

The third chapter reveals the intensity of the propaganda war relating to Kennedy's religious affiliation and questions whether it alone should have disqualified him from the presidency. Much of this analysis came from a detailed examination of the widespread anti–Catholic material emanating from numerous venues that saturated the nation and reached countless millions of voters. The print materials originated in 32 states and reached all 50. They came in a variety of formats — pamphlets, leaflets, brochures, mimeographed and crudely produced broadsides, and booklets. They came from individual churches and sermons, reprints of radio addresses, official organizational and ecclesiastical statements and reprints of articles in denominational journals. To counter this campaign of disinformation and defamation, the Kennedy campaign staff mounted a campaign aimed at religious moderates and liberals within the Protestant community as well as members of minority faiths who were acutely aware of the implications of a concerted campaign to restrict the presidency to Protestants.

Chapter 4 looks in detail at the overall results of the election, the excitement of Election Day and the vote count that dragged on until the next day. The geography of the vote reveals why this was the closest popular vote election in modern history. Looking beneath the scenes reveals an anti–Kennedy backlash that cost him numerous states, over a hundred counties that had supported the previous Democratic candidate, and a reduction in his vote share in 1,000 of the nation's 3,000 counties.

This is followed in chapter 5 by a lengthy review of election data region by region and state by state, exploring how the religious issue played out and how the vote for and against Kennedy was influenced and even determined by religion. This chapter uncovers new material that has been ignored or forgotten for five decades.

The sixth chapter is a case study of Pennsylvania and Wisconsin. It provides a bird's-eye view of how religious values shaped the vote in every precinct in these two large, important and historic states. Kennedy failed to carry 150 towns that had gone for Stevenson in 1956, revealing a shocking religious backlash that was ignored or missed by commentators a half century ago. Though most anti–Catholic bias was centered in the South or states bordering the South, there was a considerable residue in the rural North. Pennsylvania and Wisconsin were selected because of all the states they have the best history back to the Civil War era, of reporting detailed election data. They have the most diverse ethnic and religious mosaic and their vote in 1960 was close to the national one: Pennsylvania for Kennedy by two percentage points, and Wisconsin for Nixon by four percentage points.

The final chapter places the 1960 election in historical perspective and emphasizes Kennedy's role in reducing religious tensions in U.S. politics, not only through his campaign but also through the policies adopted during his all-too-brief presidency. Kennedy's "civil religion" and his role as an exemplar of a particular style and policymaker in church-state relations is considered, as is Kennedy's role in assuring Catholics that they are first-class citizens. His election is also seen as a catalyst in unleashing Catholic energy and creativity in the political realm and in supporting religious pluralism and ecumenism. A few "closing thoughts" are devoted to the present status of religion in politics a half century after the election of America's only Catholic president.

I am emboldened in this project by an observation from James Michener, who, after observing the religious issue up close when he campaigned for JFK, wrote, "If, thirty years from now, all of this can be explained away in clever articles which prove that religion played no significant role in the 1960 election, it seems to me that the writers of that age will have to blind themselves to what actually happened."[5]

CHAPTER 1

Before Kennedy

The campaign and election of John F. Kennedy in 1960 may have been the most dramatic and consequential involving religious issues, but it was not the first. Religion has played a role in several previous campaigns, going back as far as 1800 when New England clergy warned about the dangers to the Republic if the notorious infidel (in their view) Thomas Jefferson were elected president.

Religious issues influenced other campaigns and were primarily related to the nation's growing Roman Catholic community. Even though America's tiny colonial Catholic minority, residing primarily in Maryland and Pennsylvania, gave strong support to the Revolution, and individual Catholics (Charles Carroll of Maryland and Daniel Fitzsimmons of Pennsylvania) signed the Declaration of Independence and the Constitution, opposition to Catholic influences grew rapidly after the 1830s.

Organized anti–Catholicism erupted in the 1830s and 1840s, stimulated by the influx of Irish Catholics and the fear of popish invasion by militant Protestants. Journalist Samuel F.B. Morse, in a series of pseudonymous newspaper articles and a book, *A Foreign Conspiracy Against the Liberties of the United States*, promoted the view that the Catholic countries of the Holy Alliance and the papacy were conspiring to subvert Protestant America. Religious extremism characterized this period, culminating in the burning of a Charlestown, Massachusetts, convent by a Protestant mob and church burnings in Philadelphia in 1844. A flood of anti–Catholic literature and organizations is vividly described by historian Ray Allen Billington in his excellent book, *The Protestant Crusade, 1800–1860*. Bills were introduced in several state legislatures to restrict voting rights to native-born Protestants.

The 1844 election was extremely close, with Democrat James K. Polk handing Whig Henry Clay his third presidential defeat. Though no sophisticated election analysis was possible, Whigs, including future President Millard Fillmore, blamed "foreign Catholics" for their defeat, a refrain that would be heard again and again for the next century and more by the enemies of the Democratic Party.

In the 1850s a group of extremists constituted themselves as the "Know-Nothing" or Native American Party. They loathed Roman Catholics and foreigners and were convinced that American institutions were Protestant to the core and would be jeopardized if Catholics were to hold public office.

In the 1852 campaign Democrat Franklin Pierce of New Hampshire was criticized by many Catholics because his state still maintained a test act against Catholic officeholders. The voters of the strongly anti–Catholic state had declined to remove the requirement. The Whig candidate, General Winfield Scott, was accused of having hanged Irish Catholic deserters during the Mexican War. Both candidates were accused of having daughters who became nuns. Pierce won by a landslide and promptly appointed a Catholic, James Campbell of Pennsylvania, as postmaster general.

The Know-Nothings (Nativists) gained strength and were responsible for the mobbing of papal emissary Gaetano Bedini when he toured the United States in 1853. In 1854, amid rioting in Louisville and elsewhere, the Know-Nothings won eight senators out of sixty-two and 124 Congressmen out of 234, and swept local offices in Massachusetts, Delaware, Pennsylvania, Maryland, and Kentucky. Revision of immigration laws was a primary legislative goal.

In 1856 the Nativists ran former President Millard Fillmore, a Unitarian, for president. The newly formed Republican Party nominated the popular soldier-explorer John C. Frémont, who soon became the object of an absurd whispering campaign that he was a Catholic and that his daughter was educated in a convent. (He was an Episcopalian.) The Democrats nominated James Buchanan, of Pennsylvania, and adopted a platform blasting religious prejudice. Buchanan won easily, Frémont did respectably well, sweeping much of the North, and Fillmore carried only Maryland. Division among the Nativists over slavery overshadowed the religious issue. The movement vanished, only to reappear under new names and leaders in the 1890s.

The first successful Republican candidate, Abraham Lincoln,

denounced the Know-Nothings openly and wanted nothing to do with religious prejudice. However, some Republican campaigners in the North urged Protestants to vote for Lincoln because his Democratic opponent, Stephen Douglas, was married to a Catholic. Writes Richard Carwardine: "Lincoln himself never sought openly or directly to exploit religious sectarianism for electoral gain, but these scruples did not afflict Republican campaigners, who readily played on popular anti–Catholicism and branded Stephen Douglas, married to a Catholic wife, with the mark of the Beast."[1]

President Ulysses S. Grant avoided most religious issues, as he avoided religion in general, except for a ringing denunciation of attempts to gain public support for church-related schools. "Keep church and state forever separate," he told Union Army veterans meeting in Des Moines, Iowa, on September 25, 1875. Republican platforms denounced aid to parochial schools from 1876–1892.

Republican newspapers pointed out the alleged connections between Catholics and the Democratic Party throughout the late 19th century. In its July 29, 1876, issue *Harper's Weekly* charged that "the Vatican directs the policy of the ruling section of the Democratic Party." In 1880 some Republicans warned that Democratic nominee Winfield Hancock, a Baptist, was married to a Catholic.

Religion came to the fore in the 1884 election. Republican nominee James G. Blaine had proposed a federal constitutional amendment years before that would have barred aid to parochial schools and would have limited Bible reading and prayer in public schools. It was narrowly defeated, and Blaine was criticized in some circles as being anti–Catholic. Other critics warned that his mother and many family members were Catholics. Religious gossip was rampant.

An incident late in the campaign may have decided the election. In late October a weary Blaine attended a fund-raising dinner in New York City. On the morning of October 29, at the Park Avenue Hotel, several hundred Protestant clergymen gathered to hear the candidate. They selected the Rev. Samuel D. Burchard, a Presbyterian, as chairman and asked him to make a short welcoming statement. In it he said, "We expect to vote for you next Tuesday. We are Republicans and don't propose to leave our party and identify ourselves with the party whose antecedents have been rum, Romanism, and rebellion." Journalists present apparently did not hear the offensive statement or did not consider it significant.

However, a shorthand reporter, sent by the Democratic Party, recorded the statement. Within days handbills were placed in Roman Catholic parishes throughout the East. Blaine called the comment "exceedingly unfortunate," but his disclaimer probably came too late.

Blaine narrowly lost New York by 1,149 votes and, thus, the election. Whether the intemperate remark of the partisan preacher played a role in the voters' decision remains open to discussion. There were no public opinion polls and almost no viable data on which to analyze religious voting in those days. Some scholars, like historian Vincent De Santis, believed that "the importance of this incident in causing Blaine's defeat has been exaggerated."[2] Blaine may have gotten a bum rap from history. He denounced the preacher's remarks in New Haven just before the election. His autobiography indicates his displeasure with religious bias. Years later he visited the Vatican and was cordially received by Pope Leo XIII and at the North American College, an elite training ground for American priests and bishops.

These 19th century elections reveal a key difference between the two parties. Historian Robert P. Swierenga explains: "With Thomas Jefferson as its patron saint and Andrew Jackson as its titular head, the Democratic Party from its inception in the 1820s espoused egalitarian, libertarian and secularist goals. They sought a secular state that did not try to legislate social behavior and was free of church control. The Democrats easily attracted immigrants from the beginning and always stood for cultural and ethnic diversity."[3]

The American Protective Association (APA), the newest anti–Catholic group, was organized in Clinton, Iowa, in 1887. Its avowedly political aims were to oppose any Catholic candidates or Catholic political influence. The APA specialized in bogus papal encyclicals and lurid scare stories about arsenals in Catholic cathedrals, convents, churches, and schools. Virtual hysteria erupted in isolated rural areas where gossip was gospel.[4] The APA proved to be something of a flash in the pan, for, though it carried many communities in Nebraska, Iowa, Illinois, Michigan, and Ohio in 1892 and 1894, it soon dissipated and vanished from the political scene. Where it was a factor, it tended to work with and be absorbed by the Republican Party.[5]

In 1892 a minor religious issue caused some attention. The Roman Catholic Church had been the primary educator of many Indians in the

Western states, and its Indian reservation schools received some public funding under a contract of 1869. Under this arrangement the church furnished buildings, board, lodging, and clothing for the students, while the government allowed a fixed annual per capita compensation. The Bureau of Catholic Indian Missions acted as liaison with the government. Though the project began under a Republican administration, Democrat Grover Cleveland increased federal appropriations from $65,220 in 1884 to $347,672 in 1889. The Presbyterians, who maintained a few schools, received $41,825. The Republican presidential victory of 1888 augured some changes.

President Benjamin Harrison named General Thomas J. Morgan, a Baptist minister, to the post of Indian commissioner, and Dr. Daniel Dorchester, a noted Methodist preacher and author, to the position of commissioner of Indian education. Morgan promptly announced that he would withdraw government aid from the religious schools and then dismissed Catholics who were serving in the Indian office. Dorchester, who had written *Romanism Versus the Public School System* in 1888, fired almost all Catholic teachers. Catholics were outraged but were unable to reverse the policies.

President Harrison, though he admitted that he had voted the Know-Nothing ticket, claimed to be sympathetic to the Catholic Church's "stand with regard to the social order, obedience to authority, and temperance without fanaticism."[6] Harrison reiterated his opposition to religious prejudice, but refused to overrule Morgan and Dorchester, whose confirmation by the Senate had been approved.

Harry J. Sievers believed that this issue "resulted in an apparently heavy Catholic vote against President Harrison in 1892."[7] Harrison was defeated by ex–President Cleveland, and much of the Catholic press exulted. The *Courier* of Ogdensburg, New York, declared it "a great Catholic victory," while the *Catholic Herald* of New York remarked that "the Republican Party, led by bigots, invaded the sanctuary of the home, usurped parental rights and robbed the Catholic Indians of their only treasure, their faith; but the people, true to the best traditions of America, hurled it from power. Cleveland's victory was, in truth, the defeat of bigotry." Historian De Santis places the post–Civil War elections in historical perspective: "Catholicism was dragged into practically every presidential election in the post–Civil War generation. Yet as an issue it played a minor and subordinate role, and never came close to being a determining factor in the outcome of any one of these contests."[8]

William McKinley's economic policies appealed to many Catholic voters, especially after William Jennings Bryan won the Democratic nomination in 1896 and solidified the southern and western wings' control over the party. This shift of Catholics to the GOP was responsible for the McKinley landslide in every eastern state. The swing among Catholic voters in Louisville and Baltimore pushed Kentucky and Maryland into the Republican column. A similar change among Catholics and Lutherans pushed Wisconsin from a competitive state to a Republican one.

The Spanish American War brought Catholicism to the fore as a political issue once again. Since Spain was a Catholic bastion, many Protestants thought that American Catholics would be unwilling to fight against Spain. Archbishop John Ireland, a personal friend of President McKinley, was asked by the Vatican to try to convince the president not to declare war on Spain. He tried valiantly for two weeks, but, when war was declared, Ireland, who had endorsed McKinley in 1896, called upon American Catholics to accept the war effort and contribute to its success.

After the war, though, the American seizure of Cuba, Puerto Rico, and the Philippine Islands was viewed as an imperialistic land grab. Furthermore, these were almost completely Catholic nations, and Protestant missionaries seized the opportunity to "invade" them. President McKinley inadvertently insulted American Catholics by claiming that one of the reasons for the annexation of the Philippines was "to Christianize" the natives. This naïve view angered Catholics, who reminded the president that there were Christians in the islands three hundred years before there were any in Ohio.

Protestant militants saw Americanization as an opening wedge to Protestantization, beginning with mass distribution of the Protestant Bible and the opening of Protestant schools and colleges. As Thomas E. Wangler points out, "Some Protestants interpreted the new expansionism of the nation as a providentially arranged opportunity to spread a purified, reformed religion to savage peoples kept ignorant by Catholic governments and priests."[9]

Archbishop Ireland interceded with Presidents McKinley and Roosevelt to name a Catholic to the Peace Commission, to rescind the civil marriage law in Cuba, and to select Catholic teachers for the Filipino public schools. This pleased Catholics without angering Protestants unduly, since the latter were pleased with the progress they were making in the heavily Catholic lands. In addition, William Howard Taft, the newly named civil governor, negotiated a sensitive settlement of expropriated friars' lands with the Vatican. The delicacy of the church-state negotiations in this conflict showed that American domestic politics could both affect and be affected by foreign policy questions and religious conflicts.[10] As a result, McKinley's 1900 vote declined in heavily Catholic areas, from Louisville to Boston. But his overall record pleased most voters and he was reelected with an increased majority nationally.

In 1908, William Howard Taft, a Unitarian, was attacked as an infidel by some fundamentalist preachers. Taft replied that the Unitarians of this country could accept and bear the prejudice, but he wondered whether a country professing religious freedom could do so. President Theodore Roosevelt was irked by the injection of religious issues, and responded archly: "If there is one thing for which we stand in this country, it is for complete religious freedom, and it is an emphatic negation of this right to cross-examine a man on his religious views before being willing to support him for office."[11] Taft was attacked because he was civil governor of the Philippines when the U.S. government compensated some friars for land expropriated by American authorities. He was called a tool of the Vatican.

Woodrow Wilson was a progressive reformer at home and a moralist in foreign policy. Though he won a majority of Catholic votes, he never appointed a single Catholic to his cabinet or the Supreme Court. He was the first president, however, to visit the Vatican, meeting Pope Benedict XV on his triumphal 1918 tour of Europe. Wilson also appointed the first Jewish Supreme Court justice, Louis Brandeis.

The 1920s are often called the intolerant decade. Despite rapid social change, it was a time when prohibition became the law of the land despite repeated defeats by voters in many states. Malapportioned legislatures and the national Congress gave disproportionate weight to rural areas, where religious, social and cultural conservatism dominated. Rural America was soon engulfed by extremist reactionary politics and became increasingly controlled by the Ku Klux Klan, which had been reborn on Stone Mountain, Georgia, in 1915.

The Klan, in its second incarnation, was primarily anti–Catholic (though also anti–Semitic and racist), and portrayed itself as the defender of pure Americanism and Protestantism's political arm. Though never a majority, it caused trouble in government in all regions of the country and stirred up poisonous interfaith relations. The political culture of the Roaring Twenties led to immigration restrictions aimed at Catholic, Jewish and Eastern Orthodox nations, and regressive social legislation at the local, state, county and national levels.

Then there was Al Smith. The candidacy of Alfred E. Smith provoked interfaith tensions as no other previous campaign had done. Smith, whose forebears came from Ireland, was born on the Lower East Side of New York in 1873. His formal education ended before he completed the ninth grade, when he had to quit school to help support his family. He later became sheriff of New York County, president of the board of aldermen of New York City, and governor of New York in 1918. He was defeated in the Republican landslide of 1920, but was reelected in 1922, 1924, and 1926. His record was considered relatively progressive and much in tune with the needs of his urban constituents.

His record on religious affairs was somewhat mixed. In 1915 he offered an amendment to the Constitutional Convention that would have eliminated the state ban on aid to parochial schools. As governor he continued the practice of supplying four million dollars a year in state aid to parochial schools. He was also somewhat naïve about the public relations consequences of his public religious life. He made several well-publicized trips to the Vatican, where Pope Pius XI effusively praised him. He had a picture of Pope Pius XI in the governor's mansion in Albany, and he made an appearance at the 1926 Eucharistic Congress in Chicago, where he is supposed to have kissed a cardinal's ring, provoking an angry outburst from Methodist bishop Adna W. Leonard, who said, "No governor can kiss the papal ring and get within gun shot of the White House."[12]

On the other hand, Smith appointed excellent men to the state cabinet, including a reasonable balance of Protestants, Catholics, and Jews. He approved a bill extending the grounds for divorce, which the Catholic Church opposed. He objected to most forms of public censorship, though he signed the so-called Padlock Bill of 1927, which provided for the closing of any theaters for an entire year if any play presented was declared indecent by the courts. He also reorganized state government and supported social welfare and public education. He denounced the Lusk Committee, which was an early un–American activities committee which sought to expose alleged Communists in the New York state government. He won the admiration of many liberals and intellectuals, including John Dewey, who endorsed Smith in *The New Republic*.[13]

In a sense the 1928 campaign began in 1924, as Smith was one of the two leading contenders for the Democratic presidential nomination. His opponent was former secretary of the treasury William G. McAdoo, who represented the Protestant-prohibitionist rural wing of the party. Smith represented the urban anti-prohibitionist and largely Catholic and Jewish segments of the party. The Democratic convention was so bitterly divided that it narrowly defeated a resolution condemning the Ku Klux Klan and then could not make up its mind whether to nominate Smith or McAdoo. On the 103rd ballot, the weary delegates finally settled on a dull, colorless Wall Street lawyer from West Virginia, John W. Davis. The liberals were angry at the party's failure to break with the Bryan-populist tradition and deserted the party in droves to support the third-party candidacy of "Fighting Bob" La Follette of Wisconsin. The Democrats received the lowest vote in their entire history — less than 29 percent of the national total — and carried no states outside of the South. Smith was reelected governor of New York handily and began preparing for the 1928 campaign.

The first serious discussion of the religious issue arose in 1927, when Charles C. Marshall, a scholarly Episcopalian lawyer and a self-proclaimed admirer of the Roman Catholic Church, published his "Open Letter to Governor Alfred E. Smith" in the April 1927 issue of *Atlantic Monthly*. Marshall had spent years studying Catholicism and professed a "love for the Latin church." Nevertheless he was seriously concerned about Vatican policy on the relationship of church and state and its historic hostility to religious liberty. Did such policies demand a dual loyalty among prospective Roman Catholic public servants in a democratic, non–Catholic society? He questioned whether Smith could be sufficiently independent of the various papal encyclicals on church-state relations. He worried about whether religious harmony and peace could be preserved if there were constant church-state antagonisms. It was a thoughtful and serious article and Governor Smith agreed to reply in the May 1927 issue of the same journal.

Smith, who is alleged to have said after reading Marshall's article, "What the hell is a papal encyclical?" asked Father Patrick Duffy, the famous World War I chaplain, and a young priest (Francis J. Spellman, later to become cardinal), to help him prepare a response. Smith's response did not really answer most of the questions Marshall raised but Smith pledged that he was a loyal American, a genuine patriot, and a true Catholic at the same time. He professed strong support for separation of church and state and public education. He wrote: "I believe in the support of the public school as one of the cornerstones of American liberty. I believe in the right of every parent to choose whether his child shall be educated in the public school or in a religious school, supported by those of his own faith."

Unfortunately, this was to be the only rational discussion of the religious issue for the next year and a half. Most Roman Catholics objected to Smith's even being asked to respond to Marshall, and most Roman Catholic periodicals refused to discuss the issues Marshall raised. On the other hand, Protestant extremists refused to accept Smith's guarantee of good faith and began a long campaign to preserve their dominance over American public life and to keep the White House closed to Roman Catholics.

Although Smith had written in his *Atlantic Monthly* article that he recognized "no power in the institutions of my church to interfere with the operations of the Constitution of the United States or the enforcement of the law of the land," millions of Protestants refused to believe him. When Smith had written "I believe in absolute freedom of conscience for all men and in equality of all churches, all sects, and all beliefs before the law as a matter of right and not as a matter of favor," Protestants pointed to papal encyclicals that said just the opposite.

Much of the religious issue was sub rosa. Edmund Moore has written that "anti-Catholicism was indeed the silent issue in the national press and was very much more significant than the somewhat meager news or editorial space assigned to it would indicate."[14] Senator Tom Heflin of Alabama, a frock-coated demagogue, made violent anti-Catholic speeches on the floor of Congress.

The Protestant churches were politicized as never before, and almost all religious periodicals warned of the alleged dangers to religious freedom if Smith were elected.

The Republican Party was not completely immune from occasionally indulging in some anti-Catholicism for political gain. Mrs. Willie W. Caldwell, a Virginia national committeewoman, wrote to the women in her state, saying, "Mr. Hoover himself and the National Committee are depending on the women to save our country in this hour of very vital moral religious crisis. We must save the United States from being Romanized and rum-ridden, and the call is to the women to do something." Her letter outraged many Democrats and liberal Republicans. Republican officials in Florida and North Carolina distributed anti–Catholic literature. Perhaps the worst violator was Mrs. Mabel Walker Willebrandt, an assistant attorney general assigned to Prohibition enforcement. On September 7, she spoke to a delegation of Methodists in the Ohio Methodist Conference in Springfield, Ohio, and made a none-too-subtle appeal for religious bloc votes. She said, "There are two thousand pastors here. You have in your churches more than six hundred thousand members of the Methodist Church in Ohio alone. That is enough to swing the election."[15]

To his credit, Republican nominee Herbert Hoover denounced the Caldwell letter and made some appeals for religious harmony. In his memoirs, however, published after the campaign, Hoover blamed Smith for introducing the religious issue in the public arena by Smith's famous September 20 address before a boisterous crowd in Oklahoma City. This seems absurd of Hoover, since the religious issue was the most emotional and most widely discussed issue in the entire campaign.

Smith faced the crowd at Oklahoma City and lashed out at his enemies as bigots. He said that no one had a right to question his religion, that he was a loyal and patriotic American, and that his cabinet had had ten Protestants, one Jew, and only three Catholics. He talked about "the wicked motive of religious intolerance" and said that "no decent right minded, upstanding American citizen can for a moment countenance the shower of lying statements, with no basis in fact, that has been reduced to printed matter and sent broadcast through the mails of this country." Smith went on to say the following:

> I here emphatically declare that I do not wish any member of my faith in any part of the United States to vote for me on any religious grounds. I want them to vote for me only when in their hearts and consciences they become convinced that my election will promote the best interests of our country. By the same token, I cannot refrain from saying that any person who votes against me simply because of my religion is not, to my way of thinking, a good citizen. Let me remind the Democrats of this country that we belong to the party of Thomas Jefferson, whose proudest boast was that he was the author of the Virginia Statute for Religious Freedom. Let me remind the citizens of every polit-

ical faith that his Statute of Religious Freedom has become a part of the sacred heritage of our land.[16]

Smith revisited the issue at campaign's end in a speech in Baltimore on October 29. He said, "I repeat my firm adherence to the American doctrine of the absolute separation of church and state. Political activity on the part of the church is the negation of that separation."[17]

Smith's appeal, reinforced by the support of some liberal Protestant, Jewish, and Episcopalian religious leaders, was of no avail. The passionate religious antagonisms of the past were insurmountable. Smith went down to a crushing defeat, 21.4 to 15.0 million in the popular vote and 444 to 87 in electoral votes. He made substantial gains in Catholic and Jewish areas, carrying Massachusetts, Rhode Island, and most major urban areas, but he lost badly in the heartland of rural, southern, and western Protestantism. Richard Hofstadter writes:

> Even in his losing campaign Smith turned the normally huge Republican pluralities in the twelve largest cities into a slender Democratic plurality. He brought into the voting stream of the Democratic Party ethnic groups that had never taken part in politics and others that had been mainly Republican. He extricated his party from its past dependence on agrarian interests and made it known to the great urban populations. He lost a campaign that had to be lost, but in such a way as to restore his party as an effective opposition and to pave the way for the victories of F.D.R.[18]

In retrospect, Smith and his advisers were not completely blameless in the way they handled the religious issue. Smith appointed John J. Raskob, a conservative Catholic millionaire from Delaware, as chairman of the Democratic National Committee. It probably would have been wiser to have appointed a more neutral figure, but Smith was apparently unaware of the deep suspicion with which he was regarded. David Burner expresses a view that is more widely accepted today:

> For if he could not shirk his religion itself, or modify the slightest symbolic act of allegiance, he could have at least addressed himself more fully to the fears in which so many of his fellow Americans had been reared.... Smith might have acknowledged the occasional alliance between Latin Catholicism and political tyranny and then pointed to the historical American tradition of religious harmony, as embodied in Lord Baltimore; he and his supporters might even have made explicit contrast between their position, along with the position of countless of their fellow religionists in the United States, and that of Catholic reactionaries; he might have sought out the support of Protestant clergymen or outstanding laymen; he might have increased the Protestant contingent in

his campaign committee. In short, Smith might have acted as though he was aware of the anxiety, however silly or bigoted, that was felt by much of rural American Protestantism, as one who shared with it a sense of America's role in preserving religious liberty.[19]

Dr. James H. Smylie, in his trenchant essay "The Roman Catholic Church, The State and Al Smith" (*Church History*, September 1960), found a kernel of hopefulness in the rather unfortunate campaign: "Roman Catholics were slandered; of this there is no shadow of a doubt. But there is evidence that Roman Catholics themselves invited, indeed, provoked, in their own writing a discussion of the relationship between the church and the state in America. During the 1928 campaign, some Americans raised questions about the feasibility of a Roman Catholic president in an attempt to come to terms with one of the most crucial and continuing problems in American life." Another lesson of that sorry campaign is expressed by Eleanor Roosevelt: "The kind of propaganda that some of the religious groups, aided and abetted by the opposition, put forth in that campaign utterly disgusted me. If I needed anything to show me what prejudice can do to the intelligence of human beings, that campaign was the best lesson I could have had."[20]

The view of Smylie and others was superseded by the conclusion — based on a detailed analysis of voting correlated with religious affiliation — arrived at by American University professor Allan J. Lichtman. He concluded in his seminal *Prejudice and the Old Politics: The Presidential Election of 1928* the following:

> Of all possible explanations for the distinctive political alignments of 1928, religion is the best. A bitter conflict between Catholics and Protestants emerged in the presidential election of 1928: religious considerations preoccupied the public, commanded the attention of political leaders, and sharply skewed the behavior of voters. Regardless of their ethnic background, their stand on prohibition, their economic status, and other politically salient attributes, Catholics and Protestants split far more decisively in 1928 than in either previous or subsequent elections. No other division of the electorate stands out so distinctively in that presidential year. This cleft between Catholics and Protestants was not confined to particular regions of the nation, to either city or country, to either church members or nominal Protestants. Both Protestants and Catholics responded to the religious tensions of 1928.[21]

Lichtman also concluded that "the Republican presidential campaign of 1928 relied upon moralistic appeals to the mass of American voters. They exploited Protestant fears about the consequences of electing a Catholic president. The evidence suggests that both the local and national leadership of the party was heavily implicated in the effort to incite religious opposition to Al Smith."[22]

In the 809 counties that shifted party allegiance between 1924 and 1928, religion was clearly the dominant factor.

Religious Affiliation and the 1928 Swing Vote in Counties

Candidates Supported	% Protestant	% Catholic
Hoover–Davis (North)	76.7	23.3
Hoover–Davis (South)	95.0	5.0
Coolidge-Smith	46.3	53.7
La Follette-Smith	41.5	58.5
La Follette-Hoover	66.3	33.7

The Roosevelt and Truman administrations included more Catholics and Jews in influential positions than any previous Republican or Democratic ones, thus advancing pluralism and diversity, but church-state issues were marginalized by the Depression.

A major church-state controversy in the postwar years involved various forms of proposed government aid to parochial and private schools, which were mostly rejected. Another issue that surfaced was the question of U.S. diplomatic relations with the Vatican when President Truman decided to appoint Mark Clark as ambassador to the Holy See on October 20, 1951. This provoked a firestorm of organized opposition from Protestant groups that led Clark to withdraw his name in 1952, postponing the resolution to a later date.

John F. Kennedy sought the vice presidential nomination in 1956, when presidential nominee Adlai Stevenson decided to let convention delegates choose his running mate, but he lost narrowly to Tennessee Senator Estes Kefauver.

The 1958 election was a dress rehearsal for the public raising of the religious issue in 1960. The issue arose primarily in two states, California and Pennsylvania. In California a referendum on tax exemption of parochial school property was the occasion for an outpouring of verbal hostility to Catholicism. Catholic schools were called "un–American" in the literature of the forces promoting Proposition 16, to deny tax exemption. The usual anti–Catholic activists were prominent. They were opposed by many church-state separationists and political and religious liberals, including Episcopal bishop James Pike. Lutherans, Seventh-day Adventists, and Episcopalians opposed the measure, as did Catholics, and it was decisively rejected.

During the same election California attorney general Edmund Brown, the Democratic gubernatorial nominee and a Roman Catholic, was denounced by fundamentalists because he had ruled against obligatory Bible readings in public schools. The old canards about Catholic hatred of the Bible were bandied about in some of the extremist religious press. As Brown defeated his Republican opponent, Senator William Knowland, by a 60 percent to 40 percent vote landslide, the religious issue certainly must not have hurt him substantially. He won the Protestant Central Valley as well as the urban Catholic and Jewish areas.

In Pennsylvania, however, Pittsburgh mayor David Lawrence's Catholicism almost cost him the election for governor. A widely respected Stevensonian liberal, Lawrence was heavily favored to defeat a Republican pretzel dealer from Reading, businessman Arthur T. McGonigle, who had never held public office. Pennsylvania had never had a Catholic governor either, and some rural Protestant Bible Belt voters reacted with alarm. Though Lawrence won — by fewer than one hundred thousand votes out of almost four million cast — his victory came from the Catholic, Jewish, and more liberal Protestant urban and suburban areas. Lawrence ran poorly in the Protestant strongholds that had buried Al Smith under an avalanche in 1928.

The 1958 election for governor was a dress rehearsal of sorts for the religious issue in the 1960 presidential race. David Lawrence, the Democratic reform mayor of Pittsburgh and a Stevenson Democrat, was also a Catholic and many voters knew it. Thomas J. Donaghy described the issue: "Lawrence received large numbers of anti–Catholic letters. Despite his previous concerns about the religious issue in a race of that kind, Lawrence was shocked at both the volume and contents of the hate mail. Some letters were so bad he turned them over to the FBI."

A county and precinct analysis, however, shows that anti–Catholic voting was confined to a few counties and did not cause Lawrence's defeat, though it may have reduced his margin of victory. In Columbia County, where anti–Kennedy voting would prove to be rampant and decisive, there was a religious backlash. The county Democratic chairman Rollin Brewer, a Protestant, wrote to Lawrence: "Ten days before the election a splendid

Democratic victory locally seemed assured. Religion was injected into the fight and a vile whispering campaign was waged. That not only spelled defeat locally for our candidates of the Catholic faith, but materially weakened our entire ticket."[23]

The Fair Campaign Practices Committee (FCPC), in a September 1959 memorandum, concluded that there had been a shocking increase in anti–Catholicism in the 1958 elections. The FCPC was organized in 1954 to fight political chicanery and dishonest campaign tactics. Under the leadership of executive director Bruce L. Felknor and chairman Charles P. Taft, it was especially sensitive to religious and racial smears. The FCPC issued five guidelines which it hoped would influence any discussion of religion in the 1960 campaign:

1. It is proper and desirable that every public official should attempt to govern his conduct by a personal conscience informed by his religious faith.

2. No candidate for public office should be opposed or supported because of his particular religious affiliation. A campaign for a public office is not an opportunity to vote for one religion against another.

3. A candidate should be judged by his qualifications for the office he seeks, and by his position on issues relevant to that office. He may properly be questioned about such issues and about the bearing of his religious faith and conscience on them. A candidate's religion is relevant to a voter's decision, but only so far as it bears on such relevant political issues.

4. Stirring up, fostering, or tolerating religious animosity, or injecting elements of a candidate's faith not relevant to the duties of the office he seeks are unfair campaign practices.

5. Intelligent, honest, and temperate public discussion of the relation of religious faith to the public issues will, as it has already done, raise the whole level of the campaign.[24]

Despite the escalating bias, five new Catholic governors and eight new Catholic U.S. Senators were elected in the 1958 Democratic sweep. The stage was set for an extraordinary national drama two years later.

CHAPTER 2

The Kennedy Campaign and the Issue of Religion

Kennedy Enters the Race

Senator John F. Kennedy decided to seek the presidency by at least 1959. His landslide reelection to the Senate and his expanding record as a spokesman for liberal, progressive causes made him a strong possibility. He was quite different from Al Smith in almost every respect. He had been schooled almost exclusively in secular private schools. He was a Harvard University graduate and an avid student of history. His *Profiles in Courage*, a biographical study of political integrity, won a Pulitzer Prize. He was literate, urbane, and eloquent.

His legislative record was that of a moderate liberal and he had taken some bold positions on federal aid to education and the independence of Algeria. He understood the important role thrust upon the United States in the international arena and knew instinctively that democracy and liberty had to be made a reality at home before they could be exported.

Kennedy hoped that there would not be a substantial religious question in the 1960 campaign; but he soon became aware of the intensity of the issue, even in the quiescent pre–election year of 1959. In a *Look* interview (March 3, 1959) Kennedy pledged unequivocal support for the uniquely American principle of church-state separation, opposed public aid for parochial schools, and opposed an ambassador to the Vatican. Most secular journalists and pragmatic politicians applauded the young senator, but, ironically, many Catholics and some moderate Protestants criticized him for sounding too secular. Kennedy had said, "Whatever one's religion in his private life may be, for the officeholder, nothing takes precedence over his oath to uphold the Constitution and all its parts — including the First Amendment and the strict separation of church and state." Patricia Barrett commented that "some commentators thought Mr. Kennedy had gone too far in asserting the primacy of political over other loyalties and had thus deepened the cleavage between religion and public life."[1]

After announcing his candidacy, Kennedy did well in the early primaries and won convincingly in Wisconsin, where a heavy Catholic Republican crossover contributed to his victory over Senator Hubert Humphrey of Minnesota. The voting results showed a Protestant/Catholic division that would make the religious issue even more crucial. Kennedy had to win the primary on May 10 in heavily Protestant West Virginia if his credibility as a winner was to be established. He won a decisive 62 percent landslide there, forcing Humphrey's withdrawal. The last real barrier to the nomination had been overcome.

Prior to the West Virginia primary Kennedy addressed the American Society of Newspaper Editors in Washington, on April 21, 1960. He told the four hundred newsmen, "I want no votes solely on account of my religion." He warned them not to "magnify" or "oversimplify" the religious issue: "I am not the Catholic candidate for President. I do not speak for the Catholic Church on issues of public policy — and no one in that Church speaks for me." He concluded: "If there is bigotry in the country, then so be it — there is bigotry. If that bigotry is too great to prevent fair consideration of a Catholic who has made clear his complete independence and his dedication to separation of church and state, then we ought to know it. But I do not believe this is the case. I believe the American people are more concerned with a man's views and abilities than with the church to which he belongs. I believe that the founding fathers meant it when they provided in Article VI of the Constitution that there should be no religious test for public office."[2]

The Attack Begins

As early as November 1959, the Texas Baptist Convention "adopted a resolution cautioning members ... against voting for a Roman Catholic candidate," and Alabama Baptists "went on record as protesting against the election of any Roman Catholic as U.S. President." The National Association

2. The Kennedy Campaign and the Issue of Religion

W.A. Criswell, pastor of the First Baptist Church in Dallas, Texas, vigorously opposed the election of JFK (courtesy of Southern Baptist Historical Library and Archives, Nashville, Tennessee).

of Evangelicals adopted a statement that read in part, "Any country the Roman Catholic Church dominates suppresses the right of Evangelicals.... For that reason, thinking Americans view with alarm the possible election of a Roman Catholic as President of the United States."[3] On July 3, the Rev. W.A. Criswell delivered a fiery sermon in Dallas's First Baptist Church denouncing "Roman Catholicism's bloody hand" and warning that Kennedy's election would "spell the death of a free church in a free state and our hopes of continuance of full religious liberty in America."[4]

"Most Protestant periodicals were either skeptical or hostile," wrote historian Lawrence Fuchs.[5] *World Outlook* (September 11, 1960) said Kennedy's critics were engaging in "bad politics and worse religion." Typical of hostile comments even before Kennedy was nominated was *Christianity Today*'s assertion that "Protestant voters not at all irrationally would prefer to keep the White House out of the hands of someone who confesses to a foreign earthly power." The Alabama Methodist *Christian Advocate* in June 1959 blasted the state's Methodist governor, John Patterson, for supporting JFK. It said, "The people of Alabama do not intend to jeopardize their democratic liberties by opening the doors of the White House to the political machinations of a determined power-hungry Romanist hierarchy." (Apparently, these democratic liberties did not extend to the state's African American citizens.)

The Rev. Ramsey Pollard, president of the Southern Baptist Convention, announced that he would not "stand by and keep my mouth shut when a man under control of the Roman Catholic Church runs for the Presidency of the United States."[6] During the campaign he told one audience, "My church has enough members to beat Kennedy if they all vote like I tell them to."[7]

On September 7, at Washington's fashionable Mayflower Hotel, 150 conservative, evangelical, and fundamentalist Protestants of 37 denominations held a one-day national conference of the so-called Citizens for Religious Freedom. Such notables as Norman Vincent Peale, of *The Power of Positive Thinking* fame, Daniel A. Poling, editor of *Christian Herald*, L. Nelson Bell of *Christianity Today*, and Harold J. Ockenga, author and theologian, appeared. The group issued a policy statement, denying that it was bigotry to question the credentials of a Roman Catholic candidate. They felt that "it is inconceivable that a Roman Catholic president would not be under extreme pressure by the hierarchy of his church to accede to its policies." The statement drew attention to religious liberty problems in many Catholic countries and alleged canon law restrictions on a Catholic president's attendance at interfaith worship services. It pointed out

Ramsey Pollard, a Tennessee pastor and president of the Southern Baptist Convention in 1960, endorsed Nixon and said Nixon would carry Tennessee "if people vote like I tell them to" (courtesy of Southern Baptist Historical Library and Archives, Nashville, Tennessee).

that Kennedy had favored peripheral aid to parochial schools while in the 81st Congress, although it admitted that he was the only Roman Catholic senator to oppose the Morse Amendment, which would have provided partial grants and loans for parochial school construction. They claimed that "the nature of the Roman Catholic Church" created "the religious issue in the present campaign."[8]

They denounced religious persecution in Catholic countries, though they did not explain why Senator Kennedy should be blamed for these excesses. They did not blame Protestant candidates for anti–Catholic discrimination in Sweden. They drew attention to Ohio, "a state with a Roman Catholic governor," where "nuns may be placed on the public payroll as school teachers according to an attorney general's ruling." They failed, conveniently, to mention that the Ohio attorney general was a Protestant and that these conditions had occurred under several Protestant governors.

The statement was immediately denounced by Harold E. Fey, editor of *Christian Century* (September 14, 1960), and a critic of Catholicism himself: "It misrepresents the breadth of Protestant interests, the intelligence of Protestant concerns, the charity of Protestant attitudes." Scholars Reinhold Niebuhr and John C. Bennett called the piece "blind prejudice," and then noted significantly, "Most of those Protestants who have been in the forefront of this effort would oppose any liberal Democrat regardless of his religion."[9]

The Niebuhr-Bennett statement has great import. Without question, the Citizens for Religious Freedom were preponderantly Republican and conservative. They exhibited a streak of cultural snobbery, a belief that only white Protestants were good and trustworthy Americans. Peale expressed that view when he said, "Our American culture is at stake.... I don't say it won't survive, but it won't be what it was."[10] Peale, a long-time Republican, seemed unaware that America had long since become a religiously pluralistic nation. (Adlai Stevenson is supposed to have quipped in Minneapolis, "I find St. Paul appealing and St. Peale appalling.") Peale was apparently embarrassed by the publicity surrounding his participation in the conference and he later disassociated himself from it. He still disliked Kennedy, though. His biographer, Carol George, wrote that "Peale was a firm Nixon partisan, and Nixon himself worshipped at Peale's Marble Collegiate Church during the war."[11] After the election, Peale told friends,

"Kennedy is a jerk. Protestant America got its death blow on November 8th."[12]

The Speech in Houston

It was apparent to Senator Kennedy and his staff that he had to make a dramatic declaration of independence from his church's political involvement in order to allay the lingering suspicions of many Protestants. He accepted an invitation to address the Ministerial Association of Greater Houston on September 12, 1960. Before perhaps a thousand ministers and laymen and thousands more who would watch the event on television, Kennedy directly confronted the issue and pledged absolute adherence to the U.S. Constitution. He promised to resign rather than submit to clerical dictation. In words that will echo through the centuries, he made the following statements:

> I believe in an America where the separation of church and state is absolute — where no Catholic prelate would tell the President (should he be Catholic) how to act and no Protestant minister would tell his parishioners for whom to vote — where no church or church school is granted any public funds or political preference — and where no man is denied public office merely because his religion differs from the President who might appoint him or the people who might elect him.
>
> I believe in an America that is officially neither Catholic, Protestant nor Jewish — where no public official either requests or accepts instructions on public policy from the Pope, the National Council of Churches, or any other ecclesiastical source — where no religious body seeks to impose its will directly or indirectly upon the general populace or the public acts of its officials — and where religious liberty is so indivisible that an act against one church is treated as an act against all.

He reminded the listeners that prejudice against one faith should be construed as prejudice against all: "For while this year it may be a Catholic against whom the finger of suspicion is pointed, in other years it has been, and may someday be again, a Jew — or a Quaker — or a Unitarian — or a Baptist." Almost emotionally and poignantly he reminded fair-minded Americans that thousands of Catholics and Jews died fighting for the freedom we all enjoy today:

> This is the kind of America I believe in — and this is the kind of America I fought for in the South Pacific and the kind my brother died for in Europe.

No one suggested then that we might have a "divided loyalty," that we did "not believe in liberty" or that we belonged to a disloyal group that threatened "the freedom for which our forefathers died."

And in fact this is the kind of America for which our forefathers did die when they fled here to escape religious test oaths, that denied office to members of less favored churches, when they fought for the Constitution, the Bill of Rights, the Virginia Statute of Religious Freedom, and when they fought at the shrine I visited today — the Alamo. For side by side with Bowie and Crockett died Fuentes and McCafferty and Baily and Badillo and Carey — but no one knows whether they were Catholics or not. For there was no religious test there.[13]

He then answered some tough questions from the clergy, many of whom obviously opposed his candidacy.

The *New York Times* praised Kennedy's affirmations in a September 14 editorial, "The Religious Issue." The *Times* warned that "the issue of Senator John F. Kennedy's Roman Catholic religion threatens to dominate the Presidential campaign; and if it does, the harm will be irreparable to this country at home and abroad." After reviewing the relevant issues related to religion, America's leading newspaper concluded:

What more could Senator Kennedy possibly say to clarify his divorcement from any real or imputed political stand of the Catholic Church in this or any other country? How could he be more explicit or more positive? Why is he not right in insisting that to oppose him as a Catholic would now be to establish an arbitrary religious test for the Presidency that not only is disregarded for every other public office, including Chief Justice, Senator, Governor, but also is directly violative of Article VI of the Constitution of the United States and the most basic principles on which our democracy rests? In the light of his own statements Senator Kennedy's religious affiliation is irrelevant to his fitness for the Presidency. No American will be doing his duty if he votes against him because he is a Catholic, exactly as no American will be doing his duty if he votes for him because he is a Catholic.[14]

There has always been speculation over Kennedy's commitment to church-state separation. Was this posture one of political expediency or of genuine conviction? His closest aide, Theodore Sorensen, worked for Kennedy from the start of his Senate career and through his presidency and specialized in church-state matters. Sorensen's memoir *Counselor* sets the record straight: "Kennedy publicly disagreed with the church hierarchy on many public policies, was alone among the presidential hopefuls in opposing a 1960 bill that would have authorized public funds for nonpublic schools, and also opposed the U.S. government recognizing the Vatican as a state by appointing a U.S. ambassador. On the most sensitive issue of all, he opposed any attempt to reduce U.S. foreign aid to nations using public funds for birth control."[15]

Kennedy thought church-state separation was a valuable, indeed unique, American constitutional principle that he wholeheartedly endorsed. Sorensen adds that "JFK wanted to be strong in dissociating himself from centuries of Vatican doctrine inconsistent with the Jefferson-Madison principle of separating church and state."[16] During the campaign Kennedy told a reporter that separation of church and state "represents the happiest arrangement for the organization of a society."[17]

On September 12 one hundred Protestant, Catholic, Jewish, and Greek Orthodox churchmen and scholars issued a statement deploring the religious issue as a violation of Article VI of the U.S. Constitution that "no religious test shall ever be required as a qualification to any office or public trust under the United States." It denounced "the exclusion of members of any family of faith from public office on the basis of religious affiliation." Episcopal bishops were prominently identified with this declaration. The presiding bishop, the Right Rev. Arthur C. Lichtenberger, Bishops Horace Donegan of New York, Angus Dun of Washington Cathedral, James Pike of San Francisco, Henry Knox Sherrill, and Dean Francis B. Sayre of Washington Cathedral were among the signers. Methodist bishop G. Bromley Oxnam, Baptist Carlyle Marney, and Methodist Dudley Ward were included. The group listed ten principles as "guidelines for action in the 1960 election":

1. The exclusion of members of any family of faith from public office on the bases of religious affiliation violates the fundamental conditions of a free democratic society, as expressed in the spirit and letter of our Constitution.

2. The religious faith of a public officer is relevant to the conduct of his office.... Inquiry regarding this relevancy is an exercise of responsible citizenship, if conducted in such a way as not to violate the constitutional prohibition against any religious test for public office.

3. No citizen in public office dares to falsify either to his conscience or to his oath of office.... [I]f he cannot reconcile the responsibilities entailed by his oath with his conscience, then he must resign.

4. The fact that a major religious group has so far never furnished

the Nation with a candidate who won election to a particular office does not obligate the voters to elect a candidate of that faith to that office solely to demonstrate our devotion to democracy.

5. No religious organization should seek to influence and dominate public officials for its own institutional advantage.

6. Every person of every faith must be accorded full religious liberty, and no person should be coerced into accepting any religious belief or practice.

7. A candidate's faith, and his affirmations of it, as they bear upon his responsibilities in public office, should be viewed in their best light rather than their worst.

8. The public officer after his election is obligated to make his appointments to subordinate positions on a non–discriminatory basis using competence and record rather than religious affiliation as the criteria of selection.

9. If for reasons of his own he [the president] feels that participation in a particular religious ceremony is not in order, it would be contrary to the civic character of American presidency for him to feel obligated to accept the invitation.

10. He [the president] will recognize that the values in historic faiths other than his own must be brought to bear upon his problems of the day.[18]

The Smear Campaign Accelerates

Unfortunately, and not unexpectedly, the unappeasable bigots made a major effort in the campaign's home stretch to defame Kennedy and his faith. Author James Michener, who played a leading role in the Kennedy campaign in Bucks County, Pennsylvania, was sickened and shocked by the flood of anti–Catholic literature spreading throughout his well-educated and presumably enlightened county. Lurid photos of Protestants being burned and tortured by leering priests filled the mailboxes of residents. Michener feared the impact of such irrationality and thought Kennedy might lose the election because of it.[19]

The smear campaign picked up in its intensity, ironically, after Kennedy addressed the issue in Houston. Bruce L. Felknor, a Presbyterian layman who served as executive director of the Fair Campaign Practices Committee, was openly concerned about the volume of the attacks. He issued a preliminary report that warned, "We think at this point there is a substantial danger that the campaign in 1960 will be dirtier than it was in 1928. The material is showing up much earlier than it habitually does in an election."[20]

Patricia Barrett, in her methodical study of the anti–Kennedy literature, concluded that the literature was becoming "less speculative and more concrete, less rational and more emotional."[21] She added, "Many Americans thought that the worst extremes of bigotry and prejudice had been laid to rest alongside Al Smith's presidential aspirations in 1928. The record, however, shows that professional bigots were more active in 1960 than in 1928.... In the final tense days of the campaign, everyone knew that religion was a foremost concern of voters, but no one knew how it would influence their choice in the polling booths on November 8. The magnitude and virulence of the anti–Catholic material flooding the country reached unprecedented dimensions during the first week of November."[22]

Bruce L. Felknor, executive director of the Fair Campaign Practices Committee (courtesy of the Felknor family).

Some of the attacks showed paranoia and status anxiety by Kennedy's religious foes. A fringe group, the Bracken Baptist Association, said it was "unalterably opposed to the election of a Roman Catholic as president because he would appoint many Catholics to key positions in government and undermine our way of life."[23] Later books by Theodore Sorensen and Arthur Schlesinger Jr. noted that Kennedy's congressional offices had been staffed mainly by Protestants and Jews. His later appointments to the cabinet, the Supreme Court, and other top posts showed a wide range of pluralism, with no religious considerations apparent. But resolutions like these indicated that some Protestants simply did not like or respect Catholics and feared that their own privileged way of life would vanish if Catholics served in government, though Catholics had served in various capacities since the administration of Andrew Jackson.

Despite the Kennedy campaign's handling of the religious issue post–Houston, the militant wing of evangelical Protestantism and its parachurch allies decided to make a last-minute effort to defeat Kennedy through church voter registration efforts and an orgy of sermonizing on Reformation Sunday in late October. The effort was spearheaded by the National Association of Evangelicals, whose printing presses worked overtime producing anti–Catholic tracts, frank political endorsements of Nixon, and condemnations of Kennedy. Newspaper ads were mounted by the fundamentalist Church of Christ throughout the South. Radio addresses and spot announcements were sponsored by front groups working hand in glove with Republican National Committee operatives. Writes Casey: "Aided and abetted by the Nixon campaign, a spasm of anti–Catholic literature was soaking the country to an extent not seen before or since. The decentralized engines of Protestant bigotry were ramping up for the fall election, and an astonishing array of co–belligerents was plotting Kennedy's defeat."[24]

The church bodies which took an official stand against the election of a Catholic president claimed 11,139,000 members in 1960. If denominations belonging to the National Association of Evangelicals are included, the total rises to over 15 million, a formidable obstacle to overcome. Activity at the local level was still worrisome. The Missouri Baptist Women's Missionary Union prayed openly for "the Lord's blessing and assistance" in maintaining a Protestant president.[25]

Many of the ads were so vile and patently dishonest that they were denounced again by the Fair Campaign Practices Committee. Columnist David Broder exposed the inaccuracies in Texas radio broadcasts in the *Washington Star*'s September 15 issue. Several million copies of NAE literature were distributed. One made the amazing claim that "the United States will no longer be recognized as a Protestant nation in the eyes of the world," apparently ignoring the religious neutrality mandated by the Constitution's Article VI and the First Amendment of the Bill of Rights.

Kennedy campaigners encountered instances of religious bias as the campaign neared its close. Lindy Boggs, the wife of New Orleans Democratic representative Hale Boggs, campaigned for the Kennedy-Johnson ticket in western Pennsylvania, where she saw numerous signs and posters in the crowds warning that religious freedom could be lost if Kennedy won. In her memoir she remembered "Anti–Catholic flyers warning against electing a president with a connection to the Pope were under the windshield wipers of every car at our rally."[26]

Dulce and Richter noted that "the religious issue had 'gone underground' following the repercussions of the Peale controversy and the Houston speech, but it continued to add no less heat to the steadily intensified campaign."[27] Conservative Protestants attempted to make Reformation Sunday, October 30, an occasion for a last-ditch "stop Kennedy" effort. Some Catholic bishops in Puerto Rico at this time called on Catholic voters to oust Governor Munoz Marin, who supported divorce and birth control. Some Protestants seized on this local hierarchy's decision as "proof" that Kennedy could not disentangle himself from his bishops. Kennedy reportedly joked with his staff that he might lose the election if voters remembered that Puerto Rico was part of the U.S. (sort of). Puerto Rico's Catholic voters, as it turned out, repudiated the hierarchy and reelected their governor in a landslide.

Some of the attacks on Kennedy were absurd as well as unfair. One Baptist preacher in St. Louis formed an "unlock" club. His supporters wore buttons showing Baptist churches in Spain padlocked and said that they would vote against Kennedy unless Baptist churches in Spain were reopened.

Eight state Baptist conventions adopted anti–Kennedy resolutions, as did the Assemblies of God, the American Baptist Association, the Augustana Lutheran Church, and the Conservative Baptist Association of America. Most Protestant journals, notably excepting Episcopalian, expressed fear or hesitancy even after Kennedy's Houston address.[28] Many Baptist pastors in Texas, North Carolina, Arkansas, and elsewhere worked openly in Nixon's campaign and raised the religious issue.[29]

Both political and religious leaders expressed relief as the nasty campaign ended. The FCPC, in a report issued in 1962, analyzed 1,383 reports of 402 "unfair" anti–Catholic political attacks and 392 pieces of "unfair" anti–Catholic literature. The largest numbers were distributed in California,

Pennsylvania, and Minnesota, and the committee estimated that 20 to 25 million pieces of such literature were circulated in the United States. The literature was placed in four categories: vile, 5 percent; dishonest, 25 percent; unfair, 35 percent; and responsible, 35 percent. Patricia Barrett noted, "Although the volume of printed matter dealing with the religious issue in the 1960 campaign was *substantially* greater than in 1928, the quality was, on the whole, higher."[30] The *Journalism Quarterly* discovered in a survey of Southern Baptist religious journals that anti–Catholicism was even more pervasive in 1960 than it had been in 1928.[31]

Counterattack by Kennedy's Defenders

Groups seeking to counter the continuing viciousness of religious slander included the American Jewish Committee, the American Jewish Congress, the National Council of Churches, the National Conference of Christians and Jews, and the Anti-Defamation League of B'nai B'rith, which exposed the hate literature.

The general press devoted more and more space to serious discussions of the religious issue in 1960. In an appropriate July 4 issue of *Life*, Robert Coughlan shined a spotlight on the lurid history of religious bigotry in politics, mostly directed at Catholics, and called it "an un–American heritage." *Look, Newsweek, Time* and *U.S. News and World Report* chronicled the increasingly virulent intrusion of sectarianism into the political realm. *Newsweek* called it "the issue that won't die" in its September 12, 1960 issue.

Much of the commentary was sympathetic to Kennedy, beginning with Fletcher Knebel's "Democratic Forecast: A Catholic in 1960," which appeared in *Look* March 3, 1959. But *U.S. News* was distinctly anti–Kennedy, in keeping with its conservative Republican bias. Scholars looked in depth at the history of religious voting. Seymour Martin Lipset looked at the dreary history in *Commentary* (October 1960), while La Salle Woelfel argued in *America* that anti–Catholicism was "cyclical" and tended to recur every 25 to 30 years.

It should be noted in passing that America's intellectual community strongly favored Kennedy. He received the endorsements of most of the significant journals of opinion: *Harper's, Atlantic, New Republic, New Leader, Nation, Progressive*, etc.

Historian Arthur Schlesinger Jr. wrote speeches for both Stevenson and Kennedy and was a close personal friend of both. He clearly admired Stevenson: "In his eight years as titular leader, Stevenson renewed the Democratic Party. His conviction that affluence was not enough for the good life, his contempt for complacency, his impatience with clichés of the past, his demand for new ides, his respect for the people who have them, his sense of the complexity of history and the desperate need for leadership set the tone for a new era in Democratic politics." But he saw Kennedy as the appropriate heir to the Stevenson tradition and pleaded with fair-minded Stevenson supporters to support the 1960 Democratic nominee: "Kennedy shares the Stevenson vision of a new departure in American life—a time of national revival.... He knows what is required to bring it about, and his passion in life is to preside over its initiation."

In an attempt to stem any liberal defections to Nixon, Schlesinger argued that the choice in 1960 was between a mediocre present and a hopeful future: "For Nixon the Presidency seems essentially a source of private gratification. For Kennedy, it is a means of public achievement." The choice was clear:

> Kennedy and Nixon stand in sharp contrast—in their personalities, their progress, and their parties. Each asks the American people to repose in him the command of our national policy over the next four years. With Nixon, personality, programs and party combine to create the expectation of a static government dominated by the forces in our society most opposed to change. With Kennedy, personality, policies, and party combine to create the expectation of an affirmative government dominated by intelligence and vision and dedicated to abolishing the terrifying discrepancy between the American performance and the American possibility.[32]

Kennedy appointed several respected advisors to help shape his religious strategy, including liberal Catholic (and later Episcopalian) journalist John Cogley and Presbyterian lawyer James Wine, an official with the National Council of Churches. Kennedy had personally hoped the religious issue would go away but soon realized that he had to confront the fears of critics. "Kennedy had displayed a nimble and sophisticated grasp of the anti–Catholic forces he faced and showed a willingness to admit his vulnerability regarding his Catholicism," observed Shaun A. Casey.[33]

Some Baptists applauded Kennedy. Former President Harry Truman campaigned hard for JFK in the South and by his own admission "cussed out the Baptists" and brought harsh criticism upon himself from many

Baptist preachers. Walter Pope Binns, president of Baptist-related William Jewell College in Missouri, endorsed Kennedy and was given credit by Truman for JFK's razor-thin edge in that state.[34] Several prominent Baptist pastors (especially those who served university congregations) denounced religious bigotry. One was Washington's Edward Pruden, who later reflected on JFK's Houston address:

> I think I have never heard a finer delineation of our American heritage in this area of our common life. I jokingly accused one of our Baptist experts on the subject of having written the speech for Mr. Kennedy.... In view of the candidate's forthrightness and his disarming expressions of personal convictions regarding basic issues, I felt that it was unfair and un–American to suggest that he should not be considered for the Presidency because of his Catholic affiliation.... I thought it wrong to suggest that any American should be barred from any public office because of his religion.[35]

Kennedy met with C. Emanuel Carlson, the head of the Baptist Joint Committee, during the campaign. They issued this statement in August: "A frank renunciation by all churches of political power as a means to religious ends would greatly improve the political climate."[36]

E.S. James, editor of the Texas *Baptist Standard*, was so impressed by JFK and disillusioned by Nixon's equivocation on, and Lodge's open support for, tax support for parochial schools that he strongly implied support for JFK in his final pre–election editorial.[37] Casey and other scholars think that may have tipped the scales in Texas, giving Baptist voters a reason to stick with the Democratic ticket. James was an exception. Most Baptist papers opposed Kennedy. In an exhaustive doctoral study, Beryl McClerren concluded that "Southern Baptists used their state newspapers as the main organs of opposition to the presidential candidate of the Catholic faith." These newspapers existed in 28 states and collectively they devoted 485 pages of text to the religious issue in 1960.[38]

Billy Graham's Role

Evangelist Billy Graham did everything he could to elect Nixon without saying so publicly. His biographer, William Martin, recounts numerous letters of advice Graham sent to Nixon, urging the vice president to inject more religion into the campaign (as if any more was needed) and to pick a church-going evangelical like Minnesota representative Walter Judd or

Oregon governor Mark Hatfield as his running mate. Graham urged Protestant pastors to register their congregations for Nixon and said that Protestants might cast a higher vote for Nixon than for Kennedy because they were better informed about religious issues. Graham wrote Nixon:

> I have just written a letter to my mailing list of two million American families, urging them to organize their Sunday school classes and churches to get out the vote. Contrary to most people's thinking, my primary following lies in the Middle West, California, Pennsylvania and New York State. I think in these areas plus the South we can be of greatest help, though we have supporters on our list from every single post office in the United States. We are getting other religious groups throughout the Nation to do the same; thus many millions will be personally circulated. It is felt that the majority of these lists are Democratic or independent voters. It was also felt that this would bring about a favorable swing among these voters to you.[39]

Shaun Casey observed, "Thus, the most prominent leader of American evangelicalism recruited an all-star roster of clergy to plan, fund, and exe-

Senator John F. Kennedy and the Rev. Billy Graham (John F. Kennedy Presidential Library and Museum, Boston).

cute a strategy to raise the religion issue across the country on Nixon's behalf without directly endorsing Nixon."[40]

Graham further wrote Nixon: "Since the Protestant voters outnumber the Catholics three to one, you might concentrate on solidifying the Protestant vote. It is imperative for you to have as your running mate someone in the Protestant church, someone the Protestant church can rally behind enthusiastically."[41] Finally, Graham twice told Nixon that "God would give [him] supernatural wisdom" and cause him to win the election.[42]

There was monolithic sentiment for Nixon on evangelical college campuses. At Billy Graham's alma mater, Wheaton College, students and faculty voted 95 percent for Nixon (570–30). William Martin explains: "On the campus of Evangelical colleges, students expressing a preference for Kennedy were open to accusations of spiritual laxity. At Wheaton College prejudice made the short leap to overt discrimination, as students favoring Nixon were permitted free use of the college service to tout their candidate, while the few Kennedy backers were charged regular rates to mail their literature."[43]

While Graham lay low during the campaign, he turned up at a Nixon campaign rally in Columbia, South Carolina, just before Election Day and delivered the invocation. But in his autobiography, *Just As I Am* (San Francisco: Harper, 1997), Graham proclaimed that other Baptists had opposed Kennedy but that he had not.

Official Catholic Reaction

Catholic magazines kept a low profile, not wanting to be seen as partisan. *Catholic World*, the century-old Paulist Fathers monthly, put smiling pictures of both candidates on its pre–election issue. Both candidates emphasized positive values. *America* and *Commonweal*, the twin weeklies for liberal and intellectual Catholics, concentrated on church-state issues. Both hit hard at anti–Catholicism and stressed American Catholic loyalty to the American principle. *Commonweal* was pro–Kennedy but did not endorse him officially as it had Adlai Stevenson in 1952.

The *Sign* reprinted a Catholic bishop's proclamation. Archbishop Karl J. Alter of Cincinnati issued a statement denying that Catholics in America "will use religious toleration here to gain the ascendancy" or "to deprive our fellow citizens of freedom of religion or conscience.... We seek no privileged status; we proclaim our full adherence to the provisions of the Constitution as of now as well as for the future."⁴⁴

America, the distinguished Jesuit weekly, was critical of Kennedy's *Look* article in 1959 and rebuked him (as they were to do again in early 1962):

> Our own reaction to the controverted *Look* interview is one of impatience at the earnest Massachusetts Senator's efforts to appease bigots, rather than of disagreement with the positive points he made. A Catholic political candidate, if he must make a profession of his faith, should not seem to give quarter to religious bigotry, even at the risk of having his words distorted. We were somewhat taken aback, for instance, by the unvarnished statement that "whatever one's religion in his private life ... nothing takes precedence over his oath...." Mr. Kennedy doesn't really believe that. No religious man, be he Catholic, Protestant or Jew, holds such an opinion.⁴⁵

The Catholic bishops kept a low profile during the campaign, not wanting to bring more opprobrium on themselves. The words "Roman hierarchy" had become virtual swear words among anti–Kennedy zealots. A number of sophisticated and politically sagacious observers suggested that some bishops would have preferred Nixon, who was seen as more favorable to church interests than Kennedy, who was likely to be independent. Kennedy, it was thought, would bend over backwards to keep his distance from church leaders, while Nixon would seek their support. New York's Cardinal Francis Spellman almost certainly favored Nixon. He rode in the motorcade with President Eisenhower, who was making a last-minute campaign appearance for Nixon in New York.

Boston's Cardinal Richard Cushing became the semi-official Kennedy family chaplain. He frequently endorsed Kennedy's public statements on church-state relations and fought hard for a declaration favoring religious liberty as a universal principle at the Second Vatican Council. Cushing worked tirelessly for better interfaith relations. (His brother-in-law was Jewish.) When the Puerto Rican bishops issued their ill-timed and soon-to-be repudiated statement on religion in politics, Cushing shot back: "For ecclesiastical authority here to dictate the political voting of citizens ... has never been a part of our history and I pray God that it never will be."⁴⁶

On October 5 "A Statement on Religious Liberty by American Catholic laymen," signed by 166 prominent Catholics from every walk of life, was published. It was the clearest defense of religious freedom and

Senator John F. Kennedy and Cardinal Richard J. Cushing (John F. Kennedy Presidential Library and Museum, Boston).

separation of church and state ever issued by an American Catholic group. It was widely and deservedly praised.[47]

Nixon's Role

Vice President Richard Nixon's campaign was ambivalent on the religious issues. Openly he denounced religious prejudice (except against atheists) and urged voters to ignore his and Senator Kennedy's religious affiliation. But a recent study of the campaign, using long-ignored primary source documents, revealed that Nixon worked sub rosa with anti–Catholic underground groups led by an obscure former Republican congressman from the Missouri Ozarks, O.K. Armstrong. Armstrong rallied fellow Baptist businessmen to bankroll a campaign designed solely to stir up religious animosity against JFK. Armstrong "had built an impressive informal network that reaches into many corners of the Protestant world," writes professor Shaun Casey.[48] Casey notes the following: "With no sense of irony, the man who had helped the Southern Baptist Convention to pass a resolution calling for elected officials to be free of pressure and coercion from religious leaders set out a grand strategy to use religious leaders to build a grassroots campaign to pressure Protestants to vote against a Catholic."[49] Armstrong was assisted by Carr Collins, a Texas insurance man; Albert Hermann of the Republican National Committee; and W.R. Smith, an aide to Arkansas governor Orval Faubus, a segregationist Democrat. Both Collins and Hermann had direct ties to Nixon.

Nixon drew closer to clergy as the campaign entered its home stretch, receiving a mid–October endorsement from Mormon Church president David McKay. Casey summed up Nixon's role as follows: "From a purely Machiavellian perspective, Nixon had managed the issue well. By employing Armstrong to clandestinely aid the native anti–Catholicism of large swaths of the Protestant population, he had fanned those flames in secret.... By constantly saying that he would not raise the religion issue, Nixon was able to remind Protestants of their fears while preserving his innocence."[50] On the Sunday before the election, Nixon urged voters to ignore religion once again. "It was a thinly veiled means of raising Kennedy's Catholicism one last time on the eve of the election," writes Casey.[51]

Nixon's ambivalence was telling. He received the tacit support of New York's Cardinal Francis Spellman, and he retained as a close political counselor Father John Cronin, who encouraged Nixon to speak before numerous Catholic groups and to visit Pope Pius XII at the Vatican in 1957. Apparently, he hoped to win Catholic and anti–Catholic votes.

The role of New York's Cardinal Francis Spellman is revealing. Spellman's biographer, John Cooney, had this to say:

> In 1960 the Cardinal was seventy-one years old, and one of the realities of his age was that there barely seemed to be enough time to hold on to the present, let alone rush to embrace the future. The young Spellman who had excitedly awaited the emergence of a powerful America and a powerful Church had seen his desires fulfilled as reasonably as possible in a world where the future could never really be controlled. Now, Spellman wanted to support a presidential candidate who gave him guarantees, not slogans about idealism. The fact that one of the candidates was Catholic made no difference to Spellman. The Cardinal was for Richard M. Nixon.[52]

2. The Kennedy Campaign and the Issue of Religion

Senator John F. Kennedy speaks from the lectern at the Alfred E. Smith Dinner held at the Waldorf-Astoria in New York City, 19 October 1960. Also pictured (L–R): Charles H. Silver, Francis Cardinal Spellman, and Vice President Richard Nixon (photograph by Jack Schildkraut in the John F. Kennedy Presidential Library and Museum, Boston).

Cooney noted that Spellman and many conservative bishops "opposed Kennedy for his political positions," particularly his refusal to support every anti–Communist measure proposed in Congress: "Spellman and conservative Catholics generally were worried that Communism as an issue was losing its impact." Finally, he wrote, "Spellman had known Nixon since his days as a prosecutor of Alger Hiss. The Cardinal's politics had always been close to those of the Republican, who always treated Spellman with an almost exaggerated deference."[53]

Kennedy Perseveres

Kennedy himself continued to address the issue on the campaign trail, using both rational and, occasionally, emotional arguments to answer critics.

He disarmed a heckler at a rally in Modesto, California, on September 9, who asked if Kennedy believed all Protestants were heretics. Kennedy replied, "No, and I hope you don't believe all Catholics are." He constantly stressed the Constitution's no-religious-test principle in Article VI and the formal, institutional separation of religion and government in the First Amendment.

Kennedy's brother and campaign director, Robert F. Kennedy, remarked, "Right now, religion is the biggest issue in the country." His brother, he said, would try to clarify the issues "by going out and preaching religious liberty and church-state separation himself."[54] Kennedy reiterated his pledge to resign if religious convictions ever conflicted with his oath of office, however remote that might be. He told an enthusiastic crowd at the Louisville Fair Grounds on October 5 that "the President of the United States, in fact, could be impeached if he permitted improper pressures to be brought to bear upon him from any source, including a particular religious group."[55] He said it again in Manchester, New Hampshire, on election eve: "If I permitted an improper influence to be brought to bear in the conduct of my public office, if I permitted my church or Pope to attempt to direct me in meeting my public responsibility, I would properly be subject to impeachment."[56]

In the campaign's home stretch, JFK received some welcome support from religious and human relations groups. Episcopal bishop Richard Emrich of Michigan criticized the "religious underworld" that continued to harp on issues even though JFK "had made himself completely clear on church-state relations. One wonders whether those who keep bringing up the issue can read and write." Denunciations of religious bigotry came from the Chicago Board of Rabbis, the Jewish Labor Committee, the Pittsburgh City Commission on Human Relations, and the leader of the Northern Masons, George Bushnell. (Southern Masons were relentlessly anti–Kennedy). The Lancaster, Pennsylvania, Mennonite Conference also urged its 13,000 members not to be influenced by the religious issue in casting their ballots. (Leaders can say one thing, but followers don't always agree, as the huge Mennonite vote against Kennedy in Pennsylvania would suggest.) The *Wall Street Journal* also criticized Protestant clergy for doing just what they deplored, i.e., getting involved in partisan politics.

While the Republican National Committee avoided discussion of the religious issue in its publications, the Democratic National Committee issued a seven-page "Memorandum" including Kennedy's official statements on separation of church and state, an ambassador to the Vatican, aid to parochial schools, birth control programs in foreign policy and other issues of concern to voters.

One of the most exciting and historically significant campaigns for the White House had come to an end. Now the decision was in the hands of America's voters.

CHAPTER 3

The Propaganda War: An Analysis

At this juncture it might be appropriate to wonder why there was so much concern about a president's personal religious affiliation. Before Kennedy, American presidents approached religion in a variety of ways: skeptical (Jefferson), uninterested (Grant), pious (Garfield and B. Harrison), problematical (Lincoln) and many points in between. Some carefully separated their public and private religious lives. Some dealt with church-state disputes as president, in such questions as congressional chaplaincies, incorporation of churches as legal entities, distribution of federal land for churches, appointment of Catholic and Jewish chaplains to the armed forces, appropriation of federal funds for religious missions to Indians, religious messages on coinage and delicate diplomatic negotiations with the Vatican. Presidents prior to Kennedy varied greatly in what might be called religious style, use of religious rhetoric in inaugural and other addresses, church attendance and involvement in religious activities.

But all were Protestant. And that minimal statement seems to have loomed large in the everyday American citizens' conception of requirements for presidential office, despite what Article VI of the Constitution said in its forthright ban on religious tests for public office. This may have resulted, in part at least, from the undefined role of the president as the High Priest of American Civil Religion, an amorphous concept to be sure, but a real one. In a seminal essay appearing in 1967, sociologist Robert N. Bellah argued forcefully that "an elaborate and well-institutionalized civil religion" existed in America "alongside of and rather clearly differentiated from the churches."[1]

In an insightful study Robert Alley defined civil religion as "the normal expectation of a nation state ... that results from the powerful personalities of leaders in a given time, most particularly the Presidents."[2] He continues: "For the United States the rise of any civil religion is directly affected in character and form by the quality of religion exemplified by the President as chief administrator."[3] Alley was describing what had been the prevailing pattern in U.S. civil religion, faulting it at times for descending into "Messianism," a kind of blending of religion into American exceptionalism and intimations of national righteousness.[4]

Many Americans saw this vague civil religion as uniquely Protestant and as linked organically to the nation's predominant Protestant character. Whether a Catholic president could fit into an increasingly narrow mold was an unspoken question as the 1960 electoral cycle loomed. Alley asserted that "in many ways the sixties might justifiably be described as the twilight of the traditional church."[5] Therefore, "Eisenhower pietism was the last gasp of the Protestant era in America."[6] Alley also argued that "a non-doctrinal civil religion" had become "a substitute for the faded Protestant establishment."[7] As a consequence, defenders of the old establishment would do everything in their power to preserve it, especially when a serious and well qualified candidate who happened to be a Catholic was nominated for the highest office in the land.

Kennedy's stand against religious block voting was ignored by large numbers of his supporters and opponents. Many Catholics, who might otherwise not have supported JFK, voted for him to end the unspoken Protestant monopoly on the White House and to assure themselves that they were first-class citizens of the Republic. Others may have been repulsed by the shrill and irrational tone of Kennedy's religious critics and decided to cast a vote against bigotry and for inclusiveness. Many Protestants voted to prevent a member of a feared and disliked religious rival — the main one in their eyes — from becoming the nation's chief executive. Some may have felt more secure with a Protestant in the White House, while others were casting a purely religious vote and making a religious choice, a statement that their religion was the better one by voting against Kennedy. Some Protestant voters may have exemplified what sociologists call "status anxiety," which occurs when a group — religious, racial or ethnic — fears that its hard-earned status in society is threatened by another group. Sorting out political motivations is always difficult for analysts, and there were no exact polls that probed the reasons for a voter's choice in 1960.

Looking at the election returns in depth, as this book does, enables us to discern that religion outweighed income, race and ethnicity in many, if not most, instances and was a better predictor of the presidential vote outcome than other factors.

This book stresses two points. One is that the religious factor was more important in determining the outcome of the 1960 election than previous historians, political scientists or election specialists thought. Secondly, the depth of anti–Catholic, anti–Kennedy voting was much greater, particularly in rural America, than previously thought, and this religious backlash nearly cost the Massachusetts senator election as America's 35th president.

The Fair Campaign Practices Committee (FCPC) was the primary agency that collected anti–Catholic publications during the 1960 campaign. They identified 392 pamphlets and booklets, which are in the permanent special collections division of Georgetown University's Lauinger Library. FCPC leaders estimated that these materials reached 20 to 25 million people. And as good as their collection sources were, they may not have gathered all of the material that was in circulation.

FCPC officials concluded that 65 percent of the publications were either "unfair, dishonest or vile," while 35 percent were "responsible"[8] critiques of the Catholic Church. Even the allegedly responsible material took the position that Senator Kennedy's election would constitute a setback to American democracy because his church was a committed foe of enlightenment and freedom.

Some of the pamphlets addressed issues separating Catholics and Protestants in the 1950s, crudely expressed as "beer, bingo and birth control." Protestants apparently opposed the first two and favored the third, while Catholics favored or at least tolerated the first two and opposed the third. (The nonreligious favored all of them.) These differences in popular morality crept into the interreligious dialogues of the era and there was a kernel of truth to them. Protestant voters and legislatures restricted access to liquor and gambling in Kansas and Oklahoma and in other communities, while Catholic voters kept birth control illegal in a 1948 referendum in Massachusetts. Predominantly Catholic legislatures in Connecticut and Massachusetts made birth control illegal until the Supreme Court made it legal in 1965 under a new concept of privacy.

Within a decade these issues dissipated. Fewer Prohibition-style laws survived at the ballot box and in state legislatures or county councils, and lotteries became the rage in most states, where a desire for revenue outweighed moral scruples. These "culture war" issues, often central to the Protestant-Catholic clashes in politics leading up to the 1960 election, slowly vanished, only to be replaced by newer ones.

The frequent references to a Catholic takeover of America's political processes and establishment of a totalitarian government show a complete lack of knowledge of U.S. history and of fundamental civic and governmental safeguards. All of the references are to obscure Vatican documents. To the authors of these references, it is almost as if American Catholics do not exist or never existed. There is no acknowledgment that a Catholic, Charles Carroll of Carrollton, who was highly esteemed by George Washington, signed the Declaration of Independence. Catholics who signed the Constitution and served in presidential cabinets or on the Supreme Court were ignored. Nor are there any quotations from U.S. Catholic leaders who supported separation of church and state and religious liberty, such as Cardinal James Gibbons, Archbishop John England and others. The authors of these diatribes never admitted that Catholics had served in Congress, state legislatures, and state judiciaries over the years and that no credible evidence existed that they advanced hidden sectarian agendas. Constant references to past events in other lands made for a very unbalanced presentation of how the U.S. political system works.

California was the place of location for 60 of the anti–Catholic pamphlets and broadsides, followed by Pennsylvania with 41 and Minnesota with 35. These three states accounted for almost half (136) of the known locations (288) gathered by FCPC. There were 104 pieces of literature without clear geographic locations. Texas was the fourth largest distribution with 20 pieces, followed by New York (17), the District of Columbia (16), Illinois (11), New Jersey (9), Tennessee (8), Florida (6) and Missouri (6). Materials originated in 31 states and the District of Columbia, while 19 states had none. Regionally, 74 originated in the Northeast, 48 in the South, 64 on the Pacific Coast, 41 from the Midwest, 21 from the Great Lakes, 16 from the Border States, 8 from the Rocky Mountains and 16 from the District of Columbia (see Table):

Locations of Origin of Anti-Catholic Materials

State	Number	State	Number
California	60	Nebraska	4
Pennsylvania	41	Alabama	3
Minnesota	35	North Carolina	3
Texas	20	Ohio	3
New York	17	Oklahoma	3
District of Columbia	16	Arkansas	2
Illinois	11	Connecticut	2
New Jersey	9	Kansas	2
Tennessee	8	Maryland	2
Missouri	6	Michigan	2
Florida	6	Oregon	2
Colorado	5	Utah	2
Georgia	5	Washington	2
Indiana	5	Arizona	1
Kentucky	5	New Hampshire	1
Massachusetts	4	South Carolina	1

Sermons

A considerable number of the anti–Kennedy pamphlets circulating in 1960 were reprints of sermons delivered from many of the nation's pulpits — from renowned clergy and obscure alike.

W.A. Criswell's blistering July 3 attack on Kennedy, which lambasted "Roman Catholicism's bloody hand" and predicted a Kennedy victory would lead to "the death of a free church in a free state," was widely reproduced, mainly by Doniger & Raughley of Great Neck, New York, an obscure publisher in a well-to-do town on Long Island. The pamphlet was mailed anonymously, according to an investigation initiated by the U.S. Senate Subcommittee on Privileges and Elections. "The Roman Catholic institutional hierarchy is not only a religion, it is a political tyranny," the Baptist preacher thundered.

Dr. Harold A. Bosley, author and pastor of First Methodist Church in Evanston, Illinois, delivered an influential sermon, "Why I Cannot Now Vote for a Roman Catholic for President," on February 28 that was reprinted and distributed by his church. Bosley emphasized "the ambiguities if not outright contradictions which exist in Roman Catholic thought on both the principle and the practice of separation of Church and State and the meaning of religious freedom." He also cited five events in the previous two decades which undermined harmonious Protestant-Catholic relationships: "(1) in 1939, the question of Roosevelt's appointment of Myron Taylor as his personal representative at the Vatican; (2) the effort of American Catholic Bishops to have non–Catholic missionaries withdrawn from Latin America; (3) the drive for aid to parochial schools; (4) Truman's attempt in 1951 to name Mark Clark ambassador to the Vatican; and (5) the steadily worsening relations between the Roman Catholic and other churches." Bosley reiterated these points in the October 26 issue of *Christian Century.*

Herschel H. Hobbs, minister of the First Baptist Church of Oklahoma City (whose pastor in 1928, Mordecai Fowler Ham, lambasted Al Smith), claimed in "Who Is a Bigot," an August 14 sermon, that Protestants had genuine concerns about their continued religious freedom if Kennedy became president.

"Why Baptists and Protestants Fear a Catholic President," a sermon delivered on June 19 by Dr. James E. Davidson, pastor of South Avondale Baptist Church in Birmingham, Alabama, warned that Catholic leaders desire to control the government and that there would always be a "conflict of interest" between ecclesiastical directives and civil laws. The hierarchy does not really believe in religious freedom for others, Davidson charged. An odd charge is that public displays of the Catholic faith would be widespread if a Catholic were president, suggesting that the pastor did not really believe in free exercise of religion or that he feared Catholics would gain an unfair advantage in the media (echoing a charge often made at that time that Hollywood films were sympathetic to Catholicism).

"Roman Catholicism and Our Next President" is a reprint of an August 14 sermon by the Rev. Thomas Hansen, pastor of First Baptist Church in Fort Lauderdale, Florida. It emphasizes private judgment and religious liberty, which are, he says, denied to Protestants in Catholic countries. The similarly titled "Roman Catholicism and the Presidency," by the Rev. Gilbert M. Beenken, of Oliver Presbyterian Church in Minneapolis, castigates the hierarchy and warns against the specter of clericalism, or the intervention in public life by Roman Catholic clergy.

Billy Graham's father-in-law, L. Nelson Bell, was unequivocally opposed to the election of a Catholic president, and he outlined his position in a sermon delivered on August 21 at Montreat, North Carolina (which Graham's daughter described as a "home for retired Presbyterian missionaries").

Bell repeated his views at the Peale-organized meeting in Washington, D.C., on September 7. It was reprinted by the *Presbyterian Journal* in Asheville, North Carolina.

"An Issue to Be Faced" reports a sermon given some time during the election season by the Rev. Henry C. Bealty, pastor of First Methodist Church in Gering, Nebraska. It focuses on the alleged incompatibility between Protestant views and Vatican positions on the proper roles of church and state. Beatty says Catholic churchmen try to dominate political discussions in such countries as Argentina, Paraguay and Spain. Both presidential candidates, he says, should oppose public aid to faith-based schools, uphold separation of church and state, refuse to send an ambassador to the Vatican and use foreign aid funds to promote birth control programs in overpopulated countries.

Harold E. Lindsey's July 27 sermon at First Baptist Church in Waco, Texas, was reprinted as "The Issue Before Us" by the Scottish Rite Masons in Portland, Oregon, and received wide distribution in Texas. Lindsey claimed that JFK could not withstand pressures from his church, which would always insinuate itself into public issues. The First Amendment to the Constitution would be threatened, and ecclesiastical pressures would influence family life and medical care decisions.

Another famous sermon from June 5, "Religion, Politics and the Presidency," was delivered by Harold J. Ockenga at the Park Street Church in Boston, the largest evangelical church in New England. The scholarly cleric emphasized the alleged incompatibilities between Catholic teaching on the proper relationship between church and state and the American system. Ockenga claimed that a new era of Roman Catholic domination of America would surely result from Kennedy's election.

Robert P. Gates, minister of the First Presbyterian Church in Peoria, Illinois, preached "Religion and the Presidency" from his pulpit on March 13. He said that the U.S. Constitution grew out of a Protestant theological understanding and that no Catholic candidate for the presidency was acceptable (this was the sermon that Paul Simon criticized in his writings).

Gaye L. McGlothlen, pastor of Nashville's Immanuel Baptist Church, warned on September 11 that an intricate and detailed Vatican plan to dominate America would be significantly advanced if Kennedy became president. He said the Vatican must issue the following declaration: "Our policy in the U.S. will be different; we will not strive for union of church and state there; we will cease political pressure for tax funds for our schools; and we will stop receiving those political favors now granted to us."

Magazines

The *Saints Herald's* July 11 issue included "Dangers of Complacency" by Wallace Smith, which warned that Catholic leaders would dictate to Catholic officials, including the president.

The fundamentalist weekly newspaper, *The Sword of the Lord*, in Wheaton, Illinois, attacked JFK directly in its September 16 issue — "Kennedy for President?"— with evangelist Robert L. Sumner answering in the negative.

The Minneapolis-based weekly *Sunshine News* for August 25 published W.A. Criswell's "Kennedy and the Vatican," which suggested that the senator could not resist pressures from the Holy See. *Sunshine News* was published by the River Lake Tabernacle.

The Voice of Freedom, a Nashville-based monthly, lambasted Catholics in general and Kennedy in particular on four occasions. In July 1959 an editorial warned that when Catholics dominate the U.S. the voters would turn to communism. In November 1959 an editorial, "Glamour Candidates and the Dilemma of Dual Loyalty," maintained that no Catholic candidate could be a loyal American and a loyal Catholic at the same time. In September 1960 the editor officially opposed JFK's election, mixing religion with political conservatism by claiming that Kennedy was too sympathetic to labor unions and lacked experience (though his 14 years in Congress far exceeded the public service of many previous presidents). Another article in the September issue accused Kennedy of trying to deceive the American people by claiming independence from the Vatican. A final editorial in October, "Roman Catholicism Is More Than a Religion," says it all.

The Voice of Healing, a monthly published in Dallas, devoted its September issue to a review of the Inquisition and the doctrine of papal infallibility written by long-time anti–Catholic crusaders Harry Hampel and Gordon Lindsay.

The Pentecostal Evangel's October 2 issue published a sermon by Pastor Marcus Gaston of the Calvary Assembly in Inglewood, California. It was reprinted as "The Central Issue Concerning a Catholic for President," and the reverend said that Catholicism is an "aggressive, militant political body,

Typical anti–Catholic literature that circulated during the 1960 campaign (author's collection).

with the avowed intention of usurping control of government in every country possible."

The *Gospel Advocate*, a weekly published in Nashville, attacked Kennedy twice, claiming in its August 11 issue that he supported public funds for parochial schools and in September 22 that he "refuses to deny the doctrine of mental reservation," meaning that he would lie with impunity.

The monthly *Gospel Defender* in Florence, Alabama, warned that Rome had long coveted the White House, and included a long-discredited quote from Abraham Lincoln to substantiate its claim.

A Greenville, Texas, publication, *Gospel Hour News*, said on August 31 that "Kennedy's Millions has [sic] the smell of whiskey."

THE BIG QUESTION... A Vatican Victory in the U. S. A.?

By Don W. Hillis

Here is another book from the pen of Dr. Hillis, a courageous and faithful witness for Christ.

Its Table of Contents includes:

I. What Your Vote for a Roman Catholic President May Do.
II. How Fast Is Rome Moving?
III. Are There Any Protestants in Congress?
IV. Protestant Pastors Build Roman Catholic Cathedrals!
V. Except They Repent.

In this book the author takes up the outlook for public schools, evangelistic campaigns, suppression of the Bible, etc. in the event of a Vatican victory in the U.S.A.

Read this booklet for additional information.

PRICE 35c

Published by
DUNHAM PUBLISHING COMPANY
Findlay, - Ohio

Typical anti–Catholic literature that circulated during the 1960 campaign (author's collection).

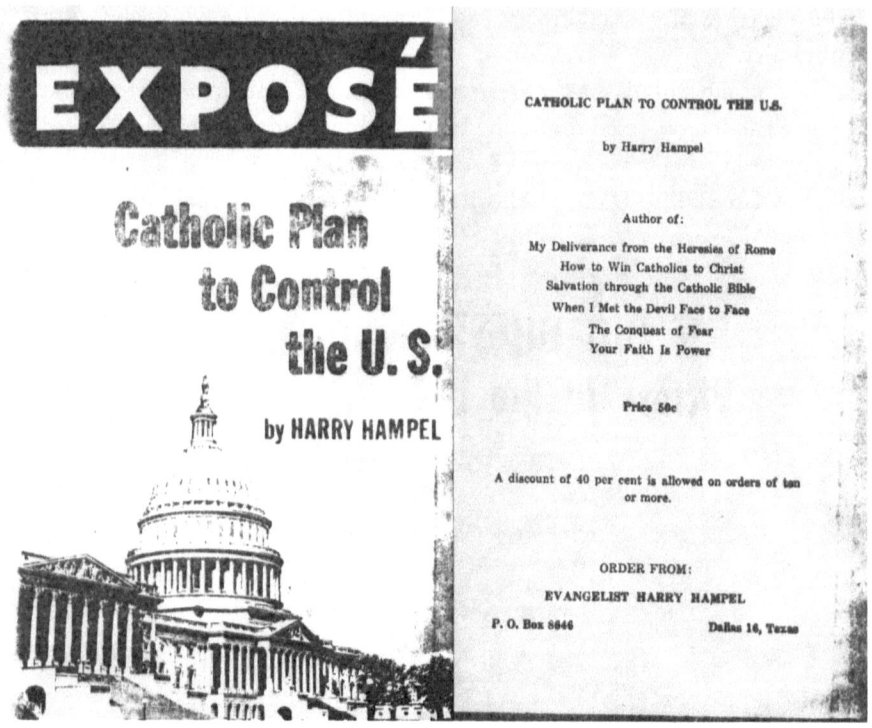

Harry Hampel was a prolific, anti–Catholic agitator whose pen was active before, during and after the 1960 campaign (Fair Campaign Practices Committee Collection, Manuscripts Division, Special Collections, Lauinger Library, Georgetown University).

The New Age, the monthly journal of the powerful Scottish Rite Masonic Order's Southern Jurisdiction, in its February issue blasted the idea of a Catholic president. The order's Sovereign Grand Commander, Luther A. Smith, argued that the blessings of civil and religious liberty bequeathed by the Founding Fathers would be compromised and lost if the Vatican controlled the U.S. presidency. Smith hit even harder in the October issue in "Is It Religion or a Trojan Horse?" Smith claimed that Catholicism yearned for material wealth and political power. The Masonic-produced materials were widely distributed by other groups in the campaign to stop Kennedy.

An old voice from the past surfaced in Los Angeles. The Rev. Robert P. Shuler, pastor of a prominent Methodist church, had been active in the anti–Al Smith campaign in 1928, lambasting the New York governor at every turn in pulpit and on radio. Thirty-two years later he was back with a similar warning in "Religion and Our Country," which appeared in the monthly journal *The Methodist Challenge* in July. Apparently, nothing had changed in Shuler's view of the unacceptability of a Catholic president.

A Dalton, Georgia, weekly, the *Southerner*, editorialized in its July 14

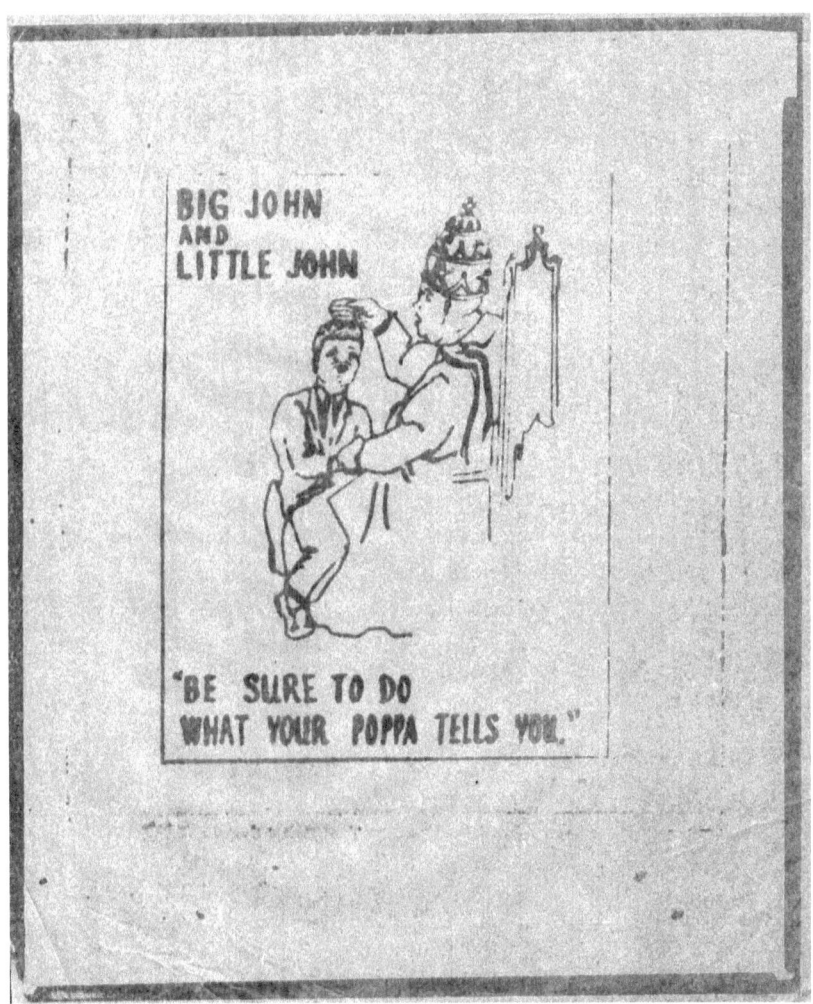

This crude anti–Catholic cartoon accusing JFK of being a papal stooge appeared in *The Challenger* and other religious publications (Fair Campaign Practices Committee Collection, Manuscripts Division, Special Collections, Lauinger Library, Georgetown University).

issue. "We Won't Vote for a Catholic" chided Protestants for not speaking out against a Catholic candidate.

The United Church Herald, early on in the campaign, before JFK had even won a primary, published "My Reservations About Voting for a Roman Catholic for U.S. President." Roy Pearson, dean of the Andover Newton Theological School, made the highly unusual, and as it turned out erroneous, charge that the liberal faction within U.S. Catholicism would be set back if Kennedy won.

The Pentecostal Free Will Baptist Messenger's August issue, published in Clinton, North Carolina, claimed that Catholics were committed to the destruction of church-state separation, while *The Prophetic Ensign*'s September issue from Eustis, Florida, charged that "Romanism" was a far greater threat to the free world than was Communism. An old anti–Catholic quarterly, *The Protestant Journal*, warned readers in its July issue that the "Roman Catholic hierarchy and the Vatican stand before the world as a secular, political state, ruled as a dictatorship by a secular ruler, an Italian politician — the Pope." Its author, Harry Hampel, was a long-time anti–Catholic crusader.

The *Watchman-Examiner*, a Baptist weekly, published two critical articles. On September 15, Gordon Palmer, past president of Eastern Baptist Theological Seminary, quoted papal encyclicals that conflicted with American constitutional ideals. The September 29 issue included "The Catholic-Protestant Dilemma," by Sterling L. Price, pastor of the Third Baptist Church in St. Louis, Missouri. Price argued that Catholic authorities would prevent Kennedy from asserting independence from church directives.

C.R. Daley's "Political Dilemma for Papists," said that Baptists would regret it if they did not oppose Kennedy but would probably be blamed for his defeat if they did. This article appeared in a Kentucky weekly, the *Western Recorder*, on August 18.

The *Baptist Examiner*'s October issue, published in Ashland, Kentucky, engaged in some rhetorical excesses in "Hail Mary" by John R. Gilpin, who wrote, "I would consider myself a traitor to the fifty million Baptists who have been killed by various means of torture at the hands of Roman Catholics if I failed to lift my voice and pen against Mr. Kennedy." Another article in the same issue, "Why I Would Not Vote for a Roman Catholic Candidate," by Bob L. Ross said that Catholics are unilaterally opposed to Baptist principles and should therefore be ineligible to receive Baptist votes.

Christian Heritage, the monthly publication of Christ's Mission, devoted its November 1960 issue to three attacks on the Catholic Church, though this was its stock in trade and not directly related to the 1960 election. Dr. Bernard Ramm's "A Critique of Authority in Roman Catholicism" criticized papal infallibility, while Francis J. Kieda's "Roman Catholic Missions in Latin America" warned that the Papal Volunteers and other Catholic missionaries are trying to check the growth of evangelical Protestantism in the region. The usual memoir of an ex–Catholic was by a Haitian, Jacques Montas, who attacked his former religion for its interference in politics. *Christian Heritage* began to warn of the dangers of a Catholic president as early as its March and April 1959 issues in articles by J.B. Rowell. Reprinted in the *Sunday School Times*, they reached a wide audience and were reissued in pamphlet form as "Shall a Roman Catholic Be President?" The answer was a resounding no.

The *Church Herald and Holiness Banner*, a fundamentalist weekly published in Overland Park, Kansas, devoted its July 7 issue to fourteen reasons why Catholicism is an enemy to American-style democracy.

The Church Speaks, a monthly published in Portland, Oregon, published a dire "warning" in its September issue from an old-time anti–Catholic zealot, Brigadier General Herbert G. Holdridge. The general, who was something of a nativist, warned against foreign-born dictators, i.e., the Vatican, who will subvert the U.S. Constitution if Catholics gain political power.

A highly unusual twist in the anti–Catholic argument was found in the October issue of *The Abaree*, published in Enid, Oklahoma. Its editor claimed that a Catholic president would lead the U.S. to a war with communist-atheist Russia in order to further the foreign policy aims of the Vatican.

The *Advent Christian Witness*, a monthly publication of the Advent Christian Church, urged in its October issue that Kennedy should seek Vatican endorsement of his positions on church-state separation.

Organizational Statements

Concordia Publishing House, the official Lutheran Church-Missouri Synod publisher, issued "A Catholic President? The Predicament" by Carl

S. Meyer, a noted Lutheran writer. It was somewhat more irenical than most, but still suggested that any Catholic has a dual allegiance and expressed concern that a Catholic president would be subject to extreme pressures from religious officials.

Another eerie voice from the past, the Book and Bible House, originally based in Toledo, Ohio, and specializing in converting Catholics, returned in 1960, this time in Gainesville, Florida. Its leader, the Rev. Fred Junior, replaced L.J. King, "a converted Catholic," as he called himself. King was obsessed with "convent slaves" and the group republished an old bogus classic, *My Life in the Convent* by Margaret Shepherd, just in time for the 1960 election. Shepherd's book had been exposed as fanciful and inaccurate decades before.

Citizens for Religious Freedom, the "Peale group," issued a ten point enunciation of its concerns called "The Religious Issue." Even after disbanding, its warning was widely distributed:

1. Roman Catholicism is not only a religion to which many of our good friends belong; it is a political force in our society as well.

2. Roman Catholic doctrine and policy are ultimately incompatible with the principle of separation of church and state, the foundation of our freedoms.

3. Wherever Roman Catholicism is the religion of the majority, it attempts to suppress all other religious faiths, and uses secular governments and institutions as a means to impose its system upon the public.

4. The hierarchy insist on controlling laymen in civic and political affairs.

5. The candidate himself has admitted, in effect, that his Church does exert pressure on men in public affairs.

6. The candidate's promise that ecclesiastical pressures would not influence his conduct of the presidency, sincere as it may be, does not prove conclusively that he could fully resist such pressure.

7. The threat of excommunication is used by the hierarchy to enforce its demands on individual members.

8. Some Catholic public officials have used their offices to procure advantages for their Church.

9. There is no evidence that the Roman Catholic hierarchy in the

U.S. has any intention of changing its announced objective of procuring public funds and other special benefits for its schools, hospitals, businesses, and other institutions.

10. American citizens must decide individually, knowing the political power of the Roman Catholic hierarchy in the U.S., whether it is wise to elect a President who gives his allegiance to that system.

Osterhus Publishing Company in Minneapolis issued a stream of anti–Catholic tracts that were obviously designed to hurt Kennedy's chances, though most were not overtly political. The fiery ex-priest Emmett McLoughlin argued in "A Message to Catholics: Can Devout Catholics Be Loyal Americans?" that "an intelligent, loyal American cannot be a sincere, devout Catholic."

Vernon Blikstad, a Minneapolis insurance agent, blasted Kennedy by claiming that all good Catholics should vote for him — an unusual twist. This leaflet was almost laughable, urging Catholics to support Kennedy in order "to make our Holy Mother Mary the true First Lady of the Land." It was so absurd that Blikstad was kicked out of the Nixon campaign offices. No slacker in the sensationalist mode, Osterhus released "Washington Under the Sway of Romanism!" compiled by the Rev. Angelo Di Domenica, D.D., which claimed to have unearthed some letters written in 1936 and 1937 by Vatican agents outlining their intrigues in America. "The Wealthiest Body in the World," by an anonymous writer, depicted the Roman Catholic Church as a financial power.

The Convert, a small anti–Catholic organization based in the western Pennsylvania town of Clairton, published numerous pamphlets and a monthly journal lambasting the Catholic Church. The group's founder was a former priest, Joseph Zacchello. Typical was "Protestants in a Spiritual Stupor Breed Strong Roman Catholicism," which claimed that Catholicism was still a criminal conspiracy spawned in the Dark Ages. Because so many Catholics served in Congress, the military, schools, the media, and the F.B.I., their church was poised to take control of America. *The Convert* went over the edge when it published Zacchello's "To Kill Protestants," claiming the Catholic Church still believed in killing heretics.

Zacchello was busy during the 1960 campaign, as were the professional anti–Catholic organizations that began decades before. "The Pope for President" attacked the hierarchy and claimed that anyone who voted for JFK was really "voting the Pope into the White House." "A Roman Catholic for President: The Strategy of the Vatican" says the Vatican had carefully planned to take over the U.S. and would do so when the country became 51 percent Catholic. In the meantime Catholics would seek entry into public and political life and hoodwink Protestants into voting for them. Zacchello claimed that the bishops allowed Kennedy to take liberal positions on church-state issues as part of their smokescreen strategy to lull Americans into complacency. Zacchello's starting point was a critique of Illinois senator Paul Douglas' article, "A Catholic Can Become President," which appeared in the March 1959 issue of the popular magazine *Coronet*.

The National Association of Evangelicals, based in Wheaton, Illinois, was the unofficial leader of the Stop Kennedy effort. Its executive director, George L. Ford, warned that a Catholic president would have a difficult time extricating himself from the demands of the hierarchy. His "A Roman Catholic President" stressed the political activities of church leaders which would be inimical to evangelical interests and values.

Going even further, the NAE Board of Administration issued "A Statement of Concern" on October 11. It expressed a final warning that Protestants should vote against Kennedy solely because of his membership in a church that is hostile to American freedoms. The statement concluded:

> The religious issue in the present political campaign has been distorted. It must be made clear that the mode of worship exercised by any candidate for public office is not in question. The manner of a man's approach to God must be a matter of his own choosing. Nevertheless, when an ecclesiastical system advocates the use of government to pursue its particular religious objectives and asserts that it has the right to control the political actions of its adherents, the religious issue must be considered by the voter. The record of the Roman Catholic Church on these two points, despite wishful thinking to the contrary, is a matter of history — fully documented and well known. Failure of the Roman Catholic hierarchy to repudiate and abandon this interference both in private conscience and in the political affairs of governments impels non–Catholics to register their position in the current campaign.

The fraternal organization, the Masons, generally steered clear of partisan politics. But the prospect of a Catholic president exercised its leaders, and numerous publications from Masonic sources reached a wide audience. Typical were "Masonic Inspiration, Free and Independent Masonic News Bulletin," published in Morris Plains, New Jersey, in September, warning that "all America is aroused by the Catholic question" and claiming that the Vatican had long planned to subvert America by taking over the presidency. A similar view was expressed by the *Masonic Home Journal*, published by the Grand Lodge of Kentucky in October.

The *Scottish Rite Torch*, a Masonic monthly in Memphis, warned readers in its September issue that the "Church would change the Constitution" if Kennedy were victorious. The authors seemed unaware of the cumbersome process to which Constitutional amendments are subjected.

The Scottish Rite's Portland, Oregon, branch sent a letter, "Election Call to Citizens" by Leslie M. Scott, claiming that Kennedy was a loyal subject of the Vatican who could not resist its mandates.

The Assemblies of God and its *Pentecostal Evangel* magazine pounded the idea of a Catholic president. Its leader, Thomas F. Zimmerman, warned in "A Statement Regarding Electing a Roman Catholic to the Presidency" that whenever the Catholic Church control led the government, other religions suffered discrimination. In a related publication, "Revival Time's Election Bulletin," C.M. Ward said that there was an inherent conflict between Kennedy's proclamations and official Vatican policy.

The American Baptist Convention's Council on Christian Social Progress stressed that official Catholic policy on church and state differed dramatically from the positions of Senator Kennedy and wondered which one could be believed in "A Roman Catholic President?"

The Church of God, Cleveland, Tennessee, published Charles W. Conn's "A Roman Catholic President?" which warned that the Catholic hierarchy sought union of church and state and would deny religious freedom to others.

Luther W. Martin's "A Roman Catholic President?" published by the Bible School Press in Athens, Georgia, said there was a parallel between Communism and Catholicism, with both being inimical to American democracy.

The Liberal League, based in Philadelphia, claimed to be a rationalist, free-thinker group opposed to all institutional religion. But its left-of-center religion espoused right-of-center politics, a blend of Ayn Rand libertarianism and extreme right nativism. The September issue of its publication, *The Liberal: Bulletin of Friendship*, was devoted to an attack on Kennedy. Martin A. Larson, author of books attacking parochial schools and later involved in Holocaust-denial, claimed in "The Vatican Over the

White House" that a Catholic president would outlaw birth control, prohibit divorce, outlaw mixed marriages, and reverse the *McCollum* and *Everson* decisions that limited church involvement in public education. A Catholic chief executive would establish a Fascist and theocratic state and would persecute humanists, secularists and Masons.

Another author, Oscar Riddle, president of the American Rationalist Federation, warned that restrictions on birth control would weaken U.S. foreign aid programs, even though it was the Eisenhower administration that refused to include family planning in its programs overseas. The magazine also published Masonic leader Luther Smith's tirade, "Catholicism and the Presidency," which claimed that Catholics had a "dual allegiance" to the Papacy and the U.S.

Of all the critiques published, the one by Larson was the most thoroughly irrational (for a self–styled rationalist), reeked of nativism and lacked nuance and sophistication. The Liberal League represented a remarkable combination of far left religion and far right politics.

Christ's Mission, then located in Sea Cliff, New York, and later in Hackensack, New Jersey, was a long-established anti–Catholic outfit that specialized in converting Catholics to evangelical Protestantism. Its flamboyant monthly, originally called *The Converted Catholic,* was renamed *Christian Heritage.* The pamphlet "While America Sleeps" warned that the Catholic Church was the "world's largest hydra-headed religio-political corporation, which has absolute control of billions of dollars worth of real estate in the U.S., completely tax exempt, while it takes every advantage of American liberty and freedom to further its relentless campaign to ruin the Democracy which protects it."

An old-time anti–Catholic agitator, Leo H. Lehmann, published "Hoodwinking Protestants" through the *Christ's Mission* apparatus. Catholics wanted religious freedom only for themselves, he said, and would eventually become dominant if Protestants didn't wake up. Lehmann had published a number of anti-Catholic books earlier in the century, including his autobiography, *Out of the Labyrinth.*

Another publication, "The White House: A Vatican Outpost," quotes Walter Montano, an ex-priest and author of *Behind the Purple Curtain,* a famous anti–Catholic diatribe published in the 1940s. Montano said the Vatican coveted the U.S. presidency and would control any candidate of its faith. "Your Church and Your Candidates," by the Rev. Stuart P. Garver,

A CATHOLIC CONSTITUTION FOR AMERICA

PAPAL DIRECTIVES FOR
RULERS AND VOTERS

A HANDBOOK FOR CATHOLICS AND
NON CATHOLICS

By
JOHN J. U. ARRIEN

— 1 9 6 0

A typical publication of quotes from papal encyclicals and other writings purporting to outline a plan for Vatican control of American life and laws (Fair Campaign Practices Committee Collection, Manuscripts Division, Special Collections, Lauinger Library, Georgetown University).

warned that church authority would be invoked against any and all Catholic candidates.

Christ's Mission published numerous hard-hitting attacks on Catholicism, often reprinted from the past. In "Lincoln's Assassins," nineteenth century Baptist preacher Justin Dewey Fulton, of Boston's Tremont Temple, claimed that Lincoln's assassination was a Jesuit plot concocted in the Vatican. Fulton wrote a slew of anti–Catholic books, one of which, *Why Priests Should Wed*, ran afoul of the Comstock Law for obscenity and was banned from the U.S. mail for a while. Reprinting material like this shows the desperation of groups like Christ's Mission.

Another group, the Conversion Center, Inc., whose specialty was converting Catholics to Protestantism and was based in the Philadelphia suburb of Havertown, published "Who Says Refusal to Vote for a Roman Catholic Presidential Candidate Is Bigotry?" by Alexander O. Dunlap. Dunlap warned that the Catholic hierarchy was cleverly disguising its true aims of uniting itself with the organs of civil power. No Catholic should be trusted because the Church allows its members to lie under "the doctrine of mental reservation."

Freelancers

Some published material seems to have been privately produced by individuals with an axe to grind but no apparent connection to any group. Many were crudely written and produced. Some were relatively sophisticated, such as "A Catholic Constitution for America," written by John Arrien of Monterey Park, California. It included numerous out–of-context quotations from papal encyclicals and out–of-date theology texts that the compiler says threatened religious freedom and independent government. the Rev. Dennis J. Brown of Riverside, California, in "Catholic Political Power vs. Religious Liberty" warns that Roman Catholic Church teaching will inevitably lead to persecution and dictatorship. Harry F. Borleis of Baltimore in "Catholic for President?" contends that a Catholic president would be bound by canon law. An unknown outfit, Protestant Action, with a post office box in Los Angeles, says it all in "A Catholic President Can Mean Vatican Control of America."

From deep in Pennsylvania Dutch country in the town of Hanover came "Catholicism on Trial" by Ethel Meadows, calling Catholicism a religion that is inimical to truth. It was published by the Full Salvation Tract Society. Norman H. Wells described "The Catholic State" as repressive in a 12-page booklet issued by Central Baptist Church in Cincinnati.

W.O. Vaught, Jr., the pastor of Immanuel Baptist Church in Little Rock, Arkansas (attended by a young Bill Clinton), led anti–Kennedy rallies throughout Arkansas. In "The Issue of a Roman Catholic President," Vaught claimed that the Catholic lobby in Washington managed to get 90 percent of the Hill-Burton Act funds for Catholic hospitals. Catholic political influence in the State Department allegedly disfavored Protestant missionaries in Central and South America, where the author visited.

Something called the Faith, Prayer and Tract League of Grand Rapids, Michigan, issued a leaflet entitled "The Menace" by Syd Youngsma, which warned that the church was totalitarian and undemocratic. This was apparently distributed in Dutch-American neighborhoods. A similar publication, "The Menace of Roman Catholicism," by Earl West, devoted 23 pages to an attack on Catholicism as a supposed threat to democracy. It was printed by "Religious Book Service" in Indianapolis.

Numerous fly-by-night "publishers," usually with post office box numbers, arrived on the scene in 1960. Roy E. Cogdill of Lufkin, Texas, produced a 35-page booklet called "The Origins and Claims of Roman Catholicism." Cogdill said he wrote it to "affirm that Catholicism originated in apostasy, that it is not just a religious institution but is political as well, that its cardinal claims are false and its aims both un–Christian and un–American." The "Book and Tract Committee" in Minneapolis issued "Is Religion Only a Campaign Issue?" This said that any candidate who owes obedience to a foreign religious potentate is unqualified for any public office in the U.S.

Many freelancers published almost book-length examinations of the religious issue, often produced at home or printed with the author's home address. One such piece was "A Roman Catholic President? A Documented Research Report on a Vital Issue," by Philip McIlnay of Minneapolis. He claimed that Catholicism would become the official state religion and would restrict worship and education for non–Catholics. Citing Harold Fey's famous series of articles for *Christian Century* a decade before, McIlnay said the trends cited by Fey had intensified since 1950 when Fey warned that "Catholicism Can Win America."

Jack Odom, who used a box number in Fort Bragg, California, suggested in "A Roman Catholic for President?" that no Catholic could ever extricate himself from thralldom to a Fascist political system controlled by the Vatican. A similar view was expounded by James M. Tolle in a 16-page booklet entitled "A Roman Catholic President?" The Denver resident said there was an inherent conflict between American Constitutionalism and Catholicism, which only pretended to accept religious liberty for all as a matter of temporary expediency.

Claiming a Ph.D., Eugene Harrison of Wheaton, Illinois (a town often called the Evangelical Vatican), blasted "the stealthy and dangerous enemy, the Church of Rome," in a 16-page booklet called "Roman Catholicism Under the Searchlight." Using an interpretation of biblical prophecy long favored by certain fundamentalists, Harrison said the Catholic Church was "clad in the garments of religion and equipped with all the tools in the arsenal of totalitarianism" and that the church's wealth proved it was wicked.

Even in JFK's home state, a couple of freelancers urged his defeat. J.F. Murphy, who called himself a "Free-thinking Catholic," cited Massachusetts as a bad example to follow in "To All Who Love America and Religious Freedom." Murphy argued that all officeholders in the state were Catholic. In a wildly ambitious publication, George W. Adams of Pittsfield labeled the Catholic Church "the most wicked crime conspiracy of all time" in his oddly titled "To Wake Up Humanity by Calling the World's Biggest Bluff."

D.N. Jackson, editor of the *American Baptist* in Jacksonville, Texas, addressed the issues in a 24-page booklet, "Twelve Reasons Why I Will Not Vote for a Catholic for President of the United States." It was a standard critique of Catholic attempts to dominate state policy through coercion. Jackson claimed that Catholics were opposed to the public school system, though a majority of Catholic children attended them. He attacked Catholic marriage rules and regulations, though what that had to do with the presidential election was never spelled out. He also claimed that when Catholicism is the dominant religion in a country, people are likely to turn to Communism. This was a frequent charge made by critics of Catholicism. While possibly true to some extent for Poland, Czechoslovakia and Hungary, that argument ignored the Eastern Orthodox majority in Russia, Bulgaria, Rumania and Yugoslavia, the Muslim majority in Albania, and the Eastern religions that once dominated China, North Korea and Vietnam, as well as Lutheran influence in East Germany.

From the Extreme Right and the Extreme Left

Gerald L.K. Smith was a long-time anti–Semite and extreme rightist who headed the Christian Nationalist Crusade in Los Angeles (before it moved to Arkansas). In "Stop Kennedy — Why?" he said Kennedy was soft on Communism, was a stooge of labor unions, and was the scion of a whiskey-dealing family. According to Smith's biographer, Glen Jeansomme, "Smith opposed the nomination of Senator John F. Kennedy by Democrats but assured his followers that Kennedy could never be nominated or elected President. According to Smith, all of the Kennedys were whiskey-drinking whoremongers, fake Catholics, soft on Communism, and puppets of international Jews."[9]

James Harvey Johnson was an outspoken atheist leader who, while despising all religion, seemed to dislike the Catholic Church the most. In three brief pamphlets — "Religion, a Gigantic Fraud," "Religious Brain Stuffing," and "The Roman Catholic Church Is a Menace to American Liberty," with a post office box number in San Diego — Johnson singled out the Catholic Church as an ecclesiastical dictatorship bent on converting America and extinguishing all religious and political liberty.

Another voice from the left was Joseph Lewis of the Freethinkers of America, located in New York's Chelsea district, who asked, "Should an Avowed Roman Catholic Be Elected President of the U.S.?" This pamphlet was based on a radio message delivered in Miami on January 30. Lewis maintained that a Catholic would place his loyalty to the Pope above the Constitution. Though Kennedy would specifically deny this assertion, this pamphlet still circulated during the campaign.

A number of pamphlets accused Kennedy of being a crypto–Communist, or some sort of Catholic Communist. Either way, according to the pamphlets, he was unfit to be president of a democratic Protestant country. Typical was a three-part series by Dan Gilbert, of Upland, California: "Kennedy Is Not Fit to Be President," "The Pink Punk Pro–Red Record of Senator Kennedy," and "The True Inside Story of the Rigging and Fixing at the Democratic Convention in Los Angeles." Gilbert said Kennedy was not patriotic. (He, of course, ignored JFK's World War II service in the Navy.)

Jos. P. Kamp's "The Greater Danger," issued by Headlines in Westport, Connecticut, said that Kennedy favored socialism, communism and the welfare state. A similar attack on Kennedy's liberalism appeared in a monthly newspaper, the *Greater Nebraskan* in August.

Many freelance productions were apparently published by individuals from their homes, since home addresses or box numbers showed no organizational or group connections. Some merely listed the towns, such as O.C. Lambert of Winfield, Alabama, who published a 31-page booklet, "A Shocking Exposé from Official Catholic Documents," which was a repetition of out-of-date and out-of-context reprints.

One murky publication—"Should a Roman Catholic Be President? Would Liberties Be Lost?"—was written by Dr. David Calderwood, who claimed to be president of the California Christian Citizens Association in Lomita. It expressed opposition "to the system of government in that church which is completely undemocratic, and therefore, un–American, for the people have no voice whatsoever in the choice of their rulers, nor in determining the church's articles of faith and the substance of its worship. They owe unquestioning obedience to an autocratic, self-perpetuating hierarch." According to researcher Patricia Barrett, this was circulated at the Democratic National Convention in Los Angeles.

Radio

The Arizona firebrand, Emmett McLaughlin, gave a radio address in Phoenix, arguing that Catholic officialdom insists that its laws are above civil laws in every country. The concept of "mental reservation" means that Catholic candidates can lie with impunity. This was issued as a pamphlet called "Senator Kennedy's Oath of Office."

General Religious Press Coverage

The Catholic press tried to maintain neutrality in an election which increased tensions between religious groups and increased the spotlight on Catholicism as a religious group seeking full participation in American civic life. The Jesuit weekly *America* devoted at least 17 articles and editorials to the religious issue, beginning in March 1959. The editors thought the singling out of Catholic candidates was unfair, but they also urged the Vatican to adopt stronger, more unequivocal statements on religious liberty. The September 24, 1960, issue was almost entirely devoted to the campaign and to Kennedy's Houston speech. One article wryly encouraged Catholics "to keep their shirts on" and not take the constant attacks on the Church personally. Several articles explored the history and cyclical nature of anti–Catholic prejudice in U.S. history. A symposium in that issue brought seven distinguished Protestant, Catholic and Jewish scholars together for a kind of roundtable discussion. The famed Jesuit theologian and specialist on religious liberty, John Courtney Murray, contributed to the conversation.

The Paulist monthly, *Catholic World*, which began publication just after the Civil War, published political scientist Lawrence Fuchs' study of religious voting in U.S. presidential election history in its October issue. In December its editor, John B. Sheerin, criticized the Puerto Rican bishops' pastoral letter that appeared to encourage a religious bloc vote in that commonwealth's elections.

The liberal weekly edited by Catholic laymen, *Commonweal*, devoted 20 articles to the religious issue from May 6 through November 4. The articles were critical both of Protestant attacks on Kennedy and of Vatican insensitivity to American concerns about noninterference by clergy in politics. The articles emphasized Catholic opposition to bigotry of all kinds, noted the widely divergent views of Catholic public officials, and explored the diverse positions taken by Protestants on the election. *Commonweal* also deplored the Puerto Rican bishops' intervention in island politics. As a liberal magazine, *Commonweal* expressed sympathy for the Democratic platform and Kennedy's positions on most issues. It had, after all, endorsed Adlai Stevenson in 1952. But it remained officially neutral in 1960, as it had in 1956.

Several popular Catholic magazines noted the growing influence of religion on the campaign. *Ave Maria*'s May 28 issue included journalist Philip Scharper's "Why Protestants Fear Us," while *Jubilee*'s December issue featured Robert Hoyt's "Kennedy, Catholicism and the Presidency." The conservative *Homiletic and Pastoral Review* noted the "pitfalls of pluralism" in its September issue, which also published John Hardon's "A Catholic in the White House." Hardon was a Jesuit priest and author.

The scholarly journal *Social Order* published four articles by Jesuit authors, beginning in December 1959 and continuing in April, November and December 1960. They explored in great depth historical and legal issues related to religion in politics. The *American Ecclesiastical Review* in its January 1961 issue hoped for improved Protestant-Catholic relations, in an article titled "Now That the Election Is Over" by Francis J. Connell.

The *Sign*, a moderately liberal Catholic monthly, devoted two articles in its July issue to the religion question. Political scientist Jerome Kerwin probed "Why This Fear of the Church," while Cincinnati Archbishop Karl Alter argued that a Catholic could honorably discharge his duties in an impartial manner as president. The fall issue of the quarterly *Cross Currents* published a serious overview of the implications of raising religion questions, in Joseph Cunneen's "The Religious Issue and the Limits of National Purpose."

On the Protestant side, views varied widely. (Much of the strident hard-line anti–Catholic presentations have already been covered in the previous section.) *Christian Century*, the mainline Protestant journal, devoted at least 19 articles to the religion issue and seemed to switch back and forth from pro–Kennedy to anti–Kennedy. (At least it did not endorse Nixon, as it had endorsed Herbert Hoover in 1928.) The *Century* explored the issues thoroughly and devoted its October 26 issue to articles defending Kennedy by Charles R. Andrews and opposing him by Harold A. Bosley.

Another liberal Protestant weekly, *Christianity and Crisis*, resolutely defended JFK, while still raising serious questions about church-state relations and interfaith dialogue. Liberal Protestant John C. Bennett wrote three of the ten articles the magazine published between March 16, 1959, and November 28, 1960. Bennett hailed the election outcome in the last issue as a "triumph for American democracy." Liberal Presbyterians Robert McAfee Brown and Henry Van Dusen suggested there were some "grounds for misgivings" about American Catholicism but did not oppose Kennedy. Liberal Catholic Daniel Callahan discussed the interplay between freedom and authority in Catholicism in the October 3 issue. In the October 17 issue Minnesota Democratic senator Eugene McCarthy, who had made an eloquent nominating speech for Adlai Stevenson at the 1960 convention, endorsed Kennedy, while New York senator Kenneth Keating endorsed Nixon. A postelection issue on November 14 deplored "what the campaign did to religion."

Surprisingly, the more conservative journals *Christian Herald* and *Christianity Today* devoted little attention to the campaign or to the prospect of a Catholic chief executive. It may be that their overall posture of opposition to Roman Catholicism on a host of issues was so well known to readers that little new commentary was necessary. *Christianity Today* had published Methodist pastor C. Stanley Lowell's "Rising Tempo of Rome's Demands" and "If America Becomes 51% Catholic" in the late 1950s. They also published Lowell's "Protestant-Catholic Dialogue" in the October 24 number. In any event, they ignored the ecumenical dialogue and interpretive articles appearing in the more liberal magazines.

Several Presbyterian journals devoted quite a bit of text to the religion issue. *Presbyterian Life*'s May 1 issue included John Sutherland Bonnell's "Religion and the Presidency," a fairly evenhanded treatment by a minister who later wrote a book-length study of the religious views of the presidents, *Presidential Profiles: Religion in the Life of American Presidents*. The weekly *Presbyterian Outlook* touched on the religious issue twice, beginning with Albert N. Wells' article, "Presidential Dilemma and Pastoral Concern," in its October 3 issue. Four weeks later the paper addressed the religious issue directly in an editorial, "Before You Vote."

Social Progress, a publication from the Board of Christian Education of the United Presbyterian Church, devoted part of its June issue to a symposium on religion in politics. Essayists included two noted academics, Murray Stedman and William Lee Miller as well as John C. Bennett, president of Union Theological Seminary, and Glenn L. Archer of Protestants and Other Americans United for Separation of Church and State.

Jewish magazines universally deplored the invocation of religious issues, seeing them as illegitimate attempts to erect a barrier to any candidates outside of the Protestant faith in aspiring to the presidency. They frequently emphasized the ban by Article VI of the Constitution on religious tests and noted, as did many Catholic journals, that other nations would be less inclined to accept America's claims of tolerance in religious matters, and the U.S. would be seen as hypocritical if the unwritten rule limiting the Oval Office to Protestants was maintained in 1960.

The American Jewish Committee's lively monthly, *Commentary*, published one of the more important articles of the campaign, Arthur Hertzberg's "The Protestant Establishment, Catholic Dogma, and the Presidency," in October. It was a scintillating overview. The beloved columnist and author Harry Golden blasted Norman Vincent Peale in the September-October issue of the *Carolina Israelite*. Golden was an unabashed admirer of JFK. The Anti-Defamation League of B'nai B'rith compiled anti–Kennedy material on two occasions in its journal, *Facts* (June-July

1960 and March 1961). These remain essential sources for historians of the campaign.

A number of Jewish magazines focused on how Jewish voters were responding to the intolerance of the campaign. Especially insightful were Rabbi Jacob Neusner's "Religion and Politics" in the *Jewish Ledger* (August 4), Albert Vorspan's "Jewish Voters and the Religious Issue" in *Jewish Frontier* (October) and "Does Religion Influence Voting in America?" in *Jewish Forum* (July).

The journals *Judaism* (Fall 1960) and *Reconstructionist* (December 30) focused on interfaith dialogue and intercommunity relations, wondering if they had been damaged by the excesses of the campaign.

General Secular Press Coverage

The secular press devoted considerable commentary, analysis and reportage to the unfolding campaign's religious dimension. Many articles were straight news stories while others were more in-depth background pieces. *Time* devoted four articles to the religious issue, including "The Power of Negative Thinking," a critique of the Peale group, on September 19, 1960, and "Faces of Bigotry" on October 31. *Newsweek*'s coverage was slim, while *U.S. News and World Report* published seven articles on the religious issue, emphasizing "The Catholic Vote" and "The Catholic Issue." The magazine was pro–Nixon and tended to sensationalize the religious issue. One such article was "The Other Side of the Catholic Issue" that appeared on July 4, written by Princeton Seminary president John Mackay, who was critical of Vatican statements on religious liberty.

The *Reporter*, a distinguished weekly noted for trenchant coverage of events, published six articles on the religious question. One, "The Protestant Issue," by Douglass Cater in the October 13 issue, was analytic and on target. Foreign correspondent Claire Sterling focused on the ambivalence of the Vatican in "The Vatican and Kennedy" in the magazine's October 27 number.

The moderately liberal *New Leader* published two insightful articles by renowned Protestant theologian Reinhold Niebuhr in its May 9 and December 12 issues. In its November 9, 1959, issue, a year before the election, Catholic scholar George N. Shuster and Lewis S. Feuer explored the possibility of a Catholic president. The liberal *New Republic*, often critical of political Catholicism in the past but sympathetic to Kennedy, devoted its March 21 issue to an overview of the religious issue, including articles by historian Arthur Schlesinger, Jr., theologians John Bennett and Jaroslav Pelikan, Catholic journalist William Clancy and Catholic critic Paul Blanshard.

The two glossy weeklies that reached immense audiences, *Life* and *Look,* provided information and enlightened coverage of the issue. *Life*'s July 4 issue included a long (for *Life*) article depicting the history of religious bigotry in U.S. politics: Robert Coughlan's "The Religious Issue: An Un–American Heritage." It shocked many readers with its depiction of the long heritage of anti–Catholicism in public life. On December 21, 1959, the magazine had published Episcopal Bishop James Pike's "Should a Catholic Be President?"

Look may have set the stage for a discussion of the issue with Fletcher Knebel's "Democratic Forecast: A Catholic in 1960," a sympathetic view in its March 3, 1959, issue. On February 16, 1960, *Look* published John O'Brien's "Can Catholics Separate Church and State?"—an affirmative answer by a priest-author noted for his books on conversion to Catholicism. A more critical Protestant view appeared in *Look*'s May 10 issue, when Presbyterian spokesman Eugene Carson Blake and Methodist Bishop G. Bromley Oxnam explored the ramifications of the issue.

Another popular journal, *Coronet,* may have been first out of the gate when it published Illinois senator Paul Douglas' "A Catholic Can Become President" in March 1959. The liberal monthly founded by Senator Bob LaFollette, *The Progressive,* which endorsed Kennedy, published Kennedy biographer and acclaimed historian James MacGregor Burns' "The Religious Issue" in November. The *Wall Street Journal*'s September 12 issue warned that "anti–Catholicism runs deeper than expected but may backfire on the GOP," in a wise observation by Philip Geyelin.

The esteemed *Saturday Review* gave pollster Elmo Roper a forum for analyzing the Catholic vote in its issues of October 31, 1959, and November 5, 1960. After initially dismissing the possibility of a partisan Catholic vote, he concluded that there had been a movement of Catholic voters to a fellow Catholic believed to be the target of unfair attacks. Finally, the feisty *Texas Observer* published a special issue on religion and politics on September 30, 1960. Its editor, Ronnie Dugger, was intensely critical of "Politicians in the Pulpit."

It should be noted that the anti–Kennedy campaign reached its crescendo on Reformation Sunday, a traditional Protestant church festival, in late October 1960. The escalation of the stop–Kennedy juggernaut prompted Bruce Felknor to issue a warning: "I am ashamed to say that this anniversary in 1960 will be perverted from a sacred to what I think is a quite profane use in many churches in our country."[10]

Some other propaganda materials appeared that reflected similar concerns. One, "If America Elects a Catholic President," was a 48-page booklet published in 1959 by an entity called Dunham Publishing Company in Findlay, Ohio, which is a small town in the northwestern part of the state. Its author was Don W. Hillis and it was "dedicated to the thousands of Christians who have suffered for Jesus' sake at the hands of Romanism." His preface tells readers that "The following pages are written to alert Christian men and women to the necessity of safeguarding the rich heritage of freedom that is ours in Protestant America."

The booklet weaves politics and religion into a tapestry of antipathy. Half the material argues that Catholicism is not a Christian faith but paganism encrusted with a thin veneer of Christianity. Catholic countries are mired in "illiteracy, poverty and moral degradation" while "nations become progressive and prosperous in proportion to their liberation from the shackles of Romanism." The United States will "face the danger of an overall degeneration if Romanism gains control." One chapter concentrates on persecution and "bloody martyrdoms perpetrated by the Vatican," claiming that U.S. Protestants are next on the list for extermination.

Hillis chided Protestants for being "Republicans or Democrats first and then Christians," while Catholics always voted for Catholic candidates. He never explained what Catholic voters did in the majority of elections in which no candidates were Catholic. Hillis was particularly incensed that California elected Pat Brown governor in 1958 because Brown, as attorney general, ruled that Bible reading and school prayer directed and mandated by the state violated the California constitution. (The U.S. Supreme Court would reach the same conclusion in 1962.) Hillis said that Brown's "apparent desire to rid the American school system of the Bible was in direct line with the avowed purpose of the Roman Catholic hierarchy." Ironically, Hillis would find himself on the same side of this issue as Cardinal Spellman a few years in the future.

Hillis, who includes few facts, no legal opinions, no historical commentaries and no political or constitutional arguments that merit notice, encouraged his readers to "pray and work toward the conversion of Catholics," presumably to his brand of fundamentalist Protestantism. Readers should also "keep posted on Catholic political, social and educational maneuvers, both national and international" and vote against any and all Catholic candidates. ("Raise your voice through your vote against Catholicism's endeavor to seek power through political office.")

A second booklet of his, "The Big Question — A Vatican Victory in the U.S.A.," continues along the same line, warning that the election of a Catholic president will lead to the suppression of Protestantism and the outlawing of the Bible and of evangelistic campaigns. One chapter asked "Are There Any Protestants in Congress?" and concluded that the few that were there were supine and cowed by "Popery." In actual fact there were 425 Protestants, 102 Catholics and 8 Jews in Congress when this book was published. The author apparently thought that no Catholics or Jews should be allowed in the club, since this represented "National Apostasy" (a term used by 19th century supporters of religious establishment in Ireland and England). Both of these booklets exhibited an appalling lack of knowledge of the political and religious history of the U.S. and an ignorance of the constitutional context in which government operates.

One of the strangest anti–Catholic documents circulating in 1960 was a 22-page mimeographed document pompously called "An Analysis of Catholic 'Power Politics' and Other Factors of Political Pressure in the First-Ballot Nomination of Sen. John F. Kennedy for President." This writer received a copy of the document about 40 years ago from an individual who was intimately involved in the anti–Kennedy campaign. Copies in libraries are exceedingly rare. No one knows for sure who wrote it. Speculation centered on a reporter for *The Christian Science Monitor* or a journalist at "Religious News Service." The author claimed to be an insider, as he says at the beginning:

> This analysis was prepared by a man who has been employed as a Washington correspondent for more than 15 years and who has been in a position where he could be particularly alert to religious influences on politics. He attended the Democratic National Convention in Los Angeles and was on the floor of the Convention when Senator Kennedy was nominated. He knows many political leaders personally and did careful research in preparing this report, including an investigation into the number of Catholic delegates attending the convention and the number of Protestant and Jewish delegates who were con-

trolled by Catholic political leaders, such as Tammany Boss, Carmine de Sapio, and others. His state-by-state analysis below is followed by a comprehensive summary of the situation that prevailed at Los Angeles, resulting in the first-ballot nomination of a man whom many delegates really didn't think was ready for the White House.

This "insider" was obsessed with the Catholic issue, and assumed that delegates voted for or against Kennedy solely on religious grounds, ignoring all other factors such as the state's primary votes, labor, special interest groups, regional affections and the like. What makes the conclusions suspect is that he claimed to know the religious affiliations of all or most of the delegates to the Democratic convention when religion was never a question asked on biographical questionnaires. This appears to be mere speculation. Even with his "insider" connections, the author listed no religious affiliation for delegates from Illinois, Washington, Wyoming, South Dakota, Wisconsin or the Virgin Islands. Of the total delegates and alternates (3,179) that are compiled, he claims that 757 were Catholic, or only 23.8 percent. If this was a Catholic plot to nominate Kennedy, it could not have succeeded without a considerable number of supporters from other faiths.

The author's state-by-state analysis is inconsistent. "Only 14 of Maryland's 62 delegates appeared to be Catholic" but they all voted for Kennedy. How does this represent Catholic abuse of power? "Religion played a very important part in swinging Illinois to Kennedy," though this is one state where the author omitted the religious affiliation of delegates.

The author delights in sarcasm: "One need mention only that the Rhode Island delegation had 38 Catholics, 4 Protestants and 7 of Eastern Orthodox or Jewish affiliation" to understand why Kennedy won those delegates. Could it not have been that this was the neighboring state to Massachusetts, where a kind of New England family loyalty was a factor? He also speculates that "Sen. Theodore Francis Green may be the last Protestant officeholder in Rhode Island in a long time." As a matter of fact, Rhode Island has continued to elect many Protestants, including incumbent senator Sheldon Whitehouse.

One wonders about the accuracy of the author's religious statistics. For example, he states that "only 8 of the 74 Louisiana delegates were Catholic," in one of the most Catholic states in the union. Given the author's loathing and disdain for Catholics, he lets that fact pass without commentary. If anything, this would suggest anti–Catholic discrimination in a state where probably 50 percent of white voters were Catholic in 1960 (and no African Americans were selected as delegates), and only 11 percent of the delegates were said to be Catholic. This shows the problem of pulling figures out of the air without proof.

The author calls Connecticut state chairman John Bailey "a fanatic Catholic." Cleveland party chairman Ray T. Miller "is as fanatic a Catholic as Connecticut's John Bailey." The author claimed, again without the slightest proof, that "Kennedy's religion definitely played an important factor in getting Governor David Lawrence to yield and in building up pressure from Kennedyites in the Pennsylvania delegation." Both of Lawrence's biographers strenuously disagree with this assessment. Governor Pat Brown of California was called a devious man who tried to "avoid the appearance of Catholic pressure": "Brown is Catholic, of course, and has a son who is a priest. He was very circumspect in not loading his delegation with Catholics."

Religious paranoia pervades this document: "Religious factors in heavily Catholic Detroit and among many heavily Catholic labor leaders contributed to Kennedy's victory in Michigan." Even though Colorado governor Steve McNichols, a Catholic, delivered only some of his state's votes to Kennedy and only 11 of 62 delegates were Catholic, "the Catholic governor was an important force for Kennedy."

As in the case of Louisiana, the underrepresentation of Catholics in many state delegations should have been noted. "Minnesota had only two Catholic members out of 57 delegates and alternates." Since the state is at least a fourth Catholic, that is very low, and one of them, Senator Eugene McCarthy, made an impassioned nominating speech for Adlai Stevenson. New Mexico had "a strong Catholic population but only 5 Catholics among 30 delegates," and Johnson defeated Kennedy 13 to 4 in the roll call vote. Shouldn't there have been more Catholic delegates in a fairly apportioned state?

If Kennedy's nomination was a Catholic plot, why did numerous Catholics support other candidates? Senator Thomas Dodd of Connecticut, Senator Mike Mansfield of Montana, and Governor John Hickey of Wyoming supported Lyndon Johnson, and Hickey seconded the nomination of Johnson.

The acidic anti–Kennedy bias in the report of this so-called insider makes good bedtime reading for fans of spy novels but one wonders about

TO ALL DELEGATES TO THE DEMOCRATIC CONVENTION

WHEREAS The United States of America is in the most serious crisis in its history, and

WHEREAS The need for unity in our land is needed more than ever before, and

WHEREAS Millions of Americans in every section of our nation cannot, in view of their unshakeable religious convictions, vote for a ROMAN CATHOLIC for President,

WE DO HEREBY PETITION DELEGATES TO THE DEMOCRATIC NATIONAL CONVENTION NOT TO NOMINATE A ROMAN CATHOLIC FOR THE OFFICE OF PRESIDENT OR VICE-PRESIDENT OF THE UNITED STATES.

Dr. Harvey Springer
Englewood, Colo.

Dr. George Norris
Ft. Worth, Texas

Dr. Ray Tatum
Lubbock, Texas

Dr. Dennis Brown
Riverside, Calif.

Dr. Bruce Powell
Chula Vista, Calif.

REPRESENTING 500,000 PROTESTANT VOTERS WHO HAVE SIGNED THE FOREGOING PETITIONS

Five fundamentalist preachers distributed this warning at the Democratic Convention in Los Angeles. All were active in anti–Catholic causes (Fair Campaign Practices Committee Collection, Manuscripts Division, Special Collections, Lauinger Library, Georgetown University)

its overall accuracy. In states with few Catholics, the report claimed, it was corruption that aided the Kennedy nomination: "Double-dealing rather than religion was the factor in getting Kansas' lukewarm votes to Kennedy."

"Some say liquor money of vast Kennedy liquor interests had something to do with the Oklahoma situation," i.e., the endorsement of JFK by Governor Edmonson. This seems absurd since all 29 Sooner votes went for Johnson and the state was a Prohibitionist stronghold. Only a fool would have thrown around liquor money in fundamentalist Oklahoma, where JFK was exceedingly weak from the start.

The author's conclusion was unsurprising: "Kennedy's religion did not handicap him. In a very real sense, it was his biggest asset because so many of the kingmakers were Catholic, and of those men, every single one who had any real votes was with Kennedy. The Catholics who held out for others, Senators McCarthy, Dodd, and Mansfield, and Governor Hickey, couldn't deliver any votes. It was a combination of Catholic power plus shrewd political deals, but it would not have succeeded had his opposition united behind one man."

But the coup de grace, proving how truly uninformed this writer was about the course and direction of American politics, comes in his last paragraph. He predicted that Catholic power would dictate a series of Catholic candidates for years to come. Of course he couldn't have been more wrong. It was 44 years before the Democrats nominated another Catholic for president, Massachusetts senator John Kerry, and Republicans have never done so.

Here is the final paragraph:

> A political lesson is apparent. If a Catholic candidate emerges who has strong support from the Catholic city bosses and Catholic governors in the North, he cannot be defeated unless the predominately Protestant Southern states unite with the other sections of the North and West to back a candidate mutually acceptable. When the South holds out for a sectional candidate, as it has the habit of doing, even for a section-within-a-section like Mississippi's Barnett, it plays into the hands of the opposition and any Catholic candidate who can line up big-state support will win. Southern sectionalism, plus Catholic control of big states, a control hard to shake because of Catholic concentrations in major cities, will equal a Catholic candidate, not just in 1960, but a succession of Catholic candidates from now on.

Another claim that JFK stole the nomination was made by evangelist Dan Gilbert, of Upland, California, who said the convention was "pre-arranged, fixed, packed, stacked and rigged in favor of John Kennedy." Gilbert's pamphlet, "The True, Inside Story of the Rigging and Fixing of the Democrat Convention in Los Angeles," claimed "the massed power of papal influence plus Papa's (Joe Kennedy) payola" stole the convention: "The leaders of even some of our Bible belt states brought shame upon themselves and their people by cowering and quailing before the brutal onslaught of the Kennedy blitzkrieg." He also claimed that governors Pat Brown of California and David Lawrence of Pennsylvania "buckled down to doing Rome's dirty work" by "betraying" Adlai Stevenson. "The intellectuals wanted Stevenson. The plain people wanted Lyndon Johnson. Rome thrust Kennedy upon them." Gilbert, of course, ignored the state primary results which were heavily for Kennedy. Gilbert concluded: "After suffering through the heart-ache and down right nausea of the Los Angeles Convention, there is only one thing I can say to my countrymen, my fellow Bible-believers ... God Help America. God save America."[11]

The Kennedy Defense Team

James W. Wine, a vice president of the National Council of Churches, as well as an attorney and active Presbyterian layman, made contact with the Kennedy campaign through a letter to Ted Sorensen on June 20, 1960. His advice for covering religious animosity stressed the importance of appealing to reasonable, moderate Protestants.[12] His recommendations so impressed Sorensen that Sorensen convinced Robert Kennedy to bring Wine aboard as Special Assistant for Community Relations, a position that Wine assumed on August 26. Wine thought that JFK should emphasize his independence, his rational, thoughtful approach to issues, and his adherence to the Constitution. The candidate should not make any direct appeals to religious leaders or seem too close to any of them.

Wine, who understood the value of communication through the press, urged the campaign to send factual statements of Kennedy's stand on specific church-state issues to denominational magazines, religious editors in the secular press and executives of state and local councils of churches. He felt that only a thorough airing of the issues would prevent the dissemination of disinformation. He also urged the campaign to make contact with Rabbi Arthur Gilbert of the Anti-Defamation League of B'nai B'rith and Monsignor George Higgins of the National Catholic Welfare Conference, who were highly regarded within their respective religious communities.

Wine's contacts within the mainstream Protestant community were valuable, as the ensuing campaign would reveal. Shaun A. Casey writes: "Wine's post at the National Council of Churches plus his activity in the Presbyterian churches put him in an ideal position to monitor the currents of Protestant thought." [13]

Wine tried to make contact with the less frenzied elements of conservative Protestantism who, while they distrusted and disliked Catholicism, did not wish to appear bigoted. Casey stresses that the national organization — Protestants and Other Americans United, or POAU — was internally divided. Some of its leaders and members were vociferously anti–Kennedy, while others thought the senator's positions on vital church-state issues were sounder than Nixon's.[14]

James W. Wine, an official with the National Council of Churches, headed the Community Relations Division of the Democratic National Committee during the Kennedy campaign (Allied Photo Service; John F. Kennedy Presidential Library and Museum, Boston).

CHAPTER 4

The National Vote

As a record 68 million Americans trooped to the polls, from snow-covered hamlets in Alaska to sleepy fishing villages in the Florida Keys, one could sense something dramatic was about to happen. Pollster George Gallup said he had never seen an election so close in his quarter century of observing and taking the pulse of the voters. No one could be certain of the outcome, he suggested. Another pollster, Elmo Roper, concurred, saying that the lead had changed hands more times during the 1960 campaign than ever before. No one could predict who would become America's 35th president.

All three television networks planned coverage from the closing of the first polls until a winner was known. Leading reporters, many of them household names, were on hand to broadcast the results. The first returns came in from the early reporting states of Indiana and Kentucky. Nixon swept Indiana as expected, but he also jumped to an early and convincing lead in Kentucky, a warning that religion was indeed affecting voter decisions. Democrats were clearly worried. Then came the eastern states, reporting solid Kennedy leads. Many states were close, suggesting that election observers were in for a long night. Kennedy led in Florida, elating Democrats for a while.

But in those halcyon days before exit polls, no one knew where the early returns were coming from. Were they from Democratic cities, which often reported late in some areas, or were they from the Republican countryside? The popular vote count was close all evening, with Kennedy clinging to a lead. Rural and western areas had not reported, it was assumed, so the outcome remained in doubt for hours. The lead shifted back and forth in key states. Absentee ballots would probably decide the outcome in California. This chapter looks at the national vote in some detail, showing the contours of the geography of the 1960 race.

4. The National Vote

The 1960 election was the closest in popular vote in the twentieth century. Massachusetts senator John F. Kennedy defeated Vice President Richard Nixon by 49.7 percent to 49.5 percent of the 68.3 million ballots cast. Kennedy carried 23 states, with 303 electoral votes, while Nixon carried 26 states, with 219 electoral votes. Mississippi gave its eight electors to a States' Rights ticket, calling itself "unpledged Democrats." These eight Mississippians, joined by six from Alabama (under a complicated unpledged electors system that deprived Kennedy, who won 57 percent of the vote in the state, of six electors) and one Nixon elector from Oklahoma, voted for Virginia senator Harry Byrd. Two new states had joined the Union: Alaska went for Nixon, and Hawaii backed Kennedy.

JFK put together his winning coalition by combining the Northeast (except upper New England), most of the South, and a few large states like Illinois and Michigan. Nixon carried the reliably Republican Midwest and far West and broke into the upper South border areas. Nixon's most impressive victories came in Nebraska, Kansas and Oklahoma (where religious prejudice hurt JFK), while Kennedy's strongest states were Rhode Island, Georgia and Massachusetts.

JFK won 61 percent of the votes in the nation's 16 largest cities, an 11-point increase over the Stevenson vote in 1956. JFK's national gain was 8 percent. The big-city votes netted Kennedy a vote margin of 2,730,000, which was reflective of the polyglot, multicultural ethos of metropolitan America. The urban megalopolis was much more religiously and racially diverse than suburbia or rural areas in 1960.

As in 1928, religion was a major factor in the voting, as JFK was the second Catholic nominated by the Democrats for president. He had to overcome the unspoken stigma that no Catholic would ever be elected U.S. president, despite an explicit ban on religious tests for public office in Article VI of the U.S. Constitution. The voting patterns and the county and state returns indicate how significant a factor religion was in 1960. While scholars disagree about the impact, an authoritative University of Michigan Survey Research Center study found that JFK lost 1.5 million more votes than he gained because of anti–Catholic voting among Protestants, especially Protestant Democrats in the South and the rural North. About 4.5 million Protestant Democrats voted for Nixon.

The percentage of the Catholic population in the states was closely correlated with the percentage gain in Kennedy support over Stevenson, but this did not guarantee a victory for JFK. He did win nine of the 12 most heavily Catholic-populated states but still lost Wisconsin, New Hampshire and Vermont. Political party heritage and tradition played a major role since JFK also carried a number of southern states with tiny Catholic populations, such as Alabama, Georgia, Arkansas and the Carolinas. A sympathetic vote for JFK by coreligionists probably shifted New Jersey, Connecticut, Maryland and New Mexico into the Kennedy column, but antipathy toward his religious faith cost him Tennessee, Kentucky, Oklahoma, and possibly Florida, Ohio and Washington.

Kennedy carried 408 counties in 46 states that had supported Eisenhower. But despite the national gain for the Democratic ticket in what was forecast to be a Democratic year, 97 counties switched from Stevenson to Nixon. These anti-trend counties were concentrated in Texas, Oklahoma, Missouri, and Kentucky but extended as far as Washington State. Furthermore, Kennedy ran weaker than Stevenson in 973 counties in 33 states—one out of three counties in the United States—even in many he carried. Most were in the South or the rural Border States. An anti–Catholic belt stretched from northern Texas through Oklahoma and into southeastern Missouri, northeastern Arkansas, west-central Kentucky and west Tennessee.

In comparison with 1928, Kennedy lost 158 counties that had supported Smith. This might have resulted from an increasing incidence of anti–Catholicism, changing social or demographic trends, or a weakening of Democratic Party loyalties. Most were predominantly Baptist counties, but some included socially conservative Catholics of German ancestry, and a few of the Smith-Nixon counties were primarily German Lutheran. Kennedy also failed to carry 28 counties that had supported all Democrats for president except Smith, another indication of anti–Catholicism. And there were 254 northern counties that had supported the five previous Democratic winners (FDR and Truman) but went for Nixon.

The persistence of anti–Catholic voting was centered in rural America. Kennedy ran well ahead of Stevenson and Smith in almost all northern and western cities and suburbs, and he did quite well in urban Florida and Texas. In the anti–Kennedy backlash areas, there was a strong religious factor. In particular, Baptists were dominant in the anti–Kennedy swing counties throughout the South, the Border States, and in Illinois and New Mexico. Lutherans composed the largest denomination in the anti–

Kennedy counties in Pennsylvania, Wisconsin, Minnesota and the Dakotas while Methodists and Dutch Reformed Christians were strongest in the anti–Kennedy counties in Iowa and Indiana.

In the counties that went for Stevenson and Nixon, only 7.7 percent of the religious population was Catholic, compared to 57.6 percent that was Baptist, according to *Churches and Church Membership in the United States, 1971*. In the counties that went for Eisenhower and Kennedy, 65.3 percent of the religious population was Catholic. JFK did well among independent and swing voters. Of the 294 counties that had switched to or against Eisenhower in 1956, Kennedy carried 188 of them, Nixon won 97, and the States' Rights splinter tickets in Dixie carried nine. Kennedy also won back 36 of the 56 counties that had cast their first Republican presidential majorities for Eisenhower in 1956. Nixon held only 17 of them, and 3 in Louisiana voted for a States' Rights party.

Nixon's geographic base was centered in the West and Midwest, with South Dakota, Iowa, Arizona, North Dakota, Indiana and Wyoming among his strongest states, in addition to Nebraska, Kansas and Oklahoma. Kennedy's geographical coalition linked lower New England (Connecticut, Massachusetts, Rhode Island) to the Mid-Atlantic (New York, Maryland, West Virginia) and to the Deep South (Georgia, Alabama, North Carolina, South Carolina). Only Nevada in the West stood out as a strong JFK state. Kennedy carried only Nevada and New Mexico in the entire West.

Geographically, the 1960 election was primarily a clash between East and West, with JFK winning in the northern and southern portions of the East while Nixon was strongest in the West and Midwest. The 8-point national gain for Kennedy was accomplished mostly in the East, though he also gained 10 points in Illinois and Wisconsin.

A major factor in 1960 was the difference in voting patterns between urban and rural areas, with the suburbs in the middle. The other story was the intense level of anti–Kennedy voting in rural America. While Kennedy ran ahead of Stevenson in popular vote percentage in 42 of the 48 states that voted in both races, he lost ground in at least one county in 33 states.

Even in states where Kennedy gained support overall, there was a backlash in rural areas. In Pennsylvania, where Kennedy gained 8 percentage points, he ran behind Stevenson in 16 rural counties. A review of local township and precinct returns (available in Pennsylvania and a few other states) found that anti–Kennedy voting occurred in 65 of the 67 counties. Even in counties where Kennedy ran a point or two ahead of the 1956 ticket (as in Berks), he ran behind in a majority of the precincts in the countryside. The same was true in Wisconsin, which also published detailed precinct data. In many towns in both states, JFK ran 10–20 points behind Stevenson. More than 100 towns in Pennsylvania and Wisconsin switched from Stevenson to Nixon.

The persistence of anti–Catholicism in rural areas has been noted by many historians. In *Strangers in the Land*, John Higham argued that "the rise of a militant rural fundamentalism coincided with the upsurge of rural nativism. Perhaps the two came partly from a common need, aggressive fundamentalism ministering to the same unfulfilled urges that sent rural Protestants crusading against popery."[1]

General mass-circulation anti–Catholic journals, which flourished during the first two decades of the twentieth century, were all published in outlying, almost isolated rural areas: *The Menace*, in Aurora, Missouri; *The Railsplitter* in Milan, Illinois; *Watson's Magazine*, in Thomson, Georgia; and the *Yellow Jacket* in Moravian Falls, North Carolina. Other, smaller, magazines were published in Magnolia, Arkansas; Iola, Kansas; Silverton, Oregon; and Barboursville, Kentucky.

In his study of anti–Catholic print culture, Justin Nordstrom writes that "the counties in which extant anti–Catholic documents were produced contained exceptionally low rates of Catholic residents."[2] Nordstrom argued, however, that "anti–Catholic writers considered themselves a fundamental part of middle-class life in their local communities"[3] and attracted readers far from their home bases. They may also have seen rural America as the last bastion of Anglo-Saxon Protestant values in a changing nation, which is why "anti–Catholic writers praised their surrounding communities not simply as sites of natural beauty but as the source of refinement, culture, and efficiency as well."[4] This tendency of rural areas to be the locale for numerous professional anti–Catholic organizations and pamphlet-producers continued to some extent in 1960. It is also where their criticisms seemed to have resonated most effectively with voters.

An examination of several demographic factors reveals that religious affiliation is the best explanation for the anti–Kennedy backlash. There was a near absence of Catholics (under 10 percent generally) in the anti–Kennedy counties, and a disproportionately large percentage of Southern

Baptists in the Southern and Border State anti–Kennedy counties, extending also into eastern New Mexico. (In Baptist Roosevelt County, Kennedy ran 16 points behind Stevenson.) In Pennsylvania, Colorado, and Iowa, Lutherans and Methodists predominated in the anti–Kennedy counties, while Lutherans were the most prominent in Minnesota, Wisconsin, South Dakota, Montana and Nebraska anti–Kennedy counties. German and Dutch ancestry were also linked to some extent with the voting patterns but were secondary to religion. In Douglas County, South Dakota, JFK dropped 11 points. The population there is a mixture of Dutch and German, and the Reformed Church and Lutherism are the dominant religions. Kennedy also ran exceptionally poorly in the Dutch counties in Michigan and Iowa. His worst Iowa decline came in Marion County, where the Dutch town of Pella is located.

There were also declines in Kennedy's strength in some metro counties. The senator lost 7 percentage points in Nashville (Davidson County), Tennessee, and Atlanta (Fulton County), Georgia. He ran weaker than Stevenson in Oklahoma City; Greenville, South Carolina; Jackson, Mississippi; and Birmingham, Alabama. In smaller metros he ran 7–10 points behind Stevenson in Paducah, Kentucky, and Macon, Georgia, and a few points weaker in Pensacola and Lakeland, Florida; Columbus, Georgia; Shreveport, Louisiana; and Chattanooga and Knoxville, Tennessee.

While Kennedy's greatest decline in support came from rural areas, he also experienced losses in about 40 small towns, mostly in the South, but also in Iowa, Indiana, New Mexico, Missouri and Oklahoma. His most significant declines (10 percent–15 percent) were centered in Georgia (Decatur, Macon and Valdosta) and South Carolina (Greenville, Columbia and Myrtle Beach). He also lost ground in Murfreesboro, Tennessee; Jonesboro, Arkansas; Paducah, Kentucky; and Meridian, Mississippi. Another ten towns gave him losses of between 7 and 9 percentage points. They included four Alabama towns (Dothan, Florence, Huntsville and Decatur) and two in Tennessee (Jackson and Columbia), as well as Blytheville, Arkansas; Jackson, Mississippi; Clovis, New Mexico; and Lawton, Oklahoma. Many of the towns were long-time centers of religious fundamentalism and were dotted with evangelical colleges.

Outside the South, JFK's support declined 4 points in York, Pennsylvania, and 1 point in Fresno, California. The States' Rights Party cost the Democrats Mississippi, where they carried 54 counties, and also placed first in 17 Louisiana counties. The 1960 States' Righters had been Democrats, since 51 of the 71 counties went for Stevenson in 1956, while 10 supported Eisenhower and 10 supported the 1956 States' Rights Party.

The majority of the counties which supported the 1956 States' Rights parties, however, went for Nixon in 1960—just as they had gone for Eisenhower in 1952. There were apparently two different strains of States' Rights voters in the rural South. These 1956 States' Rights/1960 Nixon counties included Prince Edward, Virginia, which closed its public schools rather than integrate them, Fayette, Tennessee, and Caldwell, Louisiana. In the counties in Louisiana and Mississippi which supported the States Rights' parties in *both* 1956 and 1960, Kennedy slipped into third place in 1960, suggesting that both anti-Catholicism and racism were factors influencing the electorate. In contrast, the counties that cast their first-ever Republican vote for Ike in 1952 supported Nixon. The break with the Democrats must have been more ideological and more permanent for these counties than for the 1956 Eisenhower counties, which may have been more influenced by personality.

In addition to the widespread and intense anti-Catholicism that caused nearly 100 counties to switch allegiance from Stevenson to Nixon, there were 427 counties that supported Roosevelt and Truman five times but refused to support Kennedy. Kennedy was the first Democratic *winner* to lose these counties in modern times. This reluctance to support the Democratic nominee may be linked to religious orientation. In the 254 northern and western counties, the Catholic percentage of church members was 15 points below the national figure. In the 173 southern counties that backed FDR and Truman but not Kennedy, the Catholic percentage was 30 points below the national norm. Baptists, Lutherans, Methodists and Dutch Reformed members were strongly represented in these counties, while Mormons were a significant force in Idaho and Wyoming.

The excitement of the Kennedy-Nixon race brought nearly 7 million new voters to the polls, an 11 percent increase. Every state recorded a higher presidential vote in 1960 than in 1956, ranging from 1 percent in West Virginia to 37 percent in Arizona and Florida. Other large increases, 20 percent or more, came in Louisiana, South Carolina, New Mexico and Mississippi. Increases were 15–20 percent in California, Maine, Minnesota, North Carolina and Texas. Small increases of 2–4 percent were recorded in Montana, Iowa, and South Dakota. The states with the largest increase in turnout narrowly favored Kennedy 50.5–49.5 percent in major party vote; but this was only a 5.4 percent increase over Stevenson's 1956 vote, less than Kennedy's 8 percent national vote gain.

Nixon carried 15 counties in 3 states that had never gone Republican for president before 1960. Five were in Arkansas (Clay, Craighead, Fulton, Randolph, Sharp), four in Missouri (Dunklin, Oregon, Reynolds, Shannon), and two in Oklahoma (Atoka, Garvin). Also included were Houston County, Alabama; Caldwell Parish, Louisiana; Dyer County, Tennessee; and Moore County, Texas.

Kennedy ran 10 percentage points or more behind Stevenson's 1956 vote in all but two of these counties. There was an enormous anti–Kennedy vote in northeastern Arkansas and southeastern Missouri undoubtedly related to the religious issue. Since Al Smith carried all of these counties in 1928, it can be reasonably assumed that anti–Catholicism increased as a salient political issue between 1928 and 1960 in this slice of rural America.

The religious configuration of these counties was 67 percent Baptist (mostly white Southern Baptists), 19 percent Methodist and only 4 percent Catholic. Almost 10 percent belonged to other evangelical Protestant churches. In 1926 the *U.S. Census of Religious Bodies* recorded that in these counties 40.5 percent of the religious population was Baptist, 29.5 percent was Methodist, 9 percent belonged to the Church of Christ and 3.5 percent were Catholic. About 17.5 percent belonged to other Protestant denominations. The large percentage increase in Baptists may have been a crucial factor in the 1960 vote.

Nixon was also the first Republican since 1868 to carry Marion and Scott Counties, Arkansas, and Madison County, Tennessee. He was the first Republican since 1872 to carry Barnwell County, South Carolina, and the first since 1884 to carry Fayette County, Tennessee. JFK did not have any breakthrough counties where long-time Republican voters switched to his side. He mainly revitalized the old New Deal Democratic coalition, but in a few counties his victory was quite a departure from the past. He was the first Democrat since 1836 to carry his birthplace, Norfolk County, Massachusetts, a growing and prosperous suburb south of Boston, and he was the first Democratic winner since 1912 in Niagara County, New York.

One unusual victory came in Madison County, North Carolina, where JFK was the first Democratic victor since 1876. Local factors played a role in Madison, where a long-dominant Republican machine had been ousted in the late 1950s, which may have spilled over into the 1960 presidential race. Kennedy also carried 45 counties that had been mostly Republican since 1920. He was the first Democrat since 1932 to carry Charles County, Maryland; Franklin County, New York; and Socorro County, New Mexico, all rural Catholic strongholds. In these 45 pro–Kennedy GOP counties, Catholics outnumbered Protestants 71 percent to 29 percent in 1971 data, up from 60 percent to 40 percent in 1926 data.

Scholars may disagree about the final impact of religion on the 1960 vote but one preeminent analyst of elections, V.O. Key, Jr., concluded as follows: "Of the appeals peculiar to the campaign, the religious issue evidently by far outweighed all others. For some people, it reinforced the pull of partisanship; for others, it ran counter to the tugs of party loyalty.... Probably the best guess is that Kennedy won in spite of rather than because of the fact that he was a Catholic."[5]

Other scholars generally agreed. Political scientist Philip E. Converse concluded "religion played a powerful role in shaping voting behavior in the 1960 election."[6] Dulce and Richter observed that "the election of a President of Catholic faith in 1960 gave a ringing stamp of recognition to pluralism as an indelible fact of national and political and social life.... The religious issue generated healthy discussion regarding the separation of church and state, and also raised questions as to the proper degree and the character of influence exercised by churches in the country's political affairs."[7]

THE BAPTIST VOTE

The white Baptist vote in almost all regions trended against Kennedy. In 96 Baptist majority small-town and rural counties, Kennedy dropped 2.3 percent from Stevenson (47.6 percent for JFK, 49.9 percent for Stevenson). Unlike other regions, Southern Baptist-oriented large population counties were even more anti–Kennedy than rural areas. Eight large counties in Alabama, Georgia, Louisiana, Mississippi, South Carolina, Tennessee and Texas gave Kennedy only 42.8 percent compared to Stevenson's 46.7 percent, a loss of nearly 4 percentage points. In 22 medium-sized counties from Alabama to Texas, Kennedy's decline was more modest, 50.1 percent compared to Stevenson's 50.5 percent.

RELIGION AND AMERICAN POLITICS

Political scientists Lyman Kellstedt and Mark Noll discovered that regular church attendance among evangelicals was directly correlated with a high degree of anti–Kennedy voting: "In 1960 most regular-church-attending evangelicals were unwilling to support Kennedy. Anti–Catholic sentiment among these regular churchgoers almost certainly accounted for the voting. Regularly attending Baptists, including Southern Baptists, gave Kennedy 25 percent of their votes as compared with 51 percent of Baptists who did not attend church regularly. Anti–Catholic sentiment in 1960 seems to have accounted for much of the Nixon vote among regularly attending Baptists."[8]

A survey correlating religion and church attendance among evangelicals shows this clearly. Northern evangelicals who attended church regularly gave Kennedy 14 percent of their votes compared to 44.4 percent among northern evangelicals who were not regular attendees. The same was true of southern evangelicals: 30.6 percent of regular attendees voted for Kennedy while 57.3 percent of less than regular attendees supported him.[9]

Kellstedt and Noll concluded: "Religion is an important factor — for some groups, the most important factor — in shaping political attitudes and behavior."[10]

THE NATIONAL VOTE

Election expert Richard Scammon used to say that two events largely shaped how most Americans voted: on which side their ancestors had fought in the Civil War and which side their forebears had chosen during the Reformation. That was largely true in 1960 (but far less so in succeeding decades). Theodore H. White concurred in *The Making of the President, 1960*: "There is no doubt that millions of Americans, Protestants and Catholics, voted in 1960 primordially out of instinct, kinship and past."[11]

Kennedy's election did not mean that his programs would have an easy rite of passage in Congress. Donald C. Lord discovered that Kennedy's candidacy hurt Democrats in many congressional districts: "Tragically, the young president's election was probably responsible for the defeat of twenty-two Northern Democrats who supported his campaign pledges.

Most of these defeated candidates lived in predominantly Northern Protestant areas that usually elected Democratic congressmen in close elections. But a Catholic presidential candidate on the ticket meant defeat for these Northern liberals who supported his programs."[12]

A number of other interesting facets of the 1960 election came to light after the results were studied thoroughly, the following among them: (1) Kennedy's 49 percent vote in the suburbs of the 14 largest metropolitan areas in the Northeast substantially aided his electoral vote count in that region, and reflects, most likely, his appeal to Catholic and Jewish voters. Stevenson had received 38 percent in these counties in 1956.[13] (2) Nixon's strongest subregion (59 percent support) was in what Theodore H. White called the "farm states" (Iowa, North Dakota, South Dakota, Nebraska, Kansas), reflecting "the culture of the small town and the old America, in the Protestant homesteads of traditional Republican allegiance."[14] (3) White women voted 56 percent to 44 percent for Nixon, while white men gave Kennedy a slight edge. (This should put to rest the myth that women were attracted by Kennedy's good looks.) This may well reflect the fact that women attend church more often than men — and have throughout history — and may have heard and imbibed more anti–Kennedy sermons. Women were also 8 percent more likely than men to support "churches speaking out on social and political issues," according to the Gallup Poll."[15] The so-called gender gap, in which women were much more likely to vote Democratic for president than did men, did not show up until 1980, when Ronald Reagan defeated Jimmy Carter.[16]

Top Ten States, 1960

Kennedy	*Percent*	*Nixon*	*Percent*
1. Rhode Island	63.6	1. Nebraska	62.1
2. Georgia	62.5	2. Kansas	60.4
3. Massachusetts	60.2	3. Oklahoma	59.0
4. Alabama	56.8	4. Vermont	58.6
5. Connecticut	53.7	5. South Dakota	58.2
6. Maryland	53.6	6. Maine	57.0
7. West Virginia	52.7	7. Iowa	56.7
8. New York	52.5	8. Arizona	55.5
9. North Carolina	52.1	9. North Dakota	55.4
10. South Carolina	51.2	10. Wyoming	55.0
10. Nevada	51.2	10. Indiana	55.0

Electoral Votes, 1960

States	Electoral Votes	Kennedy	Nixon	Byrd
Alabama	11	5	-	6
Alaska	3	-	3	-
Arizona	4	-	4	-
Arkansas	8	8	-	-
California	32	-	32	-
Colorado	6	-	6	-
Connecticut	8	8	-	-
Delaware	3	3	-	-
Florida	10	-	10	-
Georgia	12	12	-	-
Hawaii	3	3	-	-
Idaho	4	-	4	-
Illinois	27	27	-	-
Indiana	13	-	13	-
Iowa	10	-	10	-
Kansas	8	-	8	-
Kentucky	10	-	10	-
Louisiana	10	10	-	-
Maine	5	-	5	-
Maryland	9	9	-	-
Massachusetts	16	16	-	-
Michigan	20	20	-	-
Minnesota	11	11	-	-
Mississippi	8	-	-	8
Missouri	13	13	-	-
Montana	4	-	4	-
Nebraska	6	-	6	-
Nevada	3	3	-	-
New Hampshire	4	-	4	-
New Jersey	16	16	-	-
New Mexico	4	4	-	-
New York	45	45	-	-
North Carolina	14	14	-	-
North Dakota	4	-	4	-
Ohio	25	-	25	-
Oklahoma	8	-	7	1
Oregon	6	-	6	-
Pennsylvania	32	32	-	-
Rhode Island	4	4	-	-
South Carolina	8	8	-	-
South Dakota	4	-	4	-
Tennessee	11	-	11	-

States	Electoral Votes	Kennedy	Nixon	Byrd
Texas	24	24	-	-
Utah	4	-	4	-
Vermont	3	-	3	-
Virginia	12	-	12	-
Washington	9	-	9	-
West Virginia	8	8	-	-
Wisconsin	12	-	12	-
Wyoming	3	-	3	-
Totals	**537**	**303**	**219**	**15**

Religious Membership in the Most Anti–Kennedy Counties
South and Border

State	% Baptist	% Methodist	% Catholic	% Others
Alabama	58.1	21.7	5.0	
Arkansas	66.0	20.7	4.3	
Florida	73.2	14.4	1.0	
Georgia	50.2*	21.7	8.2	
Kentucky	65.7	14.7	7.8	
Louisiana	78.4	12.1	3.0	
Mississippi	63.5	23.6	2.6	
Missouri	61.9	11.8	3.1	
North Carolina	51.5	20.2	3.2	
Oklahoma	64.0	20.0	3.2	
South Carolina	51.4	25.9	1.0	
Tennessee	44.9	16.3	2.1	Church of Christ 15.0
Texas	55.3	19.0	18.3	
Virginia	50.3	27.4	1.3	

*This relatively low percentage reflects the statistical influence of suburban DeKalb County. In rural anti–Kennedy counties Baptists constituted 66.8 percent of members and 22.2 were Methodists. There were almost no Catholics.

Religious Membership in the Most Anti–Kennedy Counties
North and West

State	% Baptist	% Methodist	% Lutheran	% Catholic	% Others
Illinois	43.9	19.7	2.1	10.0	
Indiana	23.1	25.7	1.0	8.0	Disciples of Christ 14.2
Iowa	5.1	24.8	24.3	11.9	Dutch Reformed 13.2

State	% Baptist	% Methodist	% Lutheran	% Catholic	% Others
Minnesota	1.0	7.6	57.8	22.5	
Montana	1.2	10.2	40.3	33.6	
Nebraska	1.3	19.2	44.1	19.4	
New Mexico	47.3	15.1	0.7	23.6	
North Dakota	1.5	9.9	54.1	23.0	
Ohio	2.6	37.3	14.0	13.2	Church of Christ 9.4
Pennsylvania	2.0	22.8	29.8	14.2	United Church of Christ 13.1
South Dakota	1.1	14.2	31.5	27.2	
Washington	10.4	10.1	22.3	25.9	
Wisconsin	1.0	14.5	50.9	19.9	United Church of Christ 9.6

Counties Carried by Stevenson 1956 and Nixon 1960

Alabama: Houston

Arkansas: Clay, Craighead, Fulton, Marion, Pike, Randolph, Sharp, Stone

Florida: Desoto, Hardee

Georgia: Union, Whitfield

Illinois: Union

Indiana: Sullivan

Kentucky: Barren, Boyle, Bullitt, Clark, Grant, Livingston, McLean, Powell, Spencer

Minnesota: Isanti, Kandiyohi

Mississippi: Lowndes, Tunica

Missouri: Carter, Clay, Dent, Dunklin, Iron, Linn, Oregon, Pulaski, Reynolds, Schuyler, Scotland, Shannon, Texas, Worth

North Carolina: Jackson

Oklahoma: Atoka, Beckham, Caddo, Comanche, Garvin, Grady, Greer, Haskell, Hughes, Kiowa, Le Flore, McClain, McIntosh, Okfuskee, Pontotoc, Pottawatomie, Pushmataha, Roger Mills, Seminole, Sequoyah, Stephens, Washita

South Dakota: Miner, Spink, Todd

Tennessee: Chester, Clay, Crockett, Decatur, Dyer, Madison

Texas: Armstrong, Bailey, Childress, Collingsworth, Dallam, Dawson, Donley, Fisher, Gaines, Hale, Hardeman, Hartley, Moore, Motley, Parmer, Wheeler, Wilbarger, Wise, Yoakum

Washington: Cowlitz, Douglas, Grant

Anti–Kennedy Voting in Small Towns

Town	State	% Kennedy Decline	Town	State	% Kennedy Decline
Decatur	Georgia	-15	Pella	Iowa	-6
Greenville	South Carolina	-14	McAlister	Oklahoma	-6
Columbia	South Carolina	-12	Anderson	South Carolina	-6
Murfreesboro	Tennessee	-12	Albany	Georgia	-5
Jonesboro	Arkansas	-11	Hattiesburg	Mississippi	-5
Myrtle Beach	South Carolina	-11	Monroe	Louisiana	-5
Macon	Georgia	-10	Fayetteville	Arkansas	-4
Valdosta	Georgia	-10	Dalton	Georgia	-4
Paducah	Kentucky	-10	Columbia	Missouri	-4
Meridian	Mississippi	-10	Greenville	North Carolina	-4
Dothan	Alabama	-9	Stillwater	Oklahoma	-4
Blytheville	Arkansas	-9	Spartanburg	South Carolina	-4
Jackson	Mississippi	-9	Cleveland	Tennessee	-4
Jackson	Tennessee	-9	Lubbock	Texas	-4
Florence	Alabama	-8	Fort Myers	Florida	-3
Huntsville	Alabama	-8	Columbus	Georgia	-3
Decatur	Alabama	-8	Bloomington	Indiana	-3
Columbia	Tennessee	-8	Norman	Oklahoma	-3
Clovis	New Mexico	-7	Amarillo	Texas	-3
Lawton	Oklahoma	-7			

Note: Many of the towns have experienced considerable population growth since 1960 and are really no longer small towns.

CHAPTER 5

The Election by Region

The Northeast

The Northeast includes the six culturally distinctive New England states and the Big Three (New York, New Jersey and Pennsylvania) states called the Mid-Atlantic by the Census Bureau. Historically Republican before the New Deal, the Northeast was the economic engine that drove the nation, its symbol being Wall Street and the great metropolis of New York City. (As a result, the region was often the target of ridicule and derision from economic populists and, later, cultural conservatives in the rest of the country.) Its Republicanism was pro-business but generally libertarian and culturally tolerant. (It was the region least sympathetic to Prohibition.) It eventually became the Catholic and Jewish strongholds of the nation, and its Protestants were somewhat more moderate in theology and lifestyle than their co–religionists elsewhere (except, perhaps, in Pennsylvania Dutch country).

Virtually every European nation contributed immigrants to the Northeast. Catholics often had Italian, Irish, Polish and French Canadian backgrounds, while Protestants were often German, Scotch-Irish, Dutch and Scandinavian (there were Norwegians in Brooklyn and Swedes in Upstate New York, Maine and Massachusetts). The region was polyglot and culturally diverse (and would become even more so after 1965).

New York provided the Democrats with several presidents (Grover Cleveland, FDR) and unsuccessful candidates (Horatio Seymour, Horace Greeley, Samuel Tilden, Alfred E. Smith) but Republicans won most Northeastern electoral votes until FDR's triumphs. In 1948 the region backed its favorite son, New York governor Thomas E. Dewey, over Border-Stater Harry Truman (except in heavily Catholic and Democratic Massachusetts and Rhode Island). In two hard-fought campaigns, Eisenhower beat Stevenson in every Northeastern state.

The booming and prosperous suburbs of the Northeast became the epicenter of "modern" Eisenhower-brand Republicanism, with its internationalist posture and willingness to adapt the party to new economic and demographic realities. Little did its practitioners know that its century-long era of dominance in the party and country was coming to an end in 1960.

CONNECTICUT

Heavily Catholic and mainline Protestant Connecticut showed large Kennedy gains. No counties, and not a single one of the state's towns, gave the senator from the neighboring state a lower vote than Stevenson. Kennedy carried the state 54 percent to 46 percent.

Kennedy's highest vote (72 percent) was recorded in the blue-collar town of Griswold in New Haven County, which had also produced Stevenson's strongest support. Hartford, the state capital, was the second strongest town for both Democratic candidates. JFK's highest gain over Stevenson (32 percentage points) came in multiethnic Waterbury, a classic New England Catholic swing town. Kennedy won back New Britain, then largely Polish Catholic, which had bolted to Eisenhower in the previous election. He carried heavily Catholic Windsor Locks with 66 percent, though Al Smith had done better in 1928. A number of small towns with many French Catholic voters, such as Derby, Sprague, Enfield, Beacon Falls and Plainfield, gave Kennedy about two-thirds of their ballots. JFK carried 18 of the 20 towns that had supported Smith in 1928 and all six towns that stuck bravely with Stevenson in 1956. Stevenson had been the weakest Democratic candidate in the state since 1924.

Nixon's strongholds were in high-income suburbia, mostly in the New York City suburbs of Fairfield County, where he swept 79 percent in Darien, 74 percent in Wilton, and 72 percent in New Canaan. His other area of considerable strength was the Protestant countryside, similar in character, ethnicity and political history to other parts of rural New England. Nixon's banner town, where he received nearly 80 percent support, was the tiny village of Canaan, near the Massachusetts border in Litchfield County. Nixon's vote exceeded 70 percent in sixteen rural Protestant villages and small towns, and his support declined only about four to six points from Eisenhower's record 1956 vote.

Ethnicity and religion reinforced each other in terms of political preference. Kennedy carried towns where many voters were of Italian, French Canadian, and Polish ancestry while Nixon easily carried towns where most people claimed English or German ancestry. Irish American areas were rather close, depending more on income than on ethnicity. African American and Jewish precincts favored Kennedy. Nixon won two-thirds support in Woodstock, a town with many voters of Swedish ancestry.

Nixon carried Cornwall, Kent, West Hartford, and Westport, which all became fashionable, liberal communities decades later — a trend characteristic of the Northeast. (Connecticut's six wealthiest towns gave Kennedy 31.2 percent compared to Stevenson's 20.6 percent. In 2008 they gave Obama 54.6 percent)

MAINE

Down East was about as Republican as a state could get in 1960. Its English and Scotch-Irish Protestant orientation, with a strong Masonic movement, outweighed the French Catholic and smaller Irish and Polish Catholic communities to make the state unstoppable for any GOP candidate. Even FDR could not win the state, and Al Smith failed to win even a third of the vote. Eisenhower's landslide by 71 percent to 29 percent in 1956 offered little hope for Democrats, though Kennedy's New England residence was thought to be of some help.

JFK received 43 percent, a gain of 14 points, but he carried only two counties, French Catholic Androscoggin, and York County, where the French Catholic town of Biddeford put him over the top. But his gains were small in the most Protestant counties on the coast — Hancock, Lincoln and Washington, where Nixon piled up huge majorities. The cities also tended to vote along religious lines. Even liberal Portland narrowly favored Nixon (50.6 percent to 49.4 percent). The Democratic future was still a little short of birth.

Ethnicity, religion and tradition shaped the Maine vote in 1960. In French Catholic towns it was all JFK: 83 percent in Lewiston, 86 percent in Madawaska, 94 percent in Grand Isle, 85 percent in Saint Agatha, 87 percent in Biddeford — all solid gains over Stevenson. But in upper-income Protestant and resort areas it was all Nixon: 84 percent in Kennebunkport, 76 percent in Cape Elizabeth, and 77 percent in Bar Harbor. (These towns would drift to the Democrats decades later, supporting Barack Obama in

2008.) Rural Protestants weren't wild about JFK either. The hamlet of Meddybemps in Washington County voted 44 to 3 for Nixon. Linneus in Aroostook County gave the vice president 92 percent, up from Eisenhower's 90 percent. Kennedy ran behind Stevenson in a few of the state's 500 towns: In Stow in Knox County he dropped from 19.6 percent to 6.4 percent. In Orient in Aroostook County, Stevenson's 41.2 percent became 25.5 percent for Kennedy. Kennedy swept the American Indian vote in two counties, tiny as it was, 192–22, a 90 percent landslide. A much smaller vote in 1956 went 54–46 percent for Eisenhower.

Aroostook County has some clear-cut divisions between Catholic and Protestant. In addition, the Catholics are mostly French and inhabit the picturesque St. John Valley. The Protestants are mostly of English, Scots and Scotch-Irish heritage and somewhat evangelical and low-church. In 1960 they could not have been further apart. The French Catholic towns gave Kennedy 86.3 percent, a gain of 30 points over Stevenson's 56 percent. The Protestant villages gave Nixon 83 percent, a gain of two points. More important, the vote turnout rose 42.4 percent in Protestant areas, giving Nixon 703 additional votes to JFK's 114. For example, Kennedy was the choice of 95 percent of voters in New Canada, while Nixon received 92 percent in Linneus. These villages had similar income but different religions.

The other prong of Republicanism, upper-income towns, gave Nixon 76 percent, a loss of 11 points from Eisenhower's 87 percent. Since Protestants outnumbered Catholics better than two to one in Maine and since Masons had a higher percentage of the adult male population in Maine than in any other state, the state went easily for Nixon. Statewide, 21 towns gave Kennedy a lower vote percentage than they had given Stevenson. All were in rural areas.

David Walker of Bowdoin College found this to be true in his analysis of the data from the Pinetree State:

> In retrospect the religious issue was more important in gaining for Kennedy his unexpected support from the Franco–American group. Widely publicized efforts to defeat the Democratic candidate were initiated by fundamentalist and conservative Protestant groups. Most of the Franco–American respondents who behaved differently in November than had been expected in August did so in reaction to these efforts. In the northern-tier New England states, there was also, perhaps a growing realization that the religious campaign was having its desired effect among many of their Protestant neighbors.
>
> In Maine, the election figures indicate that the religious issue was a primary

cause for the Republican outpouring that inundated the Democrats on November 8th. Voter turnout increased 23.5 per cent over 1956 in the rural towns and by 28.5 per cent in the largely non–French cities. The Republican share of the vote in largely Protestant rural hamlets was 69 percent; the Republican share for the Yankee cities was 61 per cent. In the fourteen communities with the largest proportion of French inhabitants, the increase of votes was 11 per cent over the 1956 campaign. Kennedy received 73 per cent of this vote. When the returns from both the French and Yankee cities were compared, it was found that the increases in both groups neutralized one another, with the total "city vote" being divided between Nixon and Kennedy. The extraordinary increase in the "country vote" however, provided the needed margin for a victory for both the state and national Republican tickets. Over-all, then, in Maine, the GOP gained by the operation of the ethnic and religious factors in the campaign. But, as we have seen, the price for the victory was the loss of approximately 11 per cent of the Franco–American vote.[1]

MASSACHUSETTS

JFK easily won his home state with a shade over 60 percent, a 20-point gain over Stevenson's unusually low 1956 vote. He gained in every county, ranging from 16 points in rural Franklin County, which he lost, to 25 points in Bristol County, the most heavily Catholic county, where many Portuguese Americans resided. He lost Cape Cod (Barnstable County), where the Kennedy family estate is located in Hyannisport, as well as Martha's Vineyard and Nantucket, all of which were Yankee Protestant and unshakably Republican areas in 1960.

The town vote shows traditional partisan patterns reinforced by religious identity. Even in his home, "Kennedy lost every Protestant town," wrote political analyst Kevin Phillips.[2] He carried all of the Catholic towns, urban and small towns, and split the suburban vote. Interestingly, his number one town in the Bay State was Chelsea, then a stronghold of Eastern European Jews. Chelsea, which gave Kennedy 80 percent, was also Stevenson's strongest town, with 67 percent. JFK's biggest gain over Stevenson was registered in Provincetown, where artists, writers, artisans and Portuguese fishermen coexisted nicely (to be joined in later years by a vibrant gay community). Upper-income towns went for Nixon, since plush suburbia was still Republican in 1960, long before the party's moderate image changed dramatically. Kennedy carried upper-middle income Brookline, where he was born, with 53 percent. (Another Brookline resident and Democratic presidential candidate, Michael Dukakis, managed 74 percent in 1988, after suburbia started moving leftward.)

Religion, ethnicity and income seem to have influenced voting decisions in JFK's hometown of Boston. He carried every ward except upper-class Protestant Beacon Hill, where he received 42 percent, an increase from Stevenson's 33 percent. This was the last time Beacon Hill supported a Republican for president, joining the trend toward upper-class liberalism in inner city neighborhoods after 1964. Kennedy's vote also declined 1 percent, from 78 percent to 77 percent, in heavily Jewish precincts, though his overall Jewish vote was almost as high as among Irish and Italian Catholics. Kennedy received 85 percent in Italian precincts in the North End and in East Boston, up from Stevenson's 58 percent. His Irish support varied from 89 percent in working-class Charlestown up to 70 percent among upper-income Irish in Ward 20. His support increased 20–30 points over Stevenson's vote among the Boston Irish.[3]

Kennedy received 70 percent to 80 percent in most heavily-Catholic jurisdictions while Nixon received 75 percent to 85 percent in rural Protestant villages. In Rowe, Nixon's 84 percent was slightly higher than Eisenhower's vote. In Northfield, where evangelical evangelist Dwight Moody was born, Nixon swept to victory by 78 percent to 22 percent.

New Hampshire

Kennedy lost the Granite State 53 percent to 47 percent, but he made solid gains over Stevenson and brought the Democratic vote back to the Truman level. The state was sharply divided by religion and ethnicity. French Catholics, from rural Berlin to urban Manchester, voted for Kennedy. The Anglo-Protestants were just as solid for Nixon. Rural Carroll County turned in 80 percent for Nixon, just a few points less than Eisenhower's support. (Four years later Carroll was the only county in New England to back Barry Goldwater. In 2008 it went to Barack Obama.) Next-door Coos County, largely French Catholic, went 57 percent for Kennedy, with nearly 80 percent for JFK in the French town of Berlin. In New Hampshire there were 14 towns where Kennedy ran behind Stevenson, second only to Maine among the New England states.

There was a telling correlation between a referendum vote on expanding alcoholic beverage sales in the state, which passed easily 82 percent to 18 percent. There were 34 towns where the prohibitionist side prevailed. These Protestant, Republican jurisdictions voted three to one for Nixon, giving him 74 percent of the presidential vote. While this was nine points lower than Eisenhower's 83 percent, Nixon actually received 270 more votes than Ike in these nearly three dozen towns, a gain for Kennedy that was only about half of his statewide gain. The connection between certain social issues and Republican voting held up in the Granite State.

Heavily Catholic wards in ten New Hampshire towns and cities (including Dover, Rochester, Somersworth, Laconia, Franklin, Manchester, Nashua, Claremont, Lebanon and Berlin) gave Kennedy 75.3 percent and Stevenson 57.6 percent. Kennedy's gain of nearly 18 points was a good deal less than in many other states, possibly because Catholics were the only group in the state to stick with Adlai Stevenson in 1956.

NEW JERSEY

The Garden State was one of the few where Kennedy's Catholicism helped him eke out a narrow win, 50.4 percent to 49.6 percent, after three previous GOP victories. Kennedy ran 16 points better than Stevenson's unusually low 1956 showing, gaining in every county. JFK's biggest gains came in the New York City metro region (Hudson, Essex, Middlesex and Union), where he piled up impressive urban victories and respectable suburban results. He did well among all Catholic ethnic groups, Italians, Irish, and East Europeans, as well as among Jews and African Americans. Nixon won among German, Dutch and English ancestry voters and piled up huge margins in wealthy suburbs like Ridgewood and Saddle River.

Kennedy's weakest gains came in South Jersey (Salem, Gloucester, Camden), which are more Protestant and even southern in flavor in the rural areas. He lost decisively in the Pine Barrens, a rural area where voters resemble their counterparts in southern Delaware, and Maryland's Eastern Shore — namely white, conservative, working class and Protestant (usually Methodist). Country music is popular among the Pineys, and the Klan was strong there in the 1920s.

Kennedy ran behind Stevenson in a few towns. He dropped seven points in Audubon Park, a working-class town in Camden County (where George Wallace would receive his highest New Jersey support eight years later). In the super liberal town of Roosevelt, where artists like Ben Shahn and other intellectuals lived, JFK dropped one point, but his 87 percent and Stevenson's 88 percent made this the top Democratic town in the state. (This old left town is less liberal today, giving Democrats low-70s majorities. This is a town where Bob Dole and John McCain received twice as many votes as Dwight Eisenhower).

The religious issue showed its virulence in the Jersey Shore resort community of Ocean Grove, a kind of Methodist-revivalist theocracy where swimming, riding bicycles and Sunday newspapers were all prohibited by law until a U.S. Supreme Court ruling struck down the religious domination of civilian authority in the 1970s. Ocean Grove went for Nixon 90 percent to 10 percent.

Kennedy made 20–30 point gains in Catholic communities, ranging from small towns in Warren County (Alpha, Phillipsburg) to Italian-American areas on the Jersey Shore, e.g., Buena in Atlantic County. He trailed Stevenson in seven small Protestant towns and barely exceeded Stevenson in many others.

In middle-class Prospect Park, in Passaic County, the Dutch vote was anti–Catholic and anti–Democratic, giving Nixon 81 percent. Historian Gerald DeJong explains: "Among strict Calvinists in some eastern cities, the pro–Republican vote was, in part, a reaction to the prevailing Roman Catholic tone of the Democratic party."[4]

New York

Polyglot and multicultural New York State was made for JFK and he returned the state to the Democratic column for the first time since 1944, winning 52.6 percent. His 14-point gain over Stevenson included every county, ranging from a 26-point rise in rural French Catholic Clinton County on the Canadian border to a seven-point gain in Yankee Protestant Tioga County. His gains were greatest in upstate Catholic urban and small town areas (Albany, Buffalo, and Utica) and were smallest in central and western rural counties. Kennedy's vote ranged from 68 percent in the Bronx to 26 percent in Yates and Delaware counties, upstate rural areas. Nixon won about 55 percent in the suburbs and on Long Island, though JFK's vote was above the Democratic norm. The Hudson River Valley counties (called America's Loire Valley) gave Nixon 60 percent, reflecting its Old Dutch and English flavor.

While Kennedy did not run behind Stevenson, he still lost heavily in upstate rural counties. In six counties (Allegany, Chenango, Delaware, Hamilton, Tioga, Yates) Nixon's vote exceeded 70 percent. As for religion, Methodists ranked first in these GOP bastions, with 33 percent of churchgoers compared to 6 percent statewide. Presbyterians, Episcopalians and Baptists together were 26 percent compared to 9 percent in the state as a whole. Catholics were about a quarter of the population in these counties.

As political analyst Kevin Phillips pointed out, New York City Catholics were far less enthusiastic about JFK than their co–religionists elsewhere, giving him 55 percent to 60 percent support. This was due, he suggests, to their approval of Eisenhower-era foreign policy and the anti–Communist tenor of Republican rhetoric as well as social conservatism.[5] This may be why Staten Island (Richmond County) went for Nixon after backing Smith in 1928 (Puerto Rican Catholics were solid for Kennedy, however). Still, Kennedy won the upstate Catholic vote, possibly due to the hostility of local Protestant Republicans, and secured modest margins in the suburbs.

In heavily Catholic Buffalo, Kennedy received 65 percent, ranging from 79 percent in Polish areas and 77 percent in African American precincts to the mid–40s in German Lutheran wards.[6]

PENNSYLVANIA

Governor David Lawrence "remained skeptical about the effects of Kennedy's religion until election day," commented his biographer, Michael P. Weber. Lawrence was unusually sensitive to anti–Catholicism because he had seen the baleful effects in previous elections, including his own narrow escape from its clutches two years before. Still, "he personally campaigned extensively across the state. The Kennedy motorcade through the state drew crowds estimated at nearly one million."[7] Lawrence had been so frightened of religious bigotry that he supported a third nomination for Adlai Stevenson, though he reluctantly released the Pennsylvania delegation, which was solidly for Kennedy, at the Democratic convention. (Lawrence steadfastly maintained that Stevenson was the best man for the presidency.)

Lawrence had been through the Smith campaign of 1928 and had lost his bid to become Pittsburgh mayor in 1931, both of which he blamed on anti–Catholicism. Writes Weber: "Lawrence's own defeat in 1931 further reinforced his belief that Roman Catholicism was an insurmountable handicap for a political candidate. His concern over the issue became so strong that it bordered on paranoia."[8]

Pennsylvania was alone in the entire Northeast in that it had 16 counties where Kennedy ran behind Stevenson. (As we shall see in the next chapter, the anti–Kennedy undertow in rural areas affected 65 counties to some degree.) As had been true since the New Deal, Democrats won the state by amassing large majorities in Philadelphia and Pittsburgh and losing the rest of the state (except Scranton, Erie, Reading and a few smaller cities).

The Keystone State had been an unshakably Republican stronghold from Lincoln through Hoover, who carried the state against Roosevelt in 1932. A powerful, almost legendary Republican machine kept the state in the GOP column until widespread approval of FDR's first term led to a landslide win in 1936. Even then, the rural areas remained Republican. The luster slipped and Dewey and Eisenhower carried the state three times.

Despite widespread anti–Catholicism, Kennedy held on to a 51 percent–49 percent triumph, again with the winning formula of a 331,000-vote margin in Philadelphia and 107,000-vote margin in Allegheny County (Pittsburgh and its close-in suburbs). This 438,000-vote edge offset Nixon's 322,000-vote sweep in the other 65 counties, 53 of which he carried. Kennedy's most significant gains came from strongly Catholic counties (Elk, Cambria, and Schuylkill).

The anti–Kennedy belt was in Central Pennsylvania, from the Scotch-Irish Appalachians to heavily German Lutheran Snyder and York counties — areas which rejected Al Smith by margins ranging from four-to-one to ten-to-one. His worse declines were in rural Mifflin, Fulton and Juniata counties in Appalachia, and York, a large population county in Pennsylvania Dutch country.

In the most anti–Kennedy counties, a majority of residents were either Lutheran (29.8 percent) or Methodist (22.8 percent). Catholics were a weak third at 14.2 percent, less than half of their state average. Both Lutherans and Methodists were much stronger in these counties than they were statewide. Other religious groups overrepresented in the anti–Kennedy belt were Brethren-Mennonite (7.3 percent), and United Church of Christ (13.1 percent). (Much more detail will emerge from the precinct study in the following chapter.)

Two newspapers warned of the impending religious backlash. The October 25, 1960, *Gettysburg Times* reported: "The Harrisburg area is being covered with scurrilous anti–Kennedy religious literature." Perhaps this is why Kennedy's vote share dropped 15–20 points in rural parts of Dauphin and Cumberland counties.

In the Philadelphia suburbs the *Delaware County Daily Times* had this to say on October 17, 1960: "The word is out that Kennedy's Roman Catholic religion is hurting his chances."

RHODE ISLAND

Rhode Island, the most Catholic state, was Kennedy's top state and also the state where he gained the most. Heavily ethnic Rhode Island has many Italian, Irish, Portuguese and French Canadian ancestry residents, and also a sizable chunk of Scotch-Irish and English ancestry voters. Episcopalians are the second largest religious group. Kennedy's biggest victory was in French Catholic Woonsocket, where he received 79 percent, and in multicultural Providence (72 percent), the only two cities to support Stevenson previously. Even in Rhode Island, Kennedy dropped 1 percent in Charlestown, a Republican coastal village and agricultural area. The state's most Protestant county, Washington, was the only one to back Nixon.

The state's capital and largest city, Providence, stuck with Stevenson in 1956 though the state defected twice to Ike. Kennedy received 79 percent in Italian areas and a respectable vote among Yankee Protestants. As in Massachusetts, Yankee Protestants in Rhode Island gave their greatest support to Episcopalian Democrats like Senator Claiborne Pell. One interesting subgroup, "Catholic Negroes from the Portuguese Cape Verde Islands" (as two researchers called them), went 85 percent for JFK and 63 percent for Stevenson.[9]

VERMONT

The Green Mountain State had supported every Republican since John C. Fremont first carried the GOP banner in 1856. So it was no surprise that the Nixon-Lodge ticket easily prevailed 59 percent to 41 percent. Fellow New Englander JFK, though, gained over 13 points, especially in rural French Catholic Franklin and Grand Isle counties, and he carried Chittenden County (Burlington) by 13 points. The nation's two heaviest Congregationalist (UCC) strongholds, Lamoille and Orange counties, still voted more than three to one for Nixon and limited Kennedy's gain to under eight points.

Traditional voting patterns prevailed. While Kennedy won 70 percent or more in heavily Catholic areas, Nixon did even better in Protestant strongholds. Four towns gave Kennedy a lower vote share than Stevenson had received. It would be three decades in the future when this Old Yankee Republican State would move toward the Democrats, eventually becoming one of Barack Obama's banner states.

The New England subregion went for favorite son JFK by 56 percent to 44 percent and gave him 28 electoral votes to 12 for Nixon. The result was a sharp differentiation between southern New England for JFK and upper New England for Nixon. This was not surprising. Southern New England is somewhat more cosmopolitan and Catholic while upper New England had loyally supported the GOP since going for Fremont in 1856. It was the only subregion of a subregion to go for Landon in 1936. So even Kennedy could not dent the unshakeable Republicanism of Yankeedom. (It would take right-wing Republicans Barry Goldwater and George W. Bush to end the Republican monopoly in Maine, New Hampshire and Vermont.) Maine and Vermont were on Nixon's top ten states. They were almost always among the GOP's highest vote-getting areas.

Kennedy was immensely popular in southern New England, and all three of its states were on Kennedy's top ten in percentage of popular votes (Rhode Island 1st, Massachusetts 3rd, Connecticut 5th).

Adding to the Northeast outcome were solid, if hard-fought, victories in New York, New Jersey and Pennsylvania, giving JFK a 121–12 margin in electoral votes and nearly 53 percent of the 20 million votes cast in this vote-heavy region. Kennedy's gains over Stevenson were highest in the Northeast, exceeding double digits in every state but Pennsylvania.

Anti–Kennedy Towns in Selected Northeastern States

State	County	Town	% Anti–Kennedy
New Jersey	Atlantic	Port Republic	-0.4
	Camden	Audubon Park	-7.0
	Monmouth	Roosevelt	-1.0
	Ocean	Harvey Cedars	-1.0
	Salem	Alloway	-0.7
		Upper Pittsgrove	-1.3
	Warren	Greenwich	-0.1
Rhode Island	Washington	Charlestown	-0.3
Massachusetts	Franklin	Rowe	-0.2

5. The Election by Region   109

State	County	Town	% Anti–Kennedy
Maine	Aroostook	Amity	-3.4
		Easton	-2.2
		Mars Hill	-1.7
		Monticello	-3.7
		Orient	-15.7
		Westmanland	-3.3
	Franklin	Coplin Plantation	-15.0
		Rangeley Plantation	-7.7
		Sandy River	-3.7
	Lincoln	Alna	-1.6
	Oxford	Byron	-3.4
		Stow	-13.2
	Penobscot	Edinburg	-9.6
		Grand Falls	-11.1
	Somerset	Moose River	-8.1
		Starks	-2.4
		Dennistown	-1.5
		The Forks	-1.9
	Washington	Machiasport	-2.8
		Marshfield	-2.5
		Codyville	-17.1
New Hampshire	Rockingham	Nottingham	-0.7
	Carroll	Hart's Location	-20.8
		Eaton	-2.1
	Merrimack	Bradford	-2.2
		Sutton	-0.2
	Hillsborough	Sharon	-9.0
		Weare	-0.3
	Sullivan	Craydon	-3.2
		Washington	-1.8
	Grafton	Dorchester	-0.1
		Piermont	-0.2
		Rumney	-0.9
	Coos	Clarksville	-8.3
		Millsfield	-8.6
Vermont	Addison	Goshen	-0.6
	Orleans	Jay	-1.6
	Rutland	Tinmouth	-2.1
	Windsor	Andover	-2.1

Border States

The Border States are difficult to define. Straddling the North and South, and even the West and East, they are collectively a cultural fault line. That is why most demographers put them, reluctantly perhaps, in other regions.

Maryland and Delaware, though below the Mason-Dixon Line, increasingly belong to the Northeast politically. They went for Dewey in 1948, as did the entire Northeast, except for Massachusetts and Rhode Island; but they backed JFK in 1960, as did the entire region, save for upper New England. There are southern flavored parts of these states — in southern Delaware, on Maryland's Eastern Shore and in southern Maryland from Annapolis to the counties bordering the western shore of the Chesapeake Bay. Catholics and Methodists are the strongest groups, and Methodists are historically strong in the upper south and lower north states.

Kentucky is clearly or mostly southern, and is classified with the South (as is Oklahoma) by *Congressional Quarterly*. Kentucky is heavily Southern Baptist, with pockets of Catholic strength in the suburban counties around Cincinnati, in Louisville, and in the old Settlement areas around Bardstown. But rural Kentucky is as Baptist as parts of Alabama, Mississippi and Georgia. Historically Democratic, it occasionally bolted to the GOP, for McKinley once, for Coolidge and Hoover and for Eisenhower once before going strongly for Nixon. Its eastern rural counties operate in a kind of time warp, dividing along party lines established by the Civil War.

Missouri is another hard state to classify. St. Louis is eastern-oriented and Catholic; Kansas City faces Midwest and is divided between Protestants and Catholics. Rural areas are heavily Baptist, with pockets of Methodists and Disciples of Christ. Its "bootheel" region is as southern as Arkansas, while the Ozark region is fundamentalist and populist. Many of its presidential elections have been close, and it usually goes with the winner (though a narrow McCain victory in 2008 may have dented its barometer image).

Oklahoma is a Plains state but is so heavily Southern Baptist that it seems culturally southern. On social and cultural issues, from prohibition a century ago to abortion and gay rights, it is among the most culturally intransigent states, standing against changes popular elsewhere. It was probably the most anti–Catholic state in 1928 and 1960, though it elected a slew of Catholic Republicans to major offices decades later. Oklahoma has supported the Republican presidential candidate in 14 of the last 15 elections, beginning with Eisenhower in 1952, and was McCain's strongest state in 2008.

West Virginia remains an anomaly. Though it became a state during the Civil War to support the Union, it has never quite fit in. Is it southern or midwestern? Its population is heavily white and Protestant and mostly of Northern European descent (as are Kentucky, Indiana and Kansas). Methodists outnumbered Baptists in 1960, and it ranked with Kansas as the most Methodist states. But the state has a large number of independent fundamentalists, who do not show up in religious membership data but turn up in polling data, making it one of the most religiously conservative states. In a counterintuitive sense, this poor state, with low levels of income and education, moved Republican during the three elections in the first decade of the new century.

It was one of only five states to give Obama a lower vote than Kerry (though only by a sliver of a percentage point), and several coal-mining counties voted Republican for the first time since Hoover. Until recently, the Mountaineer State was more Democratic than the nation, going for Stevenson in 1952, Humphrey in 1968, Carter in 1980 and Dukakis in 1988. It was a loyal New Deal state until Kennedy faced considerable religion-based opposition. (Before FDR the state was staunchly Republican, even supporting Hughes over President Wilson in 1916.)

The Border States may have reached their apex of political influence in 1948, when two residents of the region, Harry Truman of Missouri and Alben Barkley of Kentucky, comprised the successful Democratic national ticket.

Delaware

Delaware's rural Methodists in Sussex County favored Nixon by small margins though JFK ran slightly ahead of Stevenson. In the state's largest city, Wilmington (New Castle County), the senator put together a winning majority in the African American, Polish and Italian neighborhoods. The part of the state that borders Maryland's rural Eastern Shore favored Nixon. Kennedy's narrow 51 percent to 49 percent victory was fueled by his seven point gain over Stevenson in the Wilmington area.

Kentucky

When the returns were coming in from Kentucky, one prominent state Democrat lamented, "It was a Democratic year and they had to go and run a Catholic." Kennedy lost this normally Democratic state 54 percent to 46 percent, a mere one-point gain over Stevenson's 1956 showing and worse than Stevenson's 1952 vote (when he barely carried the Bluegrass State) and Truman's 1948 sweep.

Kennedy's slight gain was due to urban Louisville (Jefferson County), with its large Catholic population, where the GOP margin dropped from 36,000 to 1,000; Lexington (Fayette County); and the German Catholic but Republican Cincinnati suburbs (Campbell and Kenton counties). Rural Baptist Kentucky shifted heavily toward Nixon, turning what should have been a Democratic victory in a Democratic state in a Democratic year into an 81,000-vote Nixon triumph.

In rural and small-town Kentucky, Nixon's margin was 65,000 and Eisenhower's 37,000. Kennedy ran weaker than Stevenson in 85 of the state's 120 counties. This included almost every county in the western and central regions and much of the north, extending to the Cincinnati exurbs. Only in eastern Kentucky, in the coal mining region, did Kennedy run ahead. Nine counties backed Stevenson, then shifted to Nixon. The last time they voted for a Republican was in 1928 when Hoover ran against Smith, and apparently for the same reason. The most intense anti–Kennedy tide came in the "Little Dixie" counties in the far west and in rural areas near Cincinnati, including Boone County, where the Cincinnati airport and the "Creation Museum," backed by fundamentalists, is today located. JFK dropped 18 points in Marshall County, 15 points in Calloway County and 13 points in Carlisle County, all in the far western corner, which is still Dixie in this Border State. Southern Baptists were 66 percent of the population in the anti–Kennedy counties, 17 points above their state average, while 15 percent were Methodist and 8 percent were Catholic (less than half of the 19 percent Catholic state figure).

Sharp differences in voting behavior between Catholics and Baptists occurred in a few counties where they were rivals for political influence and where they had clashed over issues involving religion in public schools. In Nelson County, home of Bardstown and one of the oldest Catholic cathedrals in the U.S., political writer Theodore H. White found that four

Baptist precincts gave Kennedy 35 percent, while five Catholic precincts gave him 88 percent — a huge gap.[10]

Kentucky

Geographic Areas	% Kennedy 1960	% Stevenson 1956	% Change
Louisville/Lexington	48	41	+7
Cincinnati Suburbs	46	39	+7
Democratic Mountains	66	63	+3
Republican Mountains	16	17	-1
Mining Counties	59	50	+9
Little Dixie	62	67	-5
Rural Baptist Democrats	54	67	-13

MARYLAND

The Old Line State is often thought of as a Catholic stronghold because of its founding as a refuge for English Catholics by Lord Baltimore, but its Catholic population has always been a bit lower than nationally (since the Civil Was era anyway). It became somewhat anti–Catholic after 1689, though Maryland Catholics later supported the Declaration of Independence. Maryland was the only state to support the American (formerly Know Nothing) Party in the 1856 election for president, and Al Smith lost decisively in 1928, particularly in rural areas. But in 1960 the moderate Border State warmed up to JFK and he won comparatively easily, sweeping Baltimore city, with its large Catholic, Jewish and African American communities, by an 88,000 vote margin, enough to win the state's electoral votes.

Kennedy lost the Methodist Eastern Shore but ran relatively well there and won in the growing suburbs around Washington, DC, sweeping Prince George's County, which almost switched to Stevenson in 1956, and affluent Montgomery County, which went Democratic for the first time since FDR in 1936.

In Montgomery, Kennedy did well in affluent and well educated areas but ran behind Stevenson in rural Protestant Damascus at the county's northern edge and lost two to one in the Seventh-day Adventist stronghold of Takoma Park. This community straddling the DC border was then the world headquarters of Adventism, anchored by a large church and Columbia Union College. It had long been Republican and was one of two precincts to support Herbert Hoover against FDR in 1932 as well as supporting prohibition in a 1933 referendum. (Takoma Park has since changed character demographically, becoming a multicultural, multiracial outpost of the political left. A town that gave only a third of its votes to Kennedy gave 93 percent to Barack Obama in 2008. In 2000 it gave Ralph Nader more votes than it did George W. Bush.)

One writer remembers growing up in the Adventist community during the 1960 election. The witty and stylish James Thompson describes his experiences among the Adventists during the campaign of 1960:

> I was sixteen years old and in the eleventh grade of an Adventist academy in Takoma Park as the campaign pushed toward its climax. Our Bible teacher that term, an elderly preacher from Mississippi named (as I shall call him) J. Hollifield Powell, devoted most of the semester to attacks on Kennedy and his Church. Day after day the Reverend Powell (or "Elder" Powell in Adventist usage) would attain a higher pitch of indignation; his face would redden and his eyes glitter with the rage of some latter-day-Jeremiah as he prophesied the doom of America should Jack Kennedy win the election. He piled atrocity upon atrocity as he exposed the depths of Roman Catholic evil; one would have thought that he alone battled to prevent America from bending the knee to Rome. About a week before Election Day Elder Powell entered the classroom carrying a tape recorder; announcing that he would once and for all convict the Catholic Church in the eyes of God-fearing Christians (as if there were any doubters among this roomful of pimply faced Catholic-haters), he threaded a tape, switched on the machine, folded his arms across his chest and peered at us with an expression of triumph. A woman's voice, quavering with suppressed emotion, identified the speaker as a former nun who had fled a Canadian convent for asylum in the United States. She proceeded to narrate a story of life behind the iron bars and impregnable walls of a nunnery; her tale contained everything guaranteed to excite our ire and confirm our suspicions (and, incidentally, goad our whelming teenage lusts as well): lascivious priests, concubinarian nuns, murdered infants — the Roman Catholic Church as repository of unspeakable depravity. The Whore of Babylon had returned in full panoply. It had taken a Catholic's run for the White House to accomplish it, but those cultured and sedate Adventists of Takoma Park had jettisoned their facts, figures and analyses for a little old-fashioned Catholic-baiting replete with scurrilous sexual imagery. I felt right at home.[11]

This fear pervaded Adventist communities nationwide. Nixon won near-unanimous support in several homogeneously Adventist towns: Keene, Texas; Berrien Springs, Michigan; Collegedale, Tennessee; College Station, Washington; and Loma Linda, California. As Thompson wryly observed, "To Adventists his candidacy threatened the verities and challenged the premises upon which the republic rested. They were not fooled by the wit and suavity: beneath that polished Harvard exterior there lurked the heart of an Inquisitor; the blood of centuries of Protestant martyrs dripped from John Kennedy's hands."[12] As he also noted, "In the face of every prediction by Adventists, the republic survived."[13]

JFK lost in rural Western Maryland, with its German Protestant and Scotch-Irish orientation, especially in Allegany and Garrett counties bordering Appalachia. He carried heavily Catholic Ellicott City, where Mount St. Mary's College, America's second oldest Catholic college is located and where St. Elizabeth Seton, the first U.S.-born saint canonized by the Vatican, is buried. And he won "Old Catholic Southern Maryland" (Charles and St. Mary's Counties), a kind of rural Southern Catholic backwater. In the counties where JFK gained the most, Catholics outnumbered Protestants about two to one, while in the counties where he gained the least, Protestants outnumbered Catholics four to one.

Southern Maryland, one of the oldest settled areas of the nation, exemplified the religious divisions found nationally. This area was settled by English Catholics in the 1630s, when Maryland was a refuge for the widely disliked Roman Catholic community. Charles and St. Mary's counties remained sleepy, tobacco-growing, almost southern areas until 1960. They voted for Kennedy, who ran well ahead of previous Democrats. But Calvert County, the other southern county, was Protestant and supported Nixon.

Kennedy ran poorly in Scotch-Irish Allegany County in the mountains, just slightly ahead of Stevenson, but much weaker than Truman. The county, which once boosted a large Socialist vote earlier in the century, went for Truman, who lost the state, but they rejected Kennedy, who carried the state—a rather typical pattern in small-town America, which moved against the national tide in 1960.

Another anomaly came in Annapolis, the state capital, where the African American ward voted for Nixon, remaining loyal to the party of Lincoln. It would be the last time a Republican candidate for president carried the ward. Kennedy did receive more than double the vote for Stevenson. However, in Baltimore's large African American wards, Kennedy drew 74 percent compared to Stevenson's 52 percent support. JFK won an impressive 85 percent in Polish and Italian Catholic Ward 2, compared to Stevenson's 61 percent. In a middle income Catholic residential-suburban ward, Kennedy received 68 percent, up from Stevenson's 46 percent.

Kennedy's support in heavily Jewish areas was 75–80 percent. Only the silk stocking Ward 12 voted for Nixon.

Maryland was often thought of as a Catholic state; but it never really was more than 20 percent Catholic, and Catholics were just beginning to break through the political barriers around 1960. Few had been elected to the Senate or the governorship. In fact, a majority of governors elected from 1790 to 1960 were Episcopalians. Rural Protestants were unenthusiastic about Catholic Democrats in statewide races. In 1958, a Democratic landslide year, the state's rural areas voted heavily enough to defeat Baltimore mayor Tommy D'Alessandro (House Speaker Nancy Pelosi's father) in the U.S. Senate race, preferring a lackluster Republican, J. Glenn Beall. All of this changed a few years after Kennedy's election.

Missouri

Religion disrupted voting patterns in Missouri in 1928 and did so again in 1960. In 1928 Smith ran worse than any Democratic candidate in history. In the counties that deserted the New York governor in droves, more than two-thirds of residents belonged to Baptist, Methodist or Disciples of Christ churches, which collectively enrolled 38 percent of the state's residents in 1926, according to a special U.S. Census.

As the 1960 campaign progressed, it appeared that history might repeat itself. It nearly did, though Kennedy in the end managed to squeak to victory by 10,000 votes out of 1.9 million. Kennedy's 50.3 percent of the vote was just an eyelash better than Stevenson's 50.1 percent four years before. Kennedy's victory came from St. Louis and its suburbs, which are substantially Catholic, and from loyal Democrats in Harry Truman's home base of Kansas City (Jackson County), though Kennedy's vote was up only slightly in Jackson. Kennedy gained in Catholic rural areas, in Osage, Ste. Genevieve, and Perry counties, and in substantially Catholic Cole County, where the capital, Jefferson City, is located.

But rural Missouri resembled 1928 in its anti–Kennedy backlash. JFK ran behind Stevenson in 92 of the Show Me State's 115 counties (80 percent of them). Fifteen counties backed Stevenson and jumped to Nixon. A dozen of them were in southeast Missouri, while three were in the north and one, Clay, was a Baptist suburb of Kansas City. Seven counties were among the most anti–Kennedy in the nation. In Dunklin County, in the far southeast Boot Heel area bordering Arkansas, Kennedy became the first

Democrat in history to lose the county, running 14 points behind Stevenson. Three nearby counties, Oregon, Reynolds and Shannon, also cast their first-ever Republican majority. (They even supported Smith in 1928, suggesting an increase in anti–Catholicism.) Five counties across the Arkansas border also joined the exodus, making this area a kind of anti–Catholic belt — which really stretched from north Texas through southeastern Oklahoma into Missouri, Arkansas, Kentucky and Tennessee.

The anti–Kennedy counties were overwhelmingly Baptist, 62 percent, with 12 percent Methodist and 3 percent Catholic. The state was roughly divided, 28 percent Catholic and 27 percent Baptist, so this subregion's religious character stands out as distinctive. Many other evangelical and fundamentalist denominations were active in these counties. In counties where Catholics were few and far between (under 10 percent) Nixon piled up a 121,000-vote majority, more than double Eisenhower's 51,000-vote lead. This religious backlash nearly cost Kennedy what should have been a reliable state.

An astute newspaper in Livingston County, the *Chillicothe Constitution-Tribune*, reported on October 31, 1960, that a deluge of anti–Kennedy material was circulating in the area: "Anti–Catholic pamphlets have been mailed to Masons in Northern Missouri, including articles attacking the Roman Catholic hierarchy and church policies that were published in the official Masonic monthly magazine." In its October 5 issue the newspaper attacked "the scurrilous anti–Catholic hate literature, extremist radio and even the sermons in some churches" and reminded voters that "there shall be no religious test for public office."

The Assemblies of God is headquartered in Springfield, the largest city in the Ozarks. Its leadership joined the fight against Kennedy, according to historian Edith L. Blumhofer: "Protestants in general and Pentecostals in particular harbored deep suspicions about Roman Catholic intrigue. During the campaign for the 1960 presidential election, Assemblies of God anti–Catholicism had become increasingly focused."[14]

The group's leader, general superintendent Thomas F. Zimmerman, published "A Protest against Electing a Roman Catholic President" in its official journal, *Pentecostal Evangel*, September 18, 1960. He explicitly called for an anti–Kennedy vote "at the polls in November."[15] This bastion of fundamentalism gave Nixon a 16,500-vote margin, almost double Eisenhower's 9,700 margin.

Oklahoma

The Sooner State may be the nation's most anti–Catholic on the presidential level. Al Smith was buried in a landslide in 1928, running 17 points weaker than the Democratic candidate in 1924. In 1960 Kennedy dropped almost four points behind Stevenson, losing the state by 163,000, almost double Eisenhower's 88,000-vote margin. Oklahoma, Truman's second strongest state in 1948, became Nixon's third strongest state just a dozen years later. Anti–Catholicism is the best explanation for this turnaround, since the state was heavily Democratic in registration and elected only Democrats to Congress and the governorship prior to 1960.

Kennedy's vote declined virtually everywhere, down in 70 of the 77 counties. More counties in Oklahoma (22) than in any other state defected from Stevenson to Nixon. Most were in the central belt from the North Texas border to the Arkansas state line. Two, Atoka (home of country singer Reba McIntyre) and Garvin, voted Republican for the first time ever. Kennedy's vote dropped 20 points in Roger Mills County and 15 points in Harmon County. He was even down two points in Oklahoma

---

RECEIVED: Thirty dirty pieces of Kennedy silver for this endorsement.
—J. Howard Quisling, Oklahoma City, Okla.

Sea-Gram

VOTE FOR
WHISKY KENNEDY
and his "100 Proof"
DAMNOCRATS!

Be sure to stagger to the polls and (1) vote, (2) Vote, (3) VOTE! Then "look for the silver lining" on the next Kennedy whisky you buy. Can a Billion Bucks be WRONG? With a Paternoster, Ave and Gloria; we shall count our Blessed Chestnuts!
—J. Howard Quisling,
Oklahoma City, Okla.

"Let's put a modern distillery in the White House!"
—Iama Kurr

This was a postcard that circulated throughout Oklahoma. At least it was funnier than the usual anti–Kennedy screeds (Fair Campaign Practices Committee Collection, Manuscripts Division, Special Collections, Lauinger Library, Georgetown University).

City but gained 2.5 points in Tulsa. In the counties where anti–Kennedy voting was most concentrated, 64 percent of residents were Baptist and 20 percent Methodist. Even in a heavily Baptist state, these counties exceeded the Baptist statewide percentage by 14 points.

WEST VIRGINIA

The Mountain State, site of Kennedy's great triumph in the primaries largely because it is overwhelmingly Protestant, gave Kennedy a comfortable 53 percent vote, up from Stevenson's 46 percent. But it was only 1 percent higher than Stevenson's 1952 vote and far lower than Truman's vote. Kennedy also ran far behind Democratic candidates for all other state offices and for Congress.

On a county level only Wirt County gave Kennedy a lower vote share than Stevenson, which would seem to indicate little anti–Catholic voting. But two large counties known for anti–Catholic organizing voted heavily for Nixon: Wood, where the Democratic vote only increased from 39 percent to 41 percent and was lower than in 1952, and Cabell, where a similar 1952–56–60 pattern prevailed.

The definitive study of West Virginia's role in 1960 comes from Dan Fleming, whose book, *Kennedy vs. Humphrey*, deals primarily with the primary election but includes a chapter on the fall campaign when religious hysteria made a comeback. He wrote that "the religious issue cost Kennedy a landslide victory against Nixon in the general election. Smear literature was much worse in the general election than in the primary and massive amounts of anti–Catholic literature were distributed against Kennedy in counties such as Cabell, Kanawha and Wood."[16] The famous and fictional "Knights of Columbus oath," the Catholic equivalent of the anti–Semitic screed "Protocols of the Elders of Zion," was even published in the *Charleston Gazette*, the state's largest newspaper. This oath, which purported to claim that Catholics were required to slaughter their Protestant neighbors, seems to have surfaced in a 1908 congressional campaign in Pennsylvania, but its true origins are murky and shrouded in mystery.

"The outpouring of anti–Catholic literature intensified as the general election drew to a close in the fall of 1960,"[17] Fleming wrote. "In Huntington County, noted for its large number of Protestant churches, there was a tremendous amount of anti–Catholic literature distributed by churches."[18] Fleming's interviews with local political leaders and campaign officials found "virulent anti–Catholic sentiment" in Huntington (Cabell County) and Parkersburg (Wood County). Kennedy supporters were shunned by friends and threatened by loss of business. Churches "whipped up" the feelings, and the Church of Christ ran several large newspaper ads denouncing Kennedy.[19] Fleming also charged that "bigotry sharply increased as the issue was inflamed for partisan motives by Republicans."[20]

Kennedy prevailed in the state, so anti–Catholicism was not triumphant, and its prevalence varied. In his summary Fleming observed that "the degree of intensity of the religious issue was quite different throughout the state. In the Protestant southern coal counties, it was generally a minor factor in both elections, and in the more Catholic northern panhandle, not nearly as much negative attention was given the religious aspect of the race. However, in other areas, including the lower Ohio Valley and the Eastern panhandle, religion permeated the campaign and definitely hurt Kennedy in the fall race against Nixon."[21] On a more positive note, he concluded, "All the evidence points to an anti–Catholic vote in parts of West Virginia and a lesser pro–Catholic vote in other sections in the 1960 primary and general elections, but Kennedy won both races by a comfortable margin. While trailing behind the rest of the ticket, he fared much better than Al Smith in 1928."[22]

Democratic leaders in the state were nonplussed at the virulence of the religious issue in the fall campaign. In a 1965 oral interview Governor Hulett C. Smith observed as follows:

> The religious issue started to pop up again; something that looked as if it had been buried in the primary in West Virginia was being promoted very strongly by outside groups. I suspect every voter in West Virginia was besieged with different types of hate literature. There was a great amount of anti–Catholic literature. Some of the border counties that Jack Kennedy didn't carry in the general election was due in part, I think, to influences from out of the state. Some of the church groups in West Virginia made an active effort to defeat Kennedy because of the religious issue.[23]

Smith added that Kennedy's loss in Cabell, Kanawha, and Wood counties was "probably due to the religious issue."[24]

A League of Women Voters official, Esther Peters, said the religious issue "was still important in the fall election" and remembered that "a great many people told me they were ashamed they had voted against him."[25] A Kennedy campaign worker, Ray De Paulo, remembered that he lost a number of friends and was eventually fired from his job for his activities in "Citizens for Kennedy" in Raleigh County. He mentioned that "the real venom came out" in the fall campaign and that "it was well financed," generally from out of state.[26]

In the Border States Kennedy won comfortably in Maryland and narrowly in Delaware, West Virginia and Missouri, while Nixon triumphed in Oklahoma and Kentucky. This gave Kennedy a 33–17 electoral vote edge even though Nixon led 51 percent to 49 percent in the popular vote, thanks to a religion-fueled landslide in Oklahoma, which was Nixon's third strongest state. Maryland, JFK's sixth strongest state, was the only Border State on Kennedy's top ten states.

The South

The eleven states of the Old Confederacy were called the "problem child" of the U.S. by John Gunther in his *Inside USA*, and have been seen as the most distinctive region by sociologist John Shelton Reed and others, possibly because the region was a separate nation for a brief period after secession. It was the primary center of operation for a bloody Civil War, and slavery and segregation affected its life and the life of the nation for a century after the restoration of the Union.

Southern leaders, particularly from Virginia, were dominant in shaping the early United States, and more presidents were born in the Old Dominion than any other state (eight have been born in Virginia, including seven of the first twelve presidents). Politically the South emerged as a Democratic stronghold after the War and Reconstruction, with race playing a central role. (Before the War, Whigs and Democrats were competitive.) The "Solid South" was a reality by the 1880 Hancock-Garfield election, with all 11 Southern states supporting the Democrat Winfield Hancock, even though he was a former Union Army general. That loyalty remained, and Woodrow Wilson, a native of Virginia, owed his 1916 reelection to the Solid South.

By the time of the Kennedy election, the Solid South was breaking up. The Democrats had lost several southern states in the three preceding elections. Dixiecrat Strom Thurmond of South Carolina carried four Deep South states in 1948, and Republican Dwight Eisenhower carried four

"Outer South" states in 1952 and five in 1956, even adding Deep South Louisiana in his reelection campaign.

The South retained an Anglo-Saxon character among its whites in addition to a large and politically untapped African American population. The region received the lowest number of immigrants from abroad. Religiously, it was the bastion of evangelical Protestantism. Southern Baptists were dominant almost everywhere. Methodists were strong, as were Presbyterians, in Virginia and North Carolina. The 1926 U.S. Census of Religious Bodies found that Greensboro, North Carolina, was the nation's most Methodist city, and Charlotte, North Carolina, was the most Presbyterian. Catholics were dominant in the French-speaking counties (called parishes) in southern Louisiana and in parts of Texas and Florida. Episcopalians were strong in the coastal regions from Virginia to Alabama, especially in Charleston and Savannah and in the resort counties of Florida. Lutherans had pockets of strength in North Carolina, South Carolina, and the "German" counties of central Texas. Smaller fundamentalist groups were well represented. The religious culture led to strong Prohibition support, as well as cultural conservatism in general, and the public schools allowed more religious activities than in most other regions.

Politically, the Democrats were still dominant at the local level, though many Southern Democrats voted Republican for president. The "Democrats for Eisenhower" campaign was stronger here than anywhere else. There were pockets of Civil War era Republicans in the mountains of Tennessee, Virginia, North Carolina, Georgia, Alabama and Arkansas but they did not affect their state outcomes. The German counties of Texas often voted Republican. Growing Republican strength was notable in the cities, where prosperity and northern migration added to the GOP strength. All of these factors made the South a real battleground in 1960.

Alabama

Kennedy took historically Democratic Alabama with 58 percent of the vote, down from Stevenson's 1956 showing. The senator did especially poorly in Birmingham (Jefferson County), where the Republican margin tripled, from 5,000 to over 15,000. Kennedy also lost Montgomery but won Mobile, with its old Catholic community, back from Eisenhower and carried the high-tech area around Huntsville.

Kennedy's poor showing in Birmingham may have been a result of that city's long heritage of anti–Catholicism. Around World War I a nativist political group, the "True Americans," and a resurgent Klan captured city hall and fired all Catholic public officials, including a long-serving police chief.[27] Then, in 1921, in a notorious trial that attracted national attention, an itinerant evangelist was acquitted, by an all-white Protestant male jury, of the brutal murder of a Catholic priest. The defense team that got the preacher off included Hugo Black, later a U.S. Supreme Court justice.[28] The political-religious climate was such that a budding politician, Lister Hill, later a prominent New Deal Democrat in the U.S. Senate, quietly changed his religion from Catholic to Methodist, believing that he could never be elected in Alabama as a Catholic. He successfully buried his religious upbringing, which was apparently unknown and never revealed until his biographer uncovered it.[29]

Historian Carl Harris describes the era. Dr. A.J. Dickinson, pastor of the city's large and influential First Baptist Church, led the True Americans, "a secret political anti–Catholic society." They campaigned for Prohibition and a crackdown on Sunday movies and attacked the favored candidate, George Ward, for mayor as "an Episcopalian and tool of the Catholics." The winner, Nathaniel Barnett, "immediately gratified the anti–Catholics by firing Birmingham's single Roman Catholic city official, police chief Martin Eagan, and replacing him with Thomas J. Shirley, a member of the anti–Catholic Ku Klux Klan that superceded the True Americans."[30] This powerful religious lobby soon succeeded in banning Sunday movies in a 1918 referendum. The Pastor's Union and the Women's Christian Temperance Union announced the following: "Our fight in Birmingham is but one sector of the great battle for the preservation, or destruction, of the American Protestant Christian Sabbath and an instrument for the conserving and preserving of our national moral life."[31] Harris noted, "By 1918 the pietistic Protestants had finally triumphed over every local group that opposed their moral regulations and had written all their major policy demands into law."[32]

Kennedy lost one South Alabama county, Houston, which voted Republican for the first time in history. Houston was in the state's far southeast corner, bordering Georgia and Florida. Five of the ten most anti–Kennedy counties were in the northwest corner, mostly bordering middle Tennessee and northeast Mississippi, where populism and prohibition sentiment were historically significant. Most voters were white and Baptist. His statewide victory came despite considerable odds.

Historian Andrew Moore described the growing anti–Catholicism in Alabama and Georgia just before Kennedy ran for president. Probing the "social fear that bred anti–Catholicism," he wrote: "In the years after World War II that type of anti–Catholicism that approached religious paranoia persisted and brought Catholics attention disproportionate to their numbers in the South. After World War II, Catholics in Alabama and Georgia expected to take advantage of new national calls for ecumenism and interdenominational brotherhood, but white Protestants in those states continued to marginalize them. Indeed, anti–Catholicism united southern white Protestants and gave them common cause with non–southern Protestants."[33]

According to Moore, the southern Protestant churches united both "cultural and theological" anti–Catholicism: "The South was the last bastion of Protestant America and the last region to flaunt religious prejudice as central to group identity." The South's cultural anti–Catholicism had political implications: "Cultural anti–Catholicism locates its roots in the belief that the Roman Catholic Church's institutional presence and hierarchy threatened American democracy and the autonomy of the individual."[34] The prejudice soon became endemic in community life:

> The 1940s and 1950s witnessed the institutionalization of anti–Catholicism. That is to say, Protestant church organizations themselves became more active in discrimination and expressions of prejudice and bigotry.... Annual celebrations of Protestant culture — in the form of Reformation Days or Protestant Heritage Days — consistently reinforced for Catholics that they were an embattled minority that needed to be constantly vigilant.... Between the late 1940s and early 1950s, cities in Alabama and Georgia alike set aside special days in which they celebrated the region's Protestant heritage.[35]

Even the secular press abetted the movement: "Newspapers and pamphlets in Alabama and Georgia regularly published anti–Catholic libel, often spreading blatant untruths and unproven rumors about Catholicism."[36] The Church of Christ sponsored a number of newspaper advertisements labeling the Catholic Church "Satanic in origin."

Ironically, southern Protestants, who felt that northern Protestants looked down on them for their racial attitudes, used anti–Catholicism as "the linchpin for Protestant identity, as well as one element that drew North and South together."[37] Moore explores this and contrasts Protestant

O.C. Lambert was a Church of Christ preacher in Alabama, noted for grinding out hard-hitting critiques of Catholicism timed for the 1960 election (Fair Campaign Practices Committee Collection, Manuscripts Division, Special Collections, Lauinger Library, Georgetown University).

feelings of belonging with Catholic marginalization in the Deep South: "Catholics were accused of not supporting freedom of religion and of being anti-democratic, mysterious and secretive, and opposed to the Bible. In the minds of many Protestants, those things equaled opposition to Protestantism itself. Those same Protestants also believed that their opposition to the Catholic Church enhanced their own patriotism and proved their American identity."[38]

Arkansas

Arkansas, with its large Baptist and evangelical character, barely favored Kennedy, whose 53.8 percent of the major party vote was about the same as Stevenson's 53.4 percent and lower than Stevenson's 56.1 percent in 1952. Including a segregationist minor party, which received 6.7

percent of all votes, Kennedy won only 50.2 percent of the entire vote, a 20th century low mark for a Democrat. Kennedy's near loss (23 of the 75 counties went for Nixon) was caused by intense anti–Catholic voting in the rural northeast, where he was the first Democrat ever to lose Clay, Craighead, Fulton, Randolph and Sharp counties. In the Ozark northwest corner he also ran poorly, even for a Democrat, running weaker than Stevenson in most counties, including Washington, where the University of Arkansas at Fayetteville is located. Only the Little Rock area (Pulaski County) and Jefferson County saved him from an embarrassing defeat.

Kennedy ran behind Stevenson in 33 counties, mostly in the northern tier, including every county that bordered Missouri. A handful of counties in the southern part of the state and along the Mississippi Delta followed suit. Eight of the state's counties switched from Stevenson to Nixon.

Opposition to Kennedy was spearheaded by clergy like Dr. W.O. Vaught, vice president of the Southern Baptist Convention, who organized a series of "religious freedom rallies throughout Arkansas" to fight Kennedy's election.[39]

FLORIDA

Just before election day *Time* commented that while "Jacksonville Old South Democrats and Miami liberals" favored Kennedy, that might not be enough to carry the Sunshine State. They were right. Huge GOP majorities in Central Florida and the Gold Coast and a decline in Democratic support in the panhandle and rural areas kept the state in the Republican column.

The state had a long heritage of anti–Catholicism, resulting in the election of a crackpot agitator, part-time preacher and shoe salesman named Sidney J. Catts as governor in 1916 on an explicit anti–Catholic platform, including convent inspection laws and other meddlesome legislation, which were ultimately shelved. Klan activity was strong and Al Smith was crushed 59 percent to 41 percent in 1928, a loss of over 25 percentage points. So it was not surprising that JFK would face a cascade of opposition based on religion.

In 18 counties in northern and western Florida and in 10 in the central region, Kennedy ran weaker than Stevenson. His urban support (Miami, Tampa and Jacksonville) helped him win 48.5 percent, up a bit from Stevenson's 43 percent but well below the FDR–Truman era. His gains were almost all on the Atlantic coast, from then-rural and substantially Catholic St. Augustine to exotic Key West.

However, many counties in the Piney Woods region in North Florida and some counties bordering Alabama and Georgia gave him the lowest support for a Democrat since Smith. Two rural counties in south central Florida's ranching and stock car region, Hardee and DeSoto, switched from Stevenson to Nixon. Both had supported every Democrat except Smith and Kennedy. Hardee was heavily Baptist, a factor in most of the highest anti–Kennedy counties, where 73 percent of voters were Baptists. In 22 white Baptist-majority rural counties, Kennedy received 65 percent, down from Stevenson's 69 percent. In Lafayette and Gilchrist counties, his support plummeted 12 points.

JFK did poorly in the Orlando-Lakeland area, falling below 29 percent in Orange County (Orlando) and losing ground in Lake County and Lee County (Fort Myers). Throughout Central Florida, small towns like Hawthorne in Alachua County and Christmas in Orange County switched from Stevenson to Nixon. In Yankee-settled, wealthy, and heavily Protestant Winter Park, Nixon matched Eisenhower's 90 percent vote.

Race interacted with religion. The anti–Kennedy counties supported segregationist candidates for governor in 1956 and 1960. African Americans in the state backed Kennedy by large margins. The Florida branches of the Ku Klux Klan, which were strongest in the rural outbacks of the panhandle and central Florida, attacked Kennedy. Its Tampa leader, William Griffin, endorsed Nixon, while Bill Hendrix, who polled over 11,000 votes for governor in 1952, urged a write-in vote for Arkansas governor Orval Faubus. As for Kennedy, a Klan statement thundered, "A vote for Kennedy is a vote against your God and Savior and your church, your country, and even yourself since the Catholic Church is directly opposed to Protestant churches, your America, and especially you as a Protestant. Heaven help your soul if you vote away your religious liberty."[40]

Precincts from Duval County, which include Jacksonville and its suburbs, showed the impact of religious voting, particularly as it intersected with and was modified by class and place of origin. The city, a large insurance and naval facility town in the northeastern part of the state, was very southern in its character, sometimes called the Capital of South Georgia, from whence many of its residents hailed. Baptists were by far the largest religious group, but Methodists, Episcopalians and Presbyterians had large followings, and there were modest-sized Catholic and Jewish communities.

The city's Hemming Park, located in the heart of downtown, attracted large political rallies for both Dwight Eisenhower and Adlai Stevenson in the 1950s. Both JFK and Nixon addressed large and enthusiastic crowds, on the same day, no less, in 1960. Eisenhower and Stevenson split the county vote almost evenly, with Stevenson winning in 1952 and Eisenhower in 1956. Kennedy was popular, but anti–Catholicism threatened his showing.

Despite considerable anti–Kennedy activity, particularly in Baptist and Church of Christ congregations, and a last-minute distribution of anti–Catholic literature throughout northern and western Florida, Kennedy prevailed 54 percent to 46 percent. The large African American vote, evenly split in 1956, went 77 percent for Kennedy, insuring his victory. White voters were divided almost evenly.

Kennedy's vote plummeted nearly 10 points in blue collar precincts, where most voters were Baptists originally from Georgia, but he still received 72 percent in the poorest white precinct around Edison Avenue and 67 percent in Woodstock. Middle income white voters moved in opposite directions. In North Shore, where many voters were city employees and where religion seemed to be the most prominent issue, Kennedy dropped to 45 percent from Stevenson's 55 percent. A similar result came in Lake Shore, on the city's west side. Kennedy split the Murray Hill neighborhood with Nixon, running six points behind Stevenson.

But in middle income neighborhoods where many voters were recent northern immigrants, Kennedy gained 5–10 points, carrying Jacksonville Beach, which had twice backed Ike. In upper middle and upper income precincts, Kennedy lost but ran 10 points ahead of Stevenson in San Marco, Avondale and Atlantic Beach, where large Catholic, Jewish and Episcopalian congregations were located. Kennedy lost 4–1 in upper class Ortega, where the Southern-born elite resided and where Democrats were not competitive.

GEORGIA

The Peach State — where Tom Watson rode a wave of anti–Catholic and populist sentiment (much of it stirred up by his ill-named *Jeffersonian* magazine) to the U.S. Senate — had a great deal of anti–Catholicism. But those sentiments were tempered by unshakable Democratic loyalties that existed through 1960 (which broke down four years later when the state went for Barry Goldwater, the States' Rights Republican who promised to slow down the civil rights movement).

Georgia in 1960 was a paradox. JFK's 62.6 percent exceeded his home state of Massachusetts and was second only to Rhode Island. But at the same time, it was 4 percent below the Stevenson marker. Kennedy won a clear majority in Baptist counties, but his support declined more in them than in less Baptist counties. Two north Georgia Baptist mountain counties, Union and Whitfield, switched from Stevenson to Nixon, but Kennedy's vote held and actually increased in some other predominantly Baptist jurisdictions.

Unlike in the North and West, it was in cities and suburbs that Nixon did best, reflecting more the prosperity-Republican connection in the emerging South, perhaps, than that of religion. Kennedy held the Atlanta area narrowly, losing 15 points in suburban DeKalb County. The Emory University precinct, a kind of elite Methodist neighborhood, went for Stevenson and Nixon. Nixon gained considerably in Macon and edged out Kennedy in Savannah and Augusta, though Kennedy ran ahead of Stevenson in Savannah.

One interesting result came from rural Effingham County, north of Savannah, where the "Salzburgers" (Austrian Lutherans), settled in the 18th century. A typical white southern Democratic area, it voted for Nixon in 1960 and Hoover in 1928, reflecting, perhaps, memories of their forebears' expulsion from Catholic Austria.

Kennedy "encountered open, even combative anti–Catholicism in Georgia," writes historian Thomas Carty. Lectures, newspaper advertisements and the mobilization of grass-roots sentiments clearly worried Democratic leaders in a state that had never supported a Republican presidential candidate and had given Stevenson his highest state support twice. Still, writes Carty, "Democratic party strength and economic class consciousness offered a potential counterbalance to anti–Catholicism in Georgia."

Democratic leaders rallied to the cause, though some endorsements were lukewarm. The newspapers exposed the religious smear campaigns, with 200 stories about the religious issue appearing in the *Atlanta Constitution*. "The mainstream Atlanta media's response to anti–Catholic attitudes showed a trend toward tolerance," says Carty.[41]

LOUISIANA

Louisiana has always been two states: the north Louisiana (Huey Long country) Baptist counties, sometimes labeled the Anglo-American belt, and "Cajun Country," the two dozen or so French Catholic counties (called parishes in this very French flavored state) in south Louisiana. Religion has always been a dividing point, though the rural areas have much in common in terms of sports, music, and historic support for segregation and states' rights. Both areas have substantial African American populations, and the French areas tend to be somewhat more tolerant, certainly in voting participation. When Kennedy faced off against Nixon, 51 percent of black residents were registered in the Cajun parishes and only 23 percent in north Louisiana. Segregationist candidates ran stronger in white Baptist areas than in Catholic areas, and a States' Rights third party carried 15 mostly Baptist parishes and only two Catholic parishes in 1960. The Catholic exceptions were St. Bernard and Plaquemines, the latter controlled by a racist political boss, Leander Perez, who was excommunicated by Catholic authorities for trying to prevent desegregation of parochial schools by force.

The 1960 vote was influenced by race and religion. JFK won 50.4 percent of the total vote and carried 34 parishes. Nixon received 28.6 percent of the total vote and carried 13 parishes. The States' Rights Party came in third with 21 percent and carried 17 parishes. The major party vote was 64 percent to 36 percent for Kennedy, which would have ranked first in the nation, had it not been for the segregationists. Kennedy swept 18 of the 20 heaviest Catholic parishes, which also included many African American Catholics. His vote reached 78 percent among the Cajuns.

Some counties in the middle parts of the state, around Baton Rouge and Alexandria, are on the fault line between North and South and between Catholic and Protestant, and their votes reflect this closeness. Twenty-two counties switched from Eisenhower to Kennedy, including Orleans Parish, reflecting gains for Kennedy among both blacks and Catholics, who narrowly favored Ike 54 percent to 46 percent in 1956.

The Baptist counties were another story. The heaviest ones were split between Nixon and the States' Rights faction (5 parishes for each), while Kennedy carried only one (Livingston, near Baton Rouge). In much of rural North Louisiana, Kennedy ran third. In Huey Long's home base,

Winn Parish, Nixon drew 45 percent, the States' Righters 28 percent and Kennedy 27 percent. In Madison Parish Kennedy received only 12 percent of the vote. In the ten parishes where Kennedy's vote declined the most, 78 percent of voters were Baptists, 12 percent Methodist and just 3 percent Catholic. Eight of these parishes were in the northeast corner of the state, with Morehouse giving Kennedy a 15-point decline from Stevenson.

One oddball result came from rural Caldwell Parish in the north, where voters backed a States' Rights Party in 1956, which carried four counties, and then voted for Nixon in 1960—the first time it had ever supported a Republican presidential ticket.

University of Alabama professor Bernard Cosman found that Kennedy received 72 percent of the total vote, including the segregationist third party, in Catholic majority parishes compared to 20 percent for Nixon and 8 percent for the States' Rights candidate. In the 30 heavily Baptist parishes, however, Kennedy ran *third* with 28 percent, Nixon 43 percent and 29 percent for the States' Rights splinter party that had put Arkansas governor Orval Faubus on the ballot. In those Baptist parishes where over 50 percent of the population was black but unable to vote, the States' Rights ticket reached 47 percent, Nixon 30 percent and Kennedy trailed with 22 percent. Kennedy made solid gains over Stevenson in Catholic strongholds but ran behind Stevenson in Baptist areas.

North Louisiana's Baptist areas resembled the rest of the Deep South, with widespread anti–Kennedy voting. Cosman also found that while 60.5 percent of nonwhites were registered to vote in 18 Catholic-majority parishes, only 8.2 percent were registered in 30 Protestant-majority parishes.[42]

MISSISSIPPI

Race overshadowed religion, though both played a role in denying Kennedy the state's electoral vote for only the second time in a century. (Truman lost to Dixiecrat Strom Thurmond in 1948 for essentially the same reasons.) The Magnolia State voted for a third-party States' Rights ticket, with Kennedy second and Nixon third. The States' Righters ran third in 1956, when Stevenson easily carried the state.

Kennedy carried the Gulf Coast counties (Hancock, Harrison, Jackson), where the state's tiny Catholic population is mostly concentrated, did well in the smaller Mississippi River cities of Vicksburg and Natchez, and won the Old South populist counties in the northeast. But the States' Rights splinter group swept the central region, especially in counties where no African Americans were allowed to vote (which was true in most of the state). Lowndes and Tunica counties switched from Stevenson to Nixon. Most other rural counties switched from Stevenson to States' Rights. Hancock, the only French Catholic county (resembling Louisiana) switched from Eisenhower to Kennedy.

Kennedy ran poorly, often third, in areas of racial conflict. The state capital, Jackson (Hinds County), which had switched from Eisenhower in 1952 to Stevenson in 1956, gave only 20 percent of its ballots to Kennedy, while the States' Rights faction edged out Nixon 42 percent to 38 percent. The States' Rights ticket carried 54 counties compared to seven when it ran a slate in 1956. Kennedy carried 25 counties, down from Stevenson's 71. Nixon carried three counties, similar to Eisenhower's four. The one loyal Republican county was Forrest, where Hattiesburg is located. The state popular vote was 39 percent States' Rights, 36 percent Kennedy and 25 percent Nixon. The most anti–Kennedy counties were 64 percent Baptist and 24 percent Methodist, a bit higher for both than statewide.

In Mississippi, Kennedy ran weaker than Stevenson in 74 of 82 counties, with the few exceptions being on the Gulf Coast, which has a moderate Catholic population, and in the counties that include Natchez and Vicksburg. The intensity of anti–Kennedy voting in the nation's most Baptist state, and arguably the most racist one at the time, is borne out by these facts: Kennedy dropped 20 percent or more in 17 counties and 10 percent to 20 percent in 35 counties. The "Black Belt" counties, where African Americans were a majority of the population but could not vote, were especially prone to anti–Kennedy voting.

NORTH CAROLINA

North Carolina, solidly Baptist along with pockets of Methodists, Presbyterians and Lutherans, was the least Catholic state in 1960. (It has since moved up a few rungs with the influx of northern migrants, and several North Carolina Catholics have been elected to Congress and even governor since then.) The Tarheel State was a Democratic bastion, loyally backing Stevenson twice. The only Democrat to lose in the 20th century was Governor Al Smith in 1928, who became a victim of anti–Catholicism and Prohibitionism. The result in 1960 was expected to be close and the campaign was bitter.

Kennedy won 52.1 percent, about a point better than Stevenson's 1956 vote but two points behind his 1952 total. Most of the vote broke along traditional lines, with JFK a winner in the staunchly Democratic east, Nixon in the mountain west, and a close result in the middle. Nixon won the more urban counties, a reverse phenomenon to the North and East, but fairly common after World War II in the South, since most of the money and prosperity were concentrated in urban areas. But Kennedy also did better than Stevenson in most of North Carolina's cities, gaining seven points in Charlotte (Mecklenburg County), the most Presbyterian city in the country at that time. He gained five points in Wilmington (New Hanover County). But the rural areas were another matter. Kennedy's vote support declined in 43 of the state's 100 counties. Most were in Democratic eastern North Carolina or in the western mountain region, where one county, Jackson, switched from Stevenson to Nixon.

In the ten most anti–Kennedy counties about 52 percent of residents were Baptists and 20 percent were Methodists, which was similar to the state average.

SOUTH CAROLINA

Kennedy barely held the Palmetto State, losing ground over religion and race. He ran weaker than Stevenson in 41 of the state's 46 counties. His only gains came in five counties in coastal or resort South Carolina (the Low Country), including the towns of Charleston, Hilton Head, Beaufort, and Georgetown. An exception was Baptist Myrtle Beach, where his vote slipped. Most of the state's Catholic, Episcopalian and Jewish residents live in these coastal counties.

In much of the Up Country region, anti–Kennedy voting was severe. He dropped 37 points in Barnwell County, which went Republican for the first time in history. His vote plummeted over 30 points in Calhoun and Clarendon counties. Fundamentalist-leaning Greenville gave Nixon 67 percent despite having gone for Stevenson in 1956. Nixon won the higher population centers (except loyally Democratic Spartanburg), but came up short, losing 51 percent to 49 percent to Kennedy.

Kennedy's vote share dropped by 10 percent or more in 28 counties; 14 of them experienced a 20 percent or greater decline. The strongest anti–

Kennedy counties were 51 percent Baptist and 26 percent Methodist. But he did receive enough of the evangelical vote, despite losses from 1956, to hold the state by 10,000 votes.

TENNESSEE

The Volunteer State gave Kennedy a rough ride. He lost the state by 75,000 votes, while Stevenson had lost to Eisenhower by fewer than 6,000. Kennedy's vote percentage fell in 73 of the 95 counties, including almost every county in West and Middle Tennessee, traditionally Democratic strongholds. His vote held in Republican East Tennessee but that wasn't much anyway, since the East had voted Republican from the time its residents flocked to join the Union Army in the Civil War.

Eight of the top ten anti–Kennedy counties were in the west, where segregationist feelings joined religious prejudice to lower the Democratic vote. Two were near Nashville — Sumner and Rutherford counties. One of the West Tennessee counties, Fayette, voted Republican for the first time since Reconstruction, after having backed a States' Rights Party in 1956. The worst anti–Kennedy voting in the state, a loss of 25 points, was in Fayette. Dyer County cast its first ever GOP majority. Madison County went Republican for the first time since General Grant carried it in 1868. Altogether, six counties switched from Stevenson to Nixon.

Southern Baptists were a powerful voice in the sixteen most anti–Kennedy counties, with 45 percent of residents, though that was slightly below the state average because the Church of Christ was the choice of 15 percent of residents, almost double their statewide adherence rate. Methodists comprised 16 percent.

Tennessee voters were unusually exercised by the religious issue, particularly in counties where Baptists and Church of Christ members predominated. "In large part this outcome may be explained by the impact of Kennedy's Catholicism — a major campaign issue in the state — upon predominantly Protestant and Fundamentalist voters," observed Dawidowicz and Goldstein.[43] Kennedy even failed to carry several counties that remained loyal to Al Smith in 1928. "In Tennessee, contrary to what is supposed to be the national trend, the religious issue has become more, not less, important since Al Smith ran," the authors added.[44]

The Churches of Christ, a fundamentalist group with many followers in Tennessee, Texas, Alabama and Indiana, produced an enormous amount of anti–Catholic and anti–Kennedy material. One of its pastors, V.E. Howard, wrote and distributed 400,000 copies of a tract called *The White House: America or Roman?* Even upscale congregations in Nashville joined the effort. On October 9 Batsell Barrett Baxter, pastor of Hillsboro Church of Christ in Nashville and a noted television personality, called on all church members to vote against Kennedy. NBC News filmed his attack. Baxter, however, did not count on the local congressman, Joe Evins, being in the congregation that morning. Evins, a Democrat and Kennedy supporter, called the sermon partisan and intolerant. The Nashville papers covered the brouhaha, and most Church of Christ members apparently sided with Reverend Baxter.[45]

Texas

Lyndon B. Johnson's home state was a battleground in 1960. Organized anti–Catholic forces had a base in Dallas, where they worked the churches, newspapers and radio stations with hard-hitting propaganda warning voters of the dangers of electing a Catholic president. Senator Johnson and Representative Sam Rayburn fought back. The results were a slender win for the Kennedy-Johnson ticket, just 51 percent–49 percent and a margin of 46,000 out of nearly 2.3 million votes cast. Still, the Democratic ticket lost ground in 57 of the 254 counties. Most of these were in the North Texas panhandle (where almost all counties were anti–Kennedy) or adjoining counties in West Texas, plus a few bordering Oklahoma or surrounding Dallas and Fort Worth.

Some of the swings against Kennedy were eye-popping. In tiny Collingsworth County bordering Oklahoma, Kennedy slid 21 points in a county Stevenson had carried. In Parmer County, bordering New Mexico, he dropped 18 points. In 13 counties his vote percentage declined 10 points or more. He failed to carry 19 counties that Stevenson had carried. Where anti–Kennedy voting was most intense, 55 percent of residents were Baptist, 19 percent Methodist and 18 percent Catholic. Most of the remaining voters belonged to the Church of Christ.

Kennedy's major gains were in South Texas, though a few were in the west and east. The Hispanic community was strong in these areas but a combination of apathy and discrimination made the Latino vote relatively small in 1960. Kennedy's vote increased in those rural counties where many voters were Czech or German by ancestry. Even in German Lutheran

Republican counties he made modest gains. In southern-oriented East Texas, his vote held and even increased in some counties.

The urban vote was closely divided. Nixon swept Baptist Dallas by almost as high a margin as Eisenhower. Texas governor Ann Richards remembered that "Dallas was big Nixon territory. Looking at yard-signs in middle class neighborhoods, you'd never have known Kennedy had a chance."[46] Kennedy won San Antonio, Austin and El Paso and made modest gains in Houston. His vote declined 4 percent in Lubbock and Amarillo, both conservative Protestant bailiwicks.

Speaker of the House Sam Rayburn may have helped stem the tide against Kennedy in East Texas. A Baptist himself (who rarely attended church, though) Rayburn despised religious prejudice and had campaigned for Al Smith, who lost Texas in 1928. "It is a terrible thing to hold a man's religion against him in a country whose very existence is based on freedom of religion," he observed.[47] He was initially convinced that no Catholic could win. His biographers Hardeman and Bacon wrote, "An enthusiastic Smith supporter, who worked hard in a losing cause, Rayburn retained in 1960 the firm belief that a Catholic candidate would lead the Democratic Party to defeat."[48] But he was impressed by Kennedy's forthright handling of the religious issue in Houston and thought the senator had demolished his opponents. As a result, "He personally campaigned for the ticket in several states."[49] His home county, Fannin County, delivered 70 percent to Kennedy.

Rayburn died on November 16, 1961, after 49 years in the House and 17 years as its Speaker. President Kennedy visited "Mr. Sam" on his deathbed and attended his funeral at First Baptist Church in Bonham, Texas. Kennedy's critics said he could not attend a Protestant service. Two years later, almost to the day, the young president was himself buried.

Virginia

The Old Dominion gradually moved toward the Republicans and gave Eisenhower solid margins of 13 points in 1952 and 17 points in 1956. Nixon won by six, 53 percent to 47 percent, a modest gain for Kennedy.

The Washington, D.C., suburbs were evenly divided, but Nixon swept the more conservative and Baptist Richmond area as well as Roanoke. Norfolk went for Kennedy. The rural areas were closely contested. The Shenandoah Valley, which began to break for Dewey in 1948, became a Republican stronghold and went solidly for Eisenhower and Nixon. It was (and remains) an Old Immigrant stronghold, having attracted many German, Scotch-Irish and English immigrants. Methodists, Presbyterians, Lutherans, Baptists and Mennonites are all well represented in the Shenandoah Valley. Southwest Virginia's mountains are divided between staunch Republicans and national Democrats in the coal mining counties. Kennedy ran weaker than Stevenson in four counties in Southside Virginia bordering North Carolina and in the cities of Bristol and Danville. Twenty-five ministers in Danville adopted a resolution that pledged to "oppose with all the powers at our command the election of a Catholic to the presidency of the United States."[50]

Virginia governor Lindsay Almond, a loyal Democrat, was incensed by these efforts and pledged to fight for the Kennedy-Johnson ticket. Almond singled out Vice President Nixon for refusing to openly condemn efforts that would clearly help his campaign and for urging people to ignore Kennedy's religion. "I think Mr. Nixon has done that by repeatedly referring to it, ostensibly to deprecate it,"[51] said the governor.

As it turned out, Kennedy held the South with a 52 percent to 48 percent margin in major party popular vote and won 81 electoral votes to Nixon's 33. The peculiarities of the Alabama voting system gave six of the state's eleven electoral votes to Virginia senator Harry Byrd, even though he did not receive a single vote in the state. An "unpledged" electors' slate carried six of the eleven congressional districts in the primaries. A State's Rights slate carried Mississippi, and its electors chose to vote for Byrd, as did one Nixon elector from Oklahoma. Segregationist State's Rights parties drew 363,543 votes in Dixie, or 3.5 percent of the total vote, compared to Kennedy's 50.5 percent and Nixon's 46 percent.

Kennedy had to fight for every vote in this religion-conscious region where opposition based on religion was intense. He gained the most over Stevenson in Lyndon Johnson's Texas, but even in the Lone Star State he failed to match his eight-point national gain. He made modest gains in Florida and Virginia, tiny gains in Arkansas and North Carolina, and lost ground in Georgia, South Carolina, Tennessee, Mississippi and Alabama. Only in Louisiana did his improvement over Stevenson exceed his national gain. Despite these losses and challenges, Georgia was Kennedy's second strongest state, and Alabama and the Carolinas were also on his top ten.

Midwest/Plains States

The Midwest is both America's breadbasket and its heartland, a region linking the Northeast to the West. Its politics are generally centrist, and presidential elections are hard fought and close most of the time. Economic unrest helped the Progressive movement in the early 20th century, making this area the center of Bob LaFolletts's strong third party effort in 1924. Isolationism in foreign policy created another source of strength, contributing to a strong Wendell Willkie vote in 1940 (though Willkie was himself an internationalist). Prohibition was popular in some areas, and its prime congressional sponsor was from Minnesota.

Immigration from Germany, Scandinavia and Holland were major factors in the population and affected the political orientation of the regions. The so-called farm vote, once thought to be pivotal in elections, was central in the Midwest. The Midwest has a clear Protestant majority and is the U.S. center of Lutheranism, particularly in Minnesota, Wisconsin, Iowa and the Dakotas. Methodists are strong in Iowa, Nebraska and Kansas. Catholics are well represented throughout the region.

IOWA

Iowa was a solid Republican state in 1960, giving Nixon a majority of 172,000 and 57 percent of its votes. This was only two points less than Eisenhower's 1956 vote, putting Iowa in the "reluctant to vote for Kennedy" category rather than the explicitly "anti" category. Nixon carried all the larger counties except German Catholic Dubuque. Kennedy ran only even with Stevenson in Polk County, the state's largest, which contains the heavily Protestant capital of Des Moines. He carried only six of the state's 99 counties and barely held on in Wapello County, a blue collar Protestant county in the southeast. Wapello was the only county Stevenson carried in 1956 — by 559 votes. Kennedy eked out an 80-vote margin.

There was considerable anti–Kennedy voting in rural and small town Iowa. JFK ran behind Stevenson in 26 counties, mostly south of Des Moines, with some in the northwest and other areas. An interesting if odd geographic pattern prevailed. Kennedy was weaker than Stevenson in six of the 10 counties bordering Missouri, a key anti–Catholic state. He also ran weaker in four of the nine counties bordering South Dakota. The most anti–Kennedy county was Marion, where he dropped six points. This county has many Dutch ancestry voters in Pella, where Central College, affiliated with the Reformed Church, is located. In Pella, noted for its annual Tulip Festival, Nixon won 78.9 percent (2,228–597), a solid gain over Eisenhower's 72.3 percent (1,889–723).

In many rural Protestant areas Kennedy was devastated. There were 135 towns in 59 counties that went for Stevenson and switched to Nixon. In 111 towns, including some of the above, Kennedy's vote dropped more than 10 percentage points and plunged 15 points in two dozen towns.

In Polk-Abington in Jefferson County Ike won 61–60 while Nixon swept Kennedy away 76–29. In the village of Oakland in Louisa County a Stevenson victory by 71–42 became a 57–51 triumph for Nixon. In East Harrison in Mahaska County a modest Eisenhower win, 88–60, turned into a Nixon romp, 105–35.

Turnout was a factor, as Democrats deserted their ticket. Kennedy drew only 11 votes compared to Stevenson's 31 in the hamlet of Settlers in Sioux County. In the same county the Democratic vote dropped from 68 to 26 in West Branch. In Fairfield in Buena Vista County, the Democratic vote plunged from 240 to 128. In sum, a group of Protestant "swing" precincts, where party registration and presidential vote are closely contested, went 67.2 percent for Nixon and only 51.8 percent for Eisenhower. While there were a number of Catholic rural enclaves where Kennedy gained, particularly in Carroll and Palo Alto counties, they were outvoted by a surge of anti–Kennedy sentiment elsewhere. Kennedy's vote declined as town size declined.

Religiously, Iowa's three strongest faiths are Catholics, Lutherans and Methodists, with the latter two groups giving Nixon a substantial win. But the "Dutch factor" was increasingly important in Iowa. Dutch Reformed adherents — affiliated with the very conservative Christian Reformed Church and the more moderate Reformed Church in America — have become the most loyally Republican voters. Six counties, mostly in the northwest — Sioux, O'Brien, Lyon, Jasper — and Mahaska and Marion are Dutch strongholds. Nixon ran ahead of Eisenhower (66.6 percent to 64.4 percent) in those six counties, receiving an even higher percentage and gain over 1956 in the most Dutch precincts.

Sioux is a Dutch-majority county where Nixon received 79 percent, one point more than Eisenhower. A higher percentage of Sioux County students attend private faith-based schools than in any other U.S. county. Two examples from Sioux County are illustrative: In Sioux Center, home of church-related Dordt College, Nixon received 93 percent and Eisenhower 92 percent. In Orange City, home of another Reformed Church school, Northwestern College, Nixon was the choice of 93 percent and Eisenhower 88 percent. In the same county, the Catholic enclave of East Orange went 91 percent for Kennedy and 70 percent for Stevenson. In 16 rural Dutch towns Kennedy's popular vote of 594 was only half of Stevenson's 1,054, and his overall support was 14 percent compared to Stevenson's 26 percent. The handful of Dutch Democrats deserted their party in droves. In the village of Capel JFK drew just 4 percent of the vote.

This "Dutch factor" is apparent in the religious configuration of the ten most anti–Kennedy counties. The Dutch Reformed voters were 13 percent in those counties compared to 3 percent statewide. Methodists edged out Lutherans (25 percent to 24 percent), with Methodists being 4 percent overrepresented compared to their statewide share and Lutherans were the same. Catholics were only 12 percent in these counties, compared to 30 percent statewide. Baptists, Presbyterians and Disciples of Christ attracted 15 percent of residents compared to 12 percent in the state as a whole.

College towns had not yet become Democratic strongholds. Kennedy took 49 percent in Johnson County and 47 percent in Iowa City, where the University of Iowa is located. This was the last time a Republican presidential candidate carried the county. In Story County, home of Iowa State University, Kennedy received 35 percent and only 30 percent in Ames, the college town. This was Nixon's highest percentage in any town that exceeded 10,000 votes. Back in 1928 Story County gave Al Smith his lowest vote in all of Iowa's 99 counties. Not much had changed by 1960 in this substantially Norwegian Lutheran county.

Ames seems to have had a long heritage of anti–Catholicism. Writer Susan Allen Toth, in her sparkling memoir, *Blooming: A Small Town Girlhood*, tells about growing up in Ames during the 1950s:

> If I was unaware that Ames was prejudiced toward blacks, I could not miss the town's feeling about Catholics.... For a Protestant to marry a Catholic in Ames produced a major social upheaval, involving parental conferences, conversions, and general disapproval on both sides. Even our liberal minister, who encouraged his Presbyterian parishioners to call him "Doctor Bob" because he didn't want to appear uppish about his advanced degree, came to our high-school fellowship group one night to lecture on Catholicism. He probably knew that

one of his deacons' daughters was going very steadily with a Catholic boy. Warning us about the autocratic nature of the Catholic Church, its iron hand, its idolatry, and most of all the way it could snatch our very children from us and bring them up in the manacles of a strange faith, Doctor Bob heated with the warmth of his topic until his cheeks glowed as he clenched and unclenched his fists.[52]

Another college precinct shows how strong religious attitudes were in 1960. Luther College in Decorah in Winneshiek County is an academic outpost of Norwegian Lutheranism. In 1960 it embraced Nixon 565–97 (85.3 percent), even more than its 520–103 (83.4 percent) vote for Eisenhower. This near-unanimous rejection of Kennedy stands out since the same precinct went for George McGovern twelve years later.

Rural Iowa was anchored in religion, and the culture reflected unitary and conformist religious values. In comparing her upbringing in Story City, another Norwegian town near Ames, with a summer in New York City, Marjorie Hart remembered: "My social life in Story City had revolved around Luther League meetings for teenagers in the basement of St. Petri Norwegian Lutheran Church, one of three Lutheran churches that anchored Story City."[53]

A joke that made its rounds shortly after the election explained what happened in Iowa. Apparently, the election in the Hawkeye State wasn't fought between Kennedy and Nixon but between Ezra Taft Benson and the Pope, and the Pope lost! Benson was Eisenhower's unpopular agriculture secretary, who, many observers thought, would tip the scales to a Democrat in the farm areas — that is, until the Democrats nominated a Catholic, thereby dooming their chances in the state.

Top Forty Towns
Anti–Kennedy Voting in Iowa

Town	County	% Kennedy Decline
Settlers	Sioux	24.4
Polk-Abingdon	Jefferson	22.0
Roscoe	Davis	19.0
Woodland	Decatur	18.6
Omega	O'Brien	18.6
Clinton	Wayne	17.9
Brooke	Buena Vista	17.4
Floyd	O'Brien	17.3
Union	Poweshiek	17.3

Town	County	% Kennedy Decline
Scott	Mahaska	16.9
Union	Polk	16.9
Silver Creek	Pottawatomie	16.8
Bethel	Fayette	16.5
Rorbeck-Clay	Shelby	16.4
Jackson	Shelby	16.3
West Harrison	Mahaska	16.2
Polk	Shelby	15.9
Independence	Appanoose	15.7
Summit	Marion	15.7
Oakland	Louisa	15.6
East Harrison	Mahaska	15.5
Garfield	Sioux	15.4
Liberty	Cherokee	15.2
Owen	Cerro Gordo	15.0
Otranto	Mitchell	15.0
Camp	Polk	15.0
Lyon	Lyon	14.6
Washington	Jasper	14.5
Jackson	Taylor	14.5
Silver	Cherokee	14.3
Polk	Marion	14.2
West Branch	Sioux	14.2
Madison	Mahaska	14.1
Coon	Buena Vista	13.8
Fairfield	Buena Vista	13.5
Wright	Wayne	13.3
Cass	Boone	13.3
Swan	Marion	13.2
Midland	Lyon	13.1
English	Iowa	13.0

KANSAS

Loyally Republican and mostly Protestant Kansans gave Nixon one of his highest percentages, 61 percent. Kennedy gained five points over Stevenson. Kansas is like Indiana, with Methodists and Catholics being the strongest groups. Kansas has pockets of Lutherans in Swedish and German counties, Baptists in the southern counties bordering Oklahoma, and Brethren-Mennonites. (The state boasts three Mennonite and Brethren colleges.) Lindsborg is a Swedish-flavored town, with a Lutheran college (Bethany) and a long-standing *Messiah* concert tradition.

Only in three rural counties (Bourbon, Cheyenne and Clark) in opposite ends of the state did Kennedy run behind Stevenson. In most other rural areas he ran only slightly ahead. Kennedy carried just two counties, Ellis, a German Catholic settlement around Hays, and Wyandotte, which includes substantially multiethnic Catholic Kansas City. All of the major population centers, including Wichita, Topeka and suburban Johnson County — which includes some of the highest income towns in the U.S.— went for Nixon, though all gave Kennedy five to six point gains.

Minnesota

Minnesota returned to the Democratic fold, after defecting to Eisenhower twice, but Kennedy's barebones' 50.7 percent was much below Truman's 59 percent. He carried St. Paul, Duluth, and Minneapolis. In rural Minnesota Kennedy slipped behind Stevenson in 16 counties, even losing two of them, Isanti and Kandiyohi. In a state that was roughly 42 percent Lutheran and 40 percent Catholic, these counties were heavily Lutheran, 58 percent to 23 percent, undoubtedly the key factor. The anti–Kennedy counties were scattered all over the state, with a half dozen on the North Dakota and Canadian borders, some in the center of the state, and two, Freeborn and Mower, in the south, bordering Iowa.

Kennedy gained and won the German Catholic counties and ran a shade better than Stevenson in the German Lutheran ones. Managing to win in a state dominated by the religious issue was an accomplishment, but he ran much weaker than Hubert Humphrey and Orville Freeman, the Protestant Democratic candidates for senator and governor.

In Scandinavian Lutheran working class precincts in Wards 9 and 12 in Minneapolis, however, the religious issue cut against Kennedy, who ran behind Stevenson. Years later Minnesota's colorful Governor Jesse Ventura, whose background was Slovak Lutheran, noted in his autobiography that his father, a staunch union Democrat, was apparently persuaded to vote for Nixon, a decision his father bitterly regretted in later years. Jesse Ventura's coolness toward religious group involvement in partisan politics seems to have stemmed from this incident: "I truly believe that my father developed his deep hatred for Nixon because he voted for him. My dad was a staunch Democrat; the old-fashioned, farmer/laborer, working-man's Democrat. He never would admit it, but I think he voted for Nixon just to vote against Kennedy, because, like many people at the time, he was afraid that if they put a Catholic in office, the pope would be running the country."[54]

A small evangelical publisher in Minneapolis announced that "demand for anti-Catholic literature has increased 400 percent," according to a report in the *Eau Claire (Wisconsin) Daily Telegraph's* October 25, 1960, edition in neighboring Wisconsin.

Minnesota is often thought of as a liberal state, largely because it has supported every Democrat for president since 1976, a record unmatched even by Massachusetts and Rhode Island. But that disguises a relatively strong conservative undertow, causing Al Gore, John Kerry and Barack Obama to expend considerable time and energy to hold the state in the first three elections of the 21st century. The state has also from time to time elected staunch conservatives to Congress, including Michelle Bachmann, *la passionaria* of the far right who represents an increasingly conservative portion of the Twin Cities suburbs. Back in Kennedy's day, Walter Judd was an evangelical Republican congressman and former Congregationalist missionary to China who took positions that foreshadowed the religious right that emerged in the late 1970s. So it is not surprising that Kennedy faced a backlash, an undertow from religious conservatives that almost cost him the Gopher State, despite its Democratic leanings since the New Deal.

One of America's most German heritage communities is New Ulm, in Brown County. A mixture of Lutherans and Catholics, as in the Old Country, it had been solidly Republican since Wendell Wilke's 1940 campaign. Kennedy received 41 percent, an improvement on Stevenson's 26 percent. JFK's gains came in two Catholic precincts, where his vote reached 57 percent, double Stevenson's 29 percent. But in Lutheran precincts JFK could manage only 29 percent compared to Stevenson's 24 percent. New Ulm was founded in the 1850s by German "freethinkers" and political radicals who fled the unsuccessful revolution of 1848. New Ulm's founders were so distrustful of religion that they prohibited religious instruction in public schools and even banned Bibles from school libraries.[55] The town cast its first presidential vote for Lincoln over Douglas by a five to one margin in 1860,[56] when the Republicans were considered the progressive party. The town largely remained Republican even when the GOP became the national conservative party.

Within a few decades, New Ulm became a conventionally conservative

German-American city, with a preponderance of Lutherans and Catholics. Both religions exercised a kind of joint political power. Sociologist Noel Iverson writes, "Since 1900 it has been plain to the astute observer that two contesting hierarchies of civic, political, and religious influence were coalescing, one Roman Catholic and the other Protestant."[57] This affected the schools as well, says Iverson: "A gentleman's agreement was reached as a result of the growth of the Roman Catholic and Lutheran population in New Ulm; the six-member school board traditionally has two freethinkers, two Roman Catholics and two Protestants."[58]

A 1958 survey showed the town to be 61 percent Protestant, 31 percent Catholic and 8 percent other or none.[59] Even with that comfortable majority, many Protestants feared Catholics were gaining political power. Iverson noted, "There is evidence to suggest that the reins of power in Germania are being taken up by Roman Catholics."[60] Thus, it is not surprising that Nixon would win the town easily.

Community Size

Size of community was almost irrelevant in Minnesota, unlike Pennsylvania, Ohio, Illinois, Wisconsin and a host of other non–southern states where the Democratic vote rose as community size increased. Kennedy received 51.6 percent of the combined vote in all towns and cities where more than 2,500 votes were cast, and 49.6 percent in communities where fewer than 2,500 votes were recorded — only a two point difference. The reason is that rural Minnesota is much more ethnically homogeneous and it experienced higher levels of religious voting than larger population centers. Many rural villages gave Kennedy or Nixon 90 percent support, largely based on religious identification or some combination of ancestry and religious tradition.

Kennedy made modest gains in the three big cities: 7 percent in St. Paul, 4 percent in Minneapolis and 3 percent in Duluth. He carried all three with a combined 56 percent compared to Stevenson's 51 percent — a 5 percent net gain for the three largest municipalities. Kennedy's overall big city vote in Minnesota was a good deal lower than in the East as was his overall gain, compared to Boston, New York, Philadelphia, Pittsburgh and Cleveland. St. Paul was more Catholic (52 percent) than Minneapolis (30 percent) or Duluth (41 percent). But all three cities had considerable numbers of Protestants, including Baptists and Presbyterians and evangelicals, who maintained seminaries, colleges and publishing companies in the Twin Cities area. Minneapolis had a strong Scandinavian flavor and was home to the Swedish American Historical Society and the largest Lutheran parish in America.

In 36 small cities (with a population above 10,000) Kennedy's vote share rose between 6 percent and 47 percent. He outperformed Stevenson in 31 cities and made solid gains in German Catholic St. Cloud (61 percent, a gain of 22 points) and in German New Ulm (up 15 points to 41 percent). He made double digit gains in Faribault, Winona and Mankato. The vote in Winona shows the importance to Kennedy of the Catholic vote — in this case, Polish Catholics on the east side of town. Kennedy beat Nixon 1757 to 537 there, for a margin of 1,220 votes, offsetting Nixon's margin of 443 in the rest of the town, which the *WPA Guide to Minnesota* described as an amalgam of "Yankees and Germans who built up fortunes in lumber, wheat, steamboating and railroading."[61]

Kennedy's vote dropped 4 percent in Willmar, a Scandinavian Lutheran community in Kandiyohi County, one of the two counties that switched from Stevenson to Nixon. Kennedy's vote also declined 2 percent in Fridley and 1 percent in Columbia Heights, both working-class suburbs of Minneapolis in Anoka County. Kennedy carried both, however.

In the small cities Kennedy triumphed in working-class suburbs of the Twin Cities, with 55 percent to 60 percent and modest gains over Stevenson's vote. His support was strong in mining towns near Duluth, such as Hibbing (home town of Bob Dylan), where JFK received 66 percent, and Virginia, where he was the choice of 60 percent.

Nixon swept 76 percent in Fergus Falls in Otter Tail County, a Lutheran stronghold, and topped 60 percent in Moorhead, Owatonna and Red Wing, other Scandinavian Lutheran areas. Nixon's best showing was his 80 percent sweep in the high-income Minneapolis suburb of Edina, down only a bit from Ike's 85 percent. North Oaks, a posh St. Paul suburb, gave Nixon 87 percent. Fashionable suburbs and prestigious inner city districts formed a core of GOP support in the Eisenhower-Nixon years, and Minnesota proved no exception. Several Edina precincts rewarded Eisenhower with 95 percent or higher support in 1956 and that level generally held up for Nixon. The 1956 Eisenhower reelection slogan, "Peace, Prosperity and Progress," resonated throughout those parts of the U.S. that prospered during his presidency. (Some of the elite commuter suburbs and bedroom communities in New York's Westchester County gave Eisenhower 90 percent or more support.) Nixon's vote was never that high, except in all-Protestant communities, but it remained constant. For example, in Edina's 1st precinct, Nixon received 90 percent.

The Rural Vote

The settlement patterns of ethnic and religious groups in Minnesota were something of a reversal of the norm for Wisconsin, Pennsylvania, Iowa and other states because a large number of rural hamlets were Catholic. This is revealed in the 1960 rural vote. There were 152 "small places" where more than 80 percent of voters supported Kennedy. One was new so we can compare the 1956 and 1960 vote in 151 towns. Kennedy's vote exceeded Stevenson's in 140 towns; in 32 of them he gained 20 percent or more. Nine even went for Eisenhower before switching to JFK.

The "swing" in some precincts was mind-boggling. In Lastrop in Morrison County voters liked Ike 35–10 but then supported JFK 52–10, a swing of 62 percentage points. In Bellechester in Wabash County the Democratic vote rose from 23 percent to 83 percent. In St. Leo Village in Yellow Medicine County, Kennedy doubled Stevenson's vote share from 48 percent to 96 percent. Of course, the vast majority of these precincts supported Stevenson, and these unusual shifts in voter sentiment were the exception rather than the rule. In 40 of these towns Stevenson was stronger than Kennedy. Most were populated by voters of Finnish or Norwegian ancestry.

In rural areas many voters clearly voted their religion and ancestry. Both parties had their ethnic champions. The Democrats could rely on Polish, Czech, Hungarian, French Canadian, Finnish and Native American voters, while Republicans found valuable allies in German Lutheran, Dutch, Mennonite, and Swedish voters. German Catholics and Norwegians were swing voters and moved in opposite directions in 1960. Religious voting was more prominent in rural areas than in cities, suburbs and small towns because of the ethnic homogeneity of the population.

In only 33 rural towns did Nixon's vote exceed 80 percent. His number one town was Pease, in Mille Lacs County, where he bested Kennedy 101–5. All these towns had fewer than a thousand votes, except Mountain Lake, a Russian Mennonite town, where Nixon swept to victory 937–137, or 87.2 percent. Nixon gained one percentage point over Eisenhower, which was typical of Mennonite towns in Pennsylvania, Ohio, Kansas and elsewhere. There was an outpouring of new votes for Nixon in Mountain Lake, where he added 180 votes to the Eisenhower total while Kennedy picked up only 16 additional ballots. Nixon received 75 percent to 80 percent of the vote in another 51 towns.

There were 148 towns throughout Minnesota that supported Stevenson in 1956 and switched to Nixon in 1960. There was at least one such town in 58 counties — a majority of the state's counties. This shows that anti–Kennedy voting in many Democratic-leaning or swing precincts existed far and wide in the Gopher State. As was true throughout the U.S., almost all of the swing precincts that moved against the national trend were rural, many of them isolated.

The only anti–Kennedy town that was not rural was Austin, a blue-collar community in Mower County in the southern part of the state, where about 12,000 votes were cast. The town's economy had been anchored for decades by the Hormel Packing Plant. Stevenson squeaked ahead by 77 votes, receiving 50.4 percent. But Kennedy fell short by 186 votes, winning 49.2 percent. The loss was due to an erosion in the Democratic vote in the working-class third ward, where, as a Wisconsin newspaper predicted, many industrial workers, lifelong Democrats, could not bring themselves to support a Catholic. Kennedy carried the ward 2,546 to 1,699, a margin of 847 votes and 60 percent support. But Stevenson won 2,423 to 1,335, a victory margin of 1,088 and 64.5 percent support. This decline of a 241-vote margin in an unshakably Democratic district cost the party the city of Austin.

Many of the Stevenson/Nixon towns experienced a considerable voter shift. Almost half (72) of these towns gave Kennedy a more than 10 percent lower share of their vote than they gave Stevenson. In 16 of these 72 towns, there was a greater than 20 percent decline in Democratic support. In Moose Park, in Carlton County, Kennedy's support plummeted 43 points. In that hamlet three-quarters of voters favored Stevenson but only one-third supported Kennedy one election later. In the tiny community of Veldt in Marshall County, five out of six voters liked Adlai (84 percent) but less than half (47 percent) embraced JFK.

In addition to the 148 towns that switched from Stevenson to Nixon, there were 129 towns where Kennedy's vote declined by 10 percent or more. Of those, 95 were Democratic and still supported Kennedy, though by a much lower margin. In Boy River in Cass County, for example, Kennedy drew 56 percent compared to Stevenson's 89 percent. In Rockwood in Hubbard County JFK could manage only 56 percent compared to Stevenson's 81 percent.

In 34 towns the Republicans were victorious in both 1956 and 1960, but Nixon ran far ahead of Eisenhower. In the Morrison County village of Upsala, Nixon was supported by 70 percent of voters and Eisenhower by 54 percent. In Waltham in Mower County, Nixon was the choice of 70 percent and Eisenhower of 54 percent. In the Yellow Medicine County village of Echo, Nixon's 71 percent was 14 percent higher than Eisenhower's support. In several super–Republican towns, the result was similar. In Rheiderland in Chippewa County, Nixon received 80 percent and Eisenhower 68 percent. In German Lutheran Plato, in McLeod County, Nixon won 86 percent compared to Eisenhower's 80 percent.

Kennedy lost ground in many Protestant swing precincts. In tiny Moose Park in Itasca County a three to one Stevenson victory (36–11) turned into a two to one Nixon romp (28–14). In Cobden in Brown County a three to two Stevenson win became a two to one Nixon triumph. The hamlet of Bungo in Cass County went three to one for Nixon (40–13) even though it had backed Stevenson four years earlier 26–21.

The decline in Kennedy support was uniform in different types of Protestant rural precincts. JFK dropped 14 points in "swing" areas with many party switchers and 14 points in Democratic precincts. But he lost 12 points in Republican Protestant strongholds as well. The vote turnout increased eight or nine point in all types of Protestant precincts. In total, there were 209 towns where Kennedy ran at least 10 percent weaker than Stevenson: 96 were for Kennedy, 113 for Nixon; Stevenson carried 168, Eisenhower 41. All were rural.

The intensity factor and the enthusiasm deficit favored Kennedy a bit in rural areas, since he made dramatic gains in many small Catholic villages and in fact ran nine points ahead of Stevenson in the strongest Democratic rural areas while Nixon ran about two points ahead of Eisenhower in heavily Republican areas. However, the vote turnout increased 14 percent in Republican precincts and 12 percent in Democratic ones. And, since Protestants outnumbered Catholics in rural Minnesota, the anti–Kennedy backlash offset pro–Kennedy voting, making the statewide outcome very close.

The "country club" Republicans were growing in size while remaining loyal to the GOP in 1960. The wealthiest suburbs of Minneapolis went for Nixon 72 percent to 28 percent, holding JFK to a modest gain of 3 percent over Stevenson's 25 percent. In super rich Minnetonka Beach and Woodland, Kennedy dropped a point to only 16 percent. These tiny enclaves of wealth favored Nixon 462–92, a little better than Eisenhower's 409–87. Nixon ran even with Ike in Minnetonka and held Kennedy to a bare gain of a percentage point or two in Deephaven and Wayzata. One demographic stood out: the presidential vote increased 38 percent in these high-income precincts between 1956 and 1960. This reflected the firm connection between economic success and Republicanism in the late 1950s.

While there was a greater "swing" in percentage points to Nixon in Protestant-Democratic and Independent-leaning areas than among Republicans, there was a large turnout in the most Republican Protestant precincts. Nixon gained 1,004 votes over Eisenhower while Kennedy added a meager 45 votes to Stevenson's total in these precincts.

The Dutch, influenced by Calvinism, have long been conservative Republicans, in Minnesota as elsewhere. Anti–Catholicism was a characteristic by-product of this ethno-cultural tradition. Dutch areas saw nothing wrong with enforcing Sunday closing statutes and Prohibition long after these issues were of no concern in most urban and suburban areas.

Prinsburg is a representative Dutch community. A *Minneapolis Tribune* report more than a decade after the Kennedy-Nixon election shows how little change occurred: "There are no beer parlors, no liquor stores, no dance halls and no billiard parlors. The town has only one church — Christian Reformed — and the only school ... is Central Minnesota Christian School."[62] Louis M. deGryse concurs: "In the Kandiyohi County settlement, the stern Calvinistic ethos has left a deep imprint on Reformed and Christian Reformed communities. Calvinist conceptions of morality, church polity, and social discipline bring heavy pressure on members to live exemplary lives, to avoid the corrupting influence of such worldly activities as gambling, dancing, theatergoing, and consuming alcoholic beverages."[63] This explains why 86 percent of Prinsburg residents voted for Nixon. This contrasted with the laid-back social mores of the Belgian Catholic town of Ghent, where Belgian-American Days were celebrated beginning in 1953.

The Finns in most parts of Minnesota adopted pro-labor, even socialist, politics in the early 20th century, though their Lutheran background, however nominal, caused them to vote against Al Smith in 1928 and only reluctantly for Franklin Roosevelt in 1932. By 1936 the Finns moved en masse to the Democrats, and they gave FDR, Truman and Stevenson some of the highest votes of any ethnic group, especially a Protestant one. Kennedy, however, ran into some suspicion over his Catholicism, and the Finnish Democratic vote remained about the same in 1960 as in 1956 and occasionally ran lower in Finnish areas outside of the Iron Range.

One reason why JFK did not do even worse was the relatively low degree of religious activity by Finnish Americans. Timo Riippa explains: "It has been estimated, however, that only one in four Finnish Americans chose to belong to any church, although practically all of them had been nominal members of the Lutheran State Church in Finland. Once in the United States, they abandoned organized religion in large numbers."[64]

Some historians preferred the designation "Old-Stock American" rather than WASP to distinguish white Protestants from people of Anglo-Saxon (British Isles) or New England descent who moved to Minnesota. These groups were staunchly Republican. Towns with a significant Old Stock population such as Owatonna, Anoka, Lake City, Austin, and Northfield all voted heavily for Nixon. An early 20th century survey found that 90 percent of Old Stock Minnesotans were Republican and two-thirds were either Methodist or Presbyterian.[65]

Norwegian-Americans in Minnesota were early participants in the state's political life. Immigrants to the Red River Valley in the northwestern part of the state were swept up into reformist third-party-movements from the 1890s until the New Deal, giving considerable support to Populists and Progressives after breaking with the Republicans. But they were reluctant to support the Democrats because the party of Jefferson and Jackson was seen as too favorable to Catholics. Jon Gjerde and Carlton C. Qualey wrote of the situation: "Significantly, Minnesota's Norwegian Americans tended not to migrate to the Democratic Party in large numbers until well into the 20th century. Whereas some retained their allegiance to the Republican banner and others joined third parties, few felt comfortable with the Democrats. According to historian Lowell J. Soike, this hesitation to become Democrats was largely due to an anti–Catholic strain among Norwegian Americans that alienated them from a party associated with Roman Catholicism."[66]

Both Norwegian and Swedish-ancestry groups have played a disproportionate role in Minnesota politics in both parties. Eventually, Norwegian dissenters became New Deal Democrats, though those in the southeastern part of the state remained Republicans. This is why Kennedy's vote varied widely in Norwegian rural areas, from 20 percent to a little over 50 percent, and in most instances lower than Stevenson's vote because of strong Lutheran Church influences.

Table 1: Sample Precincts

Town/Village	Description	% Kennedy	% Stevenson	% Change
Red Lake	American Indian	72	39	+33
Prinsburg	Dutch	14	19	-5
New Prague	Czech	75	47	+28
Leota	Dutch	32	44	-12
Embarrass	Finnish	75	77	-2
Tyler	Danish	42	43	-1
Milan	Norwegian	35	41	-6
Flensburg	Polish	86	64	+22
Gentilly	French	87	78	+9
Mountain Lake	Russian/Mennonite	13	14	-1
White Earth	American Indian	79	61	+18
Ghent	Belgian/Irish	91	60	+31
Rollingstone	Luxembourger	77	26	+51
Benson	Norwegian	51	76	-25
Hadley	Norwegian	33	42	-9
Red Lake Falls	French	70	52	+18
Cokato	Swedish/Finnish	43	51	-8
French Lake	Finnish	59	66	-7
Spring Grove	Norwegian	41	53	-12
Deer	Norwegian	29	47	-18
Lanesboro	Norwegian	30	24	+6
Clinton	Swedish/Norwegian	45	47	-2
Grove City	Swedish	27	40	-13
Lindstrom	Swedish	26	36	-10
Vasa	Swedish	44	53	-9
St. Michael	German Catholic	66	25	+41
Watkins	German Catholic	65	30	+35
Avon	German Catholic	72	50	+22

5. The Election by Region

Table 2: Rural Vote by Ethnicity*

Ethnicity	% Kennedy	% Stevenson	% Change	% Turnout Increase
French	72.9	56.7	+16.2	+28.8
Czech	72.7	49.2	+23.5	+41.5
American Indian	72.5	47.5	+25.0	+32.5
German Catholic	67.1	36.0	+31.1	+30.0
Finnish	62.4	64.9	-2.5	+8.0
Swedish	37.2	42.8	-5.6	+14.9
Mixed Scandinavian	36.7	38.0	-1.3	+7.9
Norwegian	32.7	35.8	-3.1	+7.3
Dutch	21.7	27.7	-6.0	+11.9

* A representative sample of precincts with similar ethnic characteristics.

Table 3: Summary — Rural Precincts

Precinct	% Kennedy	% Stevenson	% Change	Turnout Increase
Heavily Democratic	85.0	75.8	+9.2	+11.7
Heavily Republican	19.5	21.0	-1.5	+13.8
Protestant Republican	31.7	43.9	-12.2	+9.3
Protestant Swing	44.2	58.2	-14.0	+8.3
Protestant Democratic	58.2	72.2	-14.0	+8.3
Catholic Democrat	85.9	72.7	+13.2	+11.7
Catholic Swing	84.8	58.1	+26.7	+19.7
Catholic Republican	61.5	30.3	+31.2	+21.7
Iron Ridge Mining Towns	75.5	73.7	+1.8	+4.3
Upper Income Suburbs	28.4	25.2	+3.2	+38.0

Table 4: Kennedy Gains and Losses in Selected Cities and Towns

In Big Three

City	Pro–Kennedy
St. Paul	+7.0
Minneapolis	+4.1
Duluth	+3.0

Small Cities

City	Pro–Kennedy	City	Anti–Kennedy
St. Cloud	+22.0	Willmar	-4.4
New Ulm	+14.9	Fridley	-2.3
Faribault	+12.8	Austin	-1.2
Winona	+12.1	Columbia Heights	-1.2
Mankato	+12.0	Minnetonka	-0.1

Small towns

Town	Pro–Kennedy	Town	Anti–Kennedy
Marshall	+17.2	Chisholm	-1.9
Little Falls	+17.0	Montevideo	-0.3
Hastings	+14.6		
North Mankato	+12.1		

Table 5: Top 25 Anti–Kennedy Swing Towns

Town	County	% Anti–Kennedy
1. Moose Park	Itasca	43.3
2. Boy River	Cass	33.3
3. Pomroy	Itasca	32.4
4. Bungo	Cass	30.8
5. Veldt	Marshall	30.2
6. South Run River	Kittson	30.0
7. Lindford	Koochiching	27.3
8. Mayfield	Pennington	27.0
9. Corden	Brown	26.7
10. Wirt	Carlton	26.4
11. Bull Moose	Cass	25.8
12. Pelan	Kittson	25.7
13. Rockwood	Hubbard	25.2
14. Eagle Point	Marshall	24.7
15. Benson Township	Swift	24.6
16. Lee	Aitkin	24.2
17. Dinner Creek	Koochiching	24.1
18. Eckvoll	Marshall	23.9
19. Rabbit Lake	Crow Wing	23.2
20. Un.Dis.1	Beltrami	22.5
21. Haybrook	Kanabec	22.2
22. Nesbit	Polk	21.9
23. Jupiter	Kittson	21.7
24. Spring Brook	Kittson	21.3
25. Black River	Pennington	21.2

Table 6: Kennedy's 25 Strongest Towns

Town	County	% Kennedy
1. Wylie	St. Louis	97.7
2. Polonia	Roseau	97.6
3. Star	Pennington	97.0
4. Urbank	Otter Trail	96.9
5. Clontarf Village	Swift	96.6
6. Steenerson	Beltrami	96.6

Town	County	% Kennedy
7. Heidelberg	Le Sueur	96.0
8. St. Leo	Yellow Medicine	95.8
9. Sobieski	Morrison	94.1
10. Burton	Yellow Medicine	93.1
11. Miesville	Dakota	93.0
12. Wilmont	Nobles	92.4
13. Alden	St. Louis	92.0
14. Harding	Morrison	91.7
15. Grand View	Lyon	91.4
16. Toivola	St. Louis	91.3
17. Ghent	Lyon	91.2
18. Pulaski	Morrison	91.1
19. Goodland	Itasca	90.6
20. District 55–13	St. Louis	90.6
21. Bowlus	Morrison	90.5
22. Taunton	Lyon	90.5
23. Chester	Polk	90.3
24. Poplar Grove	Roseau	90.2
25. Lavell	St. Louis	89.9

Table 7: Nixon's 25 Strongest Towns

Town	County	% Nixon
1. Pease	Mille Lacs	95.3
2. Sunfish Lake	Dakota	88.7
3. Eitzen	Houston	88.0
4. Mountain Lake	Cottonwood	87.2
5. North Oaks	Ramsey	87.2
6. Akron	Wilkin	87.1
7. Clover	Pine	87.0
8. Northop	Martin	86.5
9. Prinsburg	Kandiyohi	86.4
10. Young America Town*	Carver	86.2
11. Clinton	Rock	85.8
12. Plato	McLeod	85.7
13. New Germany	Carver	85.4
14. New Auburn Village	Sibley	85.3
15. Hamburg	Carver	85.0
16. Wanamingo Village	Goodhue	84.9
17. Dellwood	Washington	84.8
18. Rosing	Morrison	84.2
19. Odin Village	Watonwan	84.0
20. Carson	Cottonwood	83.8
21. Nerstrand	Rice	83.6

Town	County	% Nixon
22. Woodland	Hennepin	83.6
23. Minnetonka Beach	Hennepin	83.2
24. Lester Prairie	McLeod	83.0
25. Hollandale	Freeborn	82.8

* Young America Town is now called Norwood Young America.

NEBRASKA

Loyally Republican Nebraska was Nixon's strongest state, giving the vice president 62 percent, down only a bit from Eisenhower's 65 percent. Like Iowa, Nebraska's three largest religious groups are Catholics, Lutherans and Methodists. The two large Protestant groups often live in the same counties and constitute the GOP base. Catholics are strong in Omaha (Douglas County), which is why Kennedy's vote in the state's largest city was 47 percent compared to Stevenson's 41 percent, a modest gain. Heavily Protestant Lincoln (Lancaster County), the state capital and a college town, gave Kennedy only 37 percent, up just two points.

Kennedy did well, though not as well as Smith, in the rural German and Czech Catholic counties (Cedar, Butler, Saline), usually gaining 10–16 points over Stevenson. He even gained nine points in German Lutheran Cuming County, winning a third of the vote instead of a fourth. But rural Protestant Nebraska remained firmly committed to the GOP. Kennedy's vote lagged behind Stevenson's in 28 counties scattered throughout the state.

Northeastern Nebraska's heavily Lutheran counties were quite unfriendly to the senator. He dropped seven points in 60 percent Lutheran Dixon County and three points in Swedish Lutheran Burt County. (The Swedish Lutheran anti–Kennedy vote shows up in rural Wisconsin and Minnesota as well.) In the ten most anti–Kennedy counties, 44 percent of voters were Lutheran, compared to 27 percent statewide. Catholics were underrepresented at 19 percent and Methodists a bit overrepresented, also 19 percent.

NORTH DAKOTA

The North Dakota results — 55.5 percent for Nixon — bore an eerie resemblance to 1940 when Republican Wendell Willkie received the exact same percentage against Franklin Roosevelt and a nearly identical popular vote. The differences among the state's two largest ethnic religious groups were, however, large. Norwegian Lutherans went for FDR in 1940 and Nixon in 1960. German Catholics favored Willkie and Kennedy. The third largest group, the always Republican German Lutherans, liked Willkie and Nixon.

Kennedy gained six points over Stevenson, mostly in German Catholic rural areas (Emmons County gave JFK a 31-point gain). But Nixon easily won the larger towns, with 59 percent in Lutheran Fargo. In four rural, mostly Norwegian Lutheran, counties, Kennedy ran weaker than Stevenson. He ran even in one and only slightly ahead in four others. These "anti" and "reluctant" counties were 54 percent Lutheran, nine points higher than the state, itself the most Lutheran state in the nation. These counties were 54–23 percent Lutheran over Catholic, while the state was Lutheran 45–36 percent.

South Dakota

Kennedy barely eclipsed Stevenson 41.8 percent to 41.6 percent, making the state result trends almost static. His vote share declined in 37 of the 67 counties, particularly in rural areas in the state's south and east. Three counties, Miner, Spink and Todd, shifted allegiance from Stevenson to Nixon. One of them, Todd, was a Native American county that usually votes Democratic, making the 1960 result totally out of character.

The banner anti–Kennedy county was Douglas, where JFK's vote dropped 11 points, to a miniscule 21 percent. The area is heavily Dutch (40 percent of residents belonged to the Reformed Church) and German (38 percent were Lutheran). Lutherans were the largest group in the ten counties where Kennedy's vote declined the most, and Catholics ranked fourth. Methodists, Presbyterians and Dutch Reformed members were overrepresented in these counties, but the specific denominational breakdown was less significant than in neighboring states.

Wisconsin

Wisconsin was the scene of Kennedy's first primary triumph, 58 percent to 42 percent over Hubert Humphrey. But it failed to quell the religious issue because Kennedy's victories were confined to Catholic areas of the state and Humphrey's to Protestant ones, accentuating the already apparent religious divisions. Humphrey fanned the flames after the election by singling out "Roman Catholic Republicans" who allegedly crossed over to vote for Kennedy in the open primary. He said nothing, however, about the Protestant Republicans who may have voted for him. County returns suggest that crossover votes did occur and broke along religious lines.

Wisconsin was a swing state, going for Dewey in 1944 and Truman in 1948 after backing FDR in the 1930s and Republicans most of the time since McKinley. Eisenhower won two landslides, and a postwar conservative anti–Communist trend produced Senator Joe McCarthy. Ethnicity may have overshadowed religion, as voters seem to have coalesced along ethnic lines in many elections. German-ancestry voters overwhelmed all others and the German vote had been Republican since 1940, except among some German Catholics. Scandinavians were swing voters and were not as Democratic as their counterparts in Minnesota. Catholics were more Democratic than Protestants, especially those of Polish extraction. The state has ethnic religious voting groups rarely seen in other states: Belgian Catholics, Luxembourger Catholics, Icelandic Lutherans, Cornish Methodists, Swiss Protestant liberals, Dutch Protestants *and* Dutch Catholics, to name a few.

As it turned out, Nixon beat Kennedy 52 percent to 48 percent, something of a surprise considering Kennedy's personal popularity and primary victory. He ran 10 points stronger than Stevenson, but failed to carry a state that went for Truman in 1948. County data suggest that Scandinavian and Swiss animosity toward the Catholic Church may have tipped the scales to Nixon. Another factor was that German Catholics did not give Kennedy the overwhelming support against Nixon in November that they bestowed on him against Humphrey in the spring.

More detailed precinct returns indicating the anti–Kennedy backlash will be discussed in the following chapter, but county returns give a general picture. Kennedy ran behind Stevenson in five counties — four Scandinavian Lutheran (Burnett, Polk, Jackson and Vernon) and one Swiss Protestant (Green). All are rural. Precinct returns will reveal that anti–Kennedy voting was rampant in many other counties also. Lutherans were a majority in these five counties and considerably stronger than statewide. In the state, Catholics outnumbered Lutherans among the churchgoing population 50 percent to 32 percent. In the anti–Kennedy counties, Lutherans outnumbered Catholics 51 percent to 20 percent, with 24 percent belonging to either the Methodists or the United Church of Christ, the Swiss-oriented group. Kennedy's strongest gains were in the Catholic areas surrounding Green Bay, where German, Belgian and Dutch Catholics supported their co-religionist enthusiastically.

Three newspapers reported on the intensity of religious voting. The *Sheboygan Journal* in its October 24, 1960, issue accused Nixon campaign workers of "issuing anti-Catholic literature and doing it quite openly." The paper added, "Kennedy is losing votes because of anti-Catholic prejudice among industrial workers and others who might be expected to support the Democratic ticket." The October 25, 1960, *Oshkosh Daily Northwestern* reported that "thousands of anti-Catholic pamphlets were being distributed" in its area of the state. The *Wisconsin Rapids Daily Tribune* noted on October 19, 1960 that "the fact that Kennedy is Catholic has become a big talking point in all political discussions."

Wisconsin is an ideal state to test the persistence of religious and ethnic influence on voting patterns, especially in 1960. Nixon carried all the Midwest states except Minnesota, winning 44 electoral votes to Kennedy's 11. Nebraska and Kansas were the vice president's strongest states, the only two where his support exceeded 60 percent. South Dakota, North Dakota and Iowa also appeared on his top ten states. The traditional Republicanism of the Farm Belt held up in this election, and five of Nixon's strongest states were located in this largely agricultural and small-town region, where Minneapolis-St. Paul and Milwaukee are the only really large cities. Almost one tenth of the national vote came in the Midwest, and Nixon received just under 55 percent of it. Only in Illinois did JFK exceed his national gain of 8 percent.

Great Lakes States

Ohio, Indiana, Michigan and Illinois are usually classified as Midwestern, but eastern Ohio and Michigan, and cities like Cleveland and Detroit, seem to have little in common with rural Nebraska or Kansas. Politically, these states are historically divided between Democrats and Republicans, and presidential elections are often close. This was especially true in the 1940s, when Roosevelt and Truman fought Dewey and Willkie to a virtual draw in this subregion. Industry, manufacturing and agriculture all play significant economic roles. The cities are far more Democratic than the countryside, and Democrats relied on Chicago, Detroit and Cleveland for their statewide victories.

Ohio has always appealed to Republicans, and seven GOP presidents were born in the Buckeye State. Indiana, which became increasingly Republican after 1940 when Indiana native Wendell Willkie was the Republican nominee, was once competitive and provided several Democratic vice presidential nominees. Michigan, like Pennsylvania, has had few national candidates. Lewis Cass was a Democratic candidate for president but he lost and that was in 1844! Thomas E. Dewey, GOP nominee in 1944 and 1948, was born in Michigan but migrated to New York. Illinois, of course, is the Land of Lincoln (and Douglas, too) but was ignored until its governor, Adlai Stevenson, was nominated by the Democrats in 1952.

The region has large Catholic and Protestant communities, with a huge Protestant majority in rural areas. It is ethnically diverse. Many Catholics are of Polish and other East European ancestry, while Protestants are often German or Dutch, or migrated from the border south.

While Eisenhower swept the Great Lakes, the 1960 election was expected to be close, and it was.

Illinois

Catholics were a major part of Kennedy's winning coalition, which included a large majority in Chicago and a respectable vote in Chicago's suburbs. Most of his gains over 1956 came in greater Chicago, the city and the "collar counties," along with one downstate rural area, German Catholic Clinton County. He also carried the blue-collar St. Louis suburban counties of Madison and St. Clair.

Jewish voters helped Kennedy carry Illinois, one of the most closely contested states. He was the choice of 82 percent of Jewish voters in Chicago's Ward 50, 73 percent in suburban Skokie and 64 percent in suburban Wilmette. By contrast, Swedish and German Lutheran voters in Ward 50 gave Kennedy only 38 percent.[67] But a dozen counties, all but one in Southern Illinois, moved in the opposite direction. In these culturally southern and historically Democratic counties, Southern Baptists were 44 percent of residents compared to 6 percent statewide, while 20 percent were Methodists compared to 10 percent in the state. Only 10 percent of residents were Catholic.

This pamphlet was published by the Sunday School Board of the Southern Baptist Convention and was widely distributed (Fair Campaign Practices Committee Collection, Manuscripts Division, Special Collections, Lauinger Library, Georgetown University).

Southern Illinois is a cultural and political backwater, an enclave that is truly more southern than northern in many of its attitudes. Once staunchly Democratic, it supported Stephen Douglas over Abraham Lincoln in 1860 and remained mostly Democratic for the next century. But Kennedy's Catholicism wiped those traditions away, probably because of the strong Southern Baptist identity. A key Baptist county, Union, switched from Stevenson to Nixon, and several neighboring counties showed a similar trend.

Wrote political researchers Lucy Dawidowicz and Leon Goldstein: "Political analysts have observed that downstate Illinois was affected by the religious issue. This observation is confirmed by an analysis of voting in three of the region's counties — Franklin, Jefferson and Union — where most church members are affiliated with the Southern Baptist Convention and the number of Catholics is negligible."[68] Their explanation, based on an examination of local economic and political factors, suggested religion was the deciding factor. "In the absence of other reasons, Fundamentalist anti–Catholicism would seem to account for Kennedy's poor showing here. Kennedy fared worse than Al Smith in 1928. It is possible that anti–Catholic propaganda was more widely distributed and proved more effective than in 1928."[69]

Dawidowicz and Goldstein offer another interpretation that seems to explain a great deal of the backlash vote in 1960, a kind of "status anxiety" politics that some sociologists and political scientists have advanced to explain why many downscale groups strike out against perceived changes to their cherished way of life. "In these downstate Illinois counties ... Kennedy's religion seems to be the only likely factor to account for his poor showing. Perhaps religion has become a kind of last-ditch issue with some Fundamentalists. Over the last four or five decades, they have reluctantly had to come to terms with many social and political innovations. A Catholic in the White House may well have seemed to them too stark a proof that the old America is disappearing."[70]

Paul Simon, who served in Congress for 22 years as first a congressman and then senator from Illinois, was engaged in the Kennedy campaign in fiercely Protestant Downstate Illinois. Simon, then a member of the Illinois house, was an interesting anomaly — a staunch liberal Democrat from a Lutheran family in the Missouri Synod, a branch of Lutheranism whose members are preponderantly Republican. In his memoir Simon explains another bias he grew up with but rejected: "Anti-Catholicism played a significant role in the thinking and theology of Missouri Synod Lutherans then, as well as much of the non-Catholic religious world. Anti-Catholicism was a sort of respectable Ku Klux Klanism, without the sheets and violence."[71]

An admirer of both Adlai Stevenson and John F. Kennedy, Simon and his new wife, a fellow state legislator, attended the Democratic convention in Los Angeles, where Kennedy won the nomination on the first ballot. Returning home to southern Illinois, Simon plunged headfirst into the Kennedy campaign in a region where religion was a rampant, if not dominant, issue. Simon remembered his role:

> Anti-Catholicism played a significant part in the culture of the early history of our nation, and the 1960 campaign produced the last gasp of the virulent form of anti-Catholicism. Years of indoctrination of fear and hatred collided with reality in 1960.... Sargent Shriver asked me to join Max Schrayer, a leader in the Jewish community, in heading the efforts to deal with the religious issue in Illinois. Lutherans, Baptists, and others used their pulpits to denounce the idea of a Roman Catholic becoming president. I had debates on the issue all over the state. In small communities like Steeleville (population 2,059) people packed the local school gymnasium to listen to the discussion of this issue. At Wheaton College's jammed auditorium I sensed that the only two people in the audience on my side in the debate were my wife and my mother.[72]

Simon tried to reason with Lutheran clergy, who were increasingly taking anti-Kennedy stands: "I became involved because a conference of Lutheran ministers in Wausau, Wisconsin asked me to address them on the question of Roman Catholics and politics. I submitted my address to the *Cresset*, a Lutheran journal of thought published by Valparaiso University in Indiana. Several Protestant and Catholic journals reprinted the article. Sarge Shriver distributed my article widely."[73]

Simon's articles and speeches clashed with some local clergy. Simon, who "put in campaign appearances in every corner of the state," was deluged by anti-Kennedy mail: "But I didn't expect a sermon against Kennedy in the First Presbyterian Church of Peoria, widely distributed, with the general theme that Protestants respect freedom and Catholics do not."[74]

INDIANA

The Hoosier State gave Nixon 55 percent of its votes, producing a whopping 223,000 vote majority, a margin almost as high as neighboring

Ohio. Kennedy did gain about five points over Stevenson but ran weaker than Truman or Roosevelt. He could manage only 42 percent in conservative Indianapolis but he won 63 percent in Gary (Lake County). Most of his larger gains over 1956 were recorded in the northwestern counties around Gary and South Bend, in Fort Wayne, a very German Lutheran-Catholic but Republican area, and in a couple of rural German Catholic counties in southern Indiana, Dubois and Perry. Nixon swept Elkhart County, a Mennonite-Brethren stronghold that is very Republican in its political loyalties.

But the central and southern regions — where the Ku Klux Klan dominated Indiana politics during the 1920s, burying Al Smith in a huge landslide — refused to support JFK. He ran behind Stevenson in 21 counties, including Monroe, where Indiana University is located, as well as the suburban counties around Indianapolis (which were still rural in 1960). Methodists, Baptists and Disciples of Christ (Christian Church) members predominated in the anti–Kennedy counties, while Catholics and Lutherans were underrepresented. The Disciples of Christ, which has its national headquarters in Indianapolis, is a middle-of-the-road denomination whose members were disproportionately attracted to the Klan in the 1920s and frequently opened their doors to Klan delegations. Fear of Catholicism and "foreign influence" on U.S. life were factors in that attraction, and counties with large Disciple populations in Indiana and Kentucky were anti–Smith and anti–Kennedy. The Disciples were 14 percent of church members in the top anti–Kennedy counties compared to 7 percent statewide.

Protestants from many other denominations also flocked to the Klan in the 1920s. One-fourth of all white native-born Protestant males joined the Klan in Indiana, according to one scholarly assessment.[75]

MICHIGAN

Kennedy carried the Wolverine State by 67,000 votes out of 3.3 million, a 51 percent to 49 percent edge. He gained about seven points over Stevenson, amassing close to a 380,000-vote sweep in Wayne County (Detroit and its close-in suburbs). African Americans, Jewish and Catholic voters offset the heavy Protestant vote for Nixon in most of the other counties. The all-Polish town of Hamtramck gave Kennedy a fabulous 90 percent after giving Stevenson a solid 80 percent.

Suburban Detroit split with Kennedy amassing 63 percent in somewhat blue collar and Catholic Macomb County (which had also trended to Stevenson in 1956), but only 45 percent in more affluent Oakland County. Heavily Dutch Grand Rapids (Kent County) gave Nixon 61 percent, and most German and English ancestry counties also stayed Republican. One mild surprise was Kennedy's 51 percent–49 percent loss in working-class Flint (Genesee County), where many residents haled from Kentucky and Tennessee, apparently bringing their anti–Catholic attitudes with them.

Kennedy narrowly won the Upper Peninsula 52 percent to 48 percent, one of the few rural areas of the North where Democrats do well and where presidential elections are usually close. The Upper Peninsula resembles neighboring Wisconsin, with a mix of mostly Catholics and Lutherans. Many ethnic groups reside in this isolated area. The Finns and the French dominate several counties, giving the area an unusual cultural mix.

Kennedy ran weaker than Stevenson in two Dutch counties, rural Missaukee, where he was crushed 80 percent to 20 percent and lost three points from 1956, and more urban Ottawa County, where he was defeated more than three to one. Some Dutch towns, like Zeeland, gave Nixon 90 percent. In a number of "Waspish" counties, where Methodists, Presbyterians, Congregationalists and other evangelicals were prominent, Kennedy's gains were minimal, as they were in Dutch-flavored Allegan and Kalamazoo counties.

Jewish voters contributed to Kennedy's relatively slender majority in Michigan. African American and Polish Catholic voters were also supportive. Kennedy received a whopping 93 percent of the Jewish vote in the northwest Detroit suburb of Oak Park, up a bit from Stevenson's 86 percent. In the same community 71 percent of Catholics (up 22 points) and 47 percent of Protestants (up 10 points) went for Kennedy.

Religious voting was intense in Harper Woods, a suburb northeast of Detroit. Catholics were 88 percent for Kennedy, while Protestants were 80 percent for Nixon. Kennedy gained 36 points over Stevenson among Catholics but lost six points among Protestants. Two researchers found that "Catholics and Protestants expressed their mutual apprehensions in a highly rigid political fashion."[76]

The *Herald Press* of Saint Joseph reported in its October 24, 1960, edition: "As election day draws nearer, increasing numbers of anti–Catholic pamphlets turn up in the *Herald Press* mail box. Many are inflammatory, while others are totally inaccurate." Berrien County, where Saint Joseph is located, gave Kennedy only 39 percent of its vote, a small gain over Stevenson.

OHIO

Ohio, a classic swing state that usually favors the winning presidential candidate, departed from tradition by going for Nixon, and by a thumping margin of 273,000 votes, or 53.3 percent. This was Nixon's largest statewide margin. Kennedy did gain eight points over Stevenson's lower than average 1956 vote but Kennedy fell short of Truman's squeaker victory.

Religion was clearly a factor. Kennedy's vote declined in four counties, one of which, Holmes, is a Mennonite–Amish stronghold. (The nation's largest Amish community is located in this county, though the Amish generally do not vote.) Holmes, once Democratic, revolted against Al Smith in 1928 and became Republican. By 1960 Kennedy was the least popular Democrat since Smith. The four anti–Kennedy counties and four others where his vote was about even with Stevenson were strongly Protestant. Methodists were far in the lead with 37 percent, followed by 14 percent Lutheran, 9.4 percent Church of Christ, 7.3 percent Presbyterian and 3.1 percent Mennonite and Brethren. Much of central Ohio (40 counties) includes bastions of old immigration Protestantism, with Catholic populations under 10 percent. Nixon won the state in these counties, piling up a huge majority, and offsetting Kennedy victories in Cleveland, Toledo and other industrial cities.

Akron (Summit County) shows how the anti–Kennedy undertow reduced what should have been a comfortable Democratic margin. Kennedy barely gained two points and squeaked ahead with 50.4 percent. But that was less than Stevenson's 1952 margin and much lower than that of the Truman-Roosevelt era. The town has a large evangelical community from Appalachia and resembles Flint, Michigan.[77]

In southern Ohio Kennedy ran behind Stevenson in Adams County, a Prohibition stronghold, and barely exceeded Stevenson's vote in five nearby counties (Fayette, Gallia, Highland, Jackson and Pike), where Methodists, Lutherans, and assorted evangelicals of German, Welsh, English and Scottish ancestry resided. Kennedy ran far behind Democratic candidates for governor and senator. Dawidowicz and Goldstein concluded: "In the absence of any more persuasive factor, we may be justified in concluding that some Protestants hesitated to vote Democratic because they did not want a Catholic as President. If religion had not been a factor, the six counties' vote for Kennedy probably would have been 2 to 6 percentage points higher."[78]

Heavily Catholic and German Cincinnati narrowly backed Kennedy (50.4 percent to 49.6 percent), up from Stevenson's 37 percent. Kennedy gained 26 points in German Catholic Ward 25, won in some other Catholic areas, and received 84 percent in African American wards. Upper and middle income Protestant areas remained solid for Nixon.[79]

The four Great Lakes states were about as close as the nation was, splitting two states each. Kennedy carried Michigan and Illinois, thanks to Detroit and Chicago, and gained 47 electoral votes while Nixon took Indiana and Ohio for 38. More than 14 million votes—over 20 percent of the national total—were cast in these four states. Nixon edged out Kennedy 51 percent to 48 percent in popular vote because of huge margins in Ohio and Indiana that came mostly from the heavily Protestant rural counties. Indiana was one of Nixon's ten strongest states, the only Great Lakes state to go that heavily for either candidate.

Pacific Coast States

The Pacific Coast, the region of second chances, of restless migration and the "la-la" world of Hollywood and its dream factory, is noted for political extremes. California Democrats were far to the left of the national party, and its Republicans were increasingly far to the right, as would soon be seen by Barry Goldwater's victory over Nelson Rockefeller in the 1964 presidential primary and the election of Ronald Reagan as governor. This represented a major departure from the liberal Republican tradition of Governor Earl Warren, who was the party's 1948 candidate for vice president. In 1916, California also had provided the GOP with a liberal nominee for vice president.

Oregon, despite its secular orientation in religious matters, was the most Republican state on the West Coast, almost an extension of New England. It went for Dewey in 1948. But it also elected Wayne Morse, an outspoken liberal, to the Senate, where his mid–1950s switch from Republican to Democrat affected the national political balance of power. To make matters even more confusing, Oregon was a northern stronghold of the Ku Klux Klan in the 1920s; and its voters tried to outlaw private, mainly Catholic, religious schools in a 1922 referendum that led to a famous Supreme Court decision upholding the right of private schools to exist.

Washington State had a radical Scandinavian populist tradition that gave the state to Teddy Roosevelt's third party in 1912 and a strong second-place finish for Bob LaFollette's third party in 1924.

All Pacific Coast states turned rightward and rejected Al Smith by 2–1 in 1928, before supporting Roosevelt and Eisenhower, showing a tendency to go with the national winner. Huge population increases made all three states up for grabs in 1960. In 1956 Stevenson gained in the Pacific Coast region with an emphasis on public power and environmental and conservation policies.

The Pacific Coast states were noted for their openness to new religious movements, as well as their tolerance for nonaffiliation and secularity. Buddhists, Catholics, and Russian Orthodox Christians were found in large numbers in Hawaii, Alaska and California.

Alaska

Alaska first voted as a state in 1960, so comparison is not possible with 1956. But Kennedy's narrow defeat was a surprise, given that Democrats had completely dominated the vote in Territory days and that Kennedy was the only Democrat to lose in 1960, while Democrats easily prevailed in races for governor, senator and Congress. Alaska was religiously diverse in 1960, but Protestants far outnumbered Catholics. The Russian Orthodox vote in Sitka and on Kodiak Island favored Kennedy.

Alaska in 1960 had not moved as far to the right as it would in succeeding decades. Historian Raymond Gastil noted, "Although Alaska is a center of extreme individualism, of both aggressive and retiring varieties, it is supported to a remarkable extent by the activities of the federal government."[80]

Gastil observed that religious diversity was a fact of Alaskan life and may have influenced the 1960 vote: "Religiously, the people of Alaska cover the full spectrum, with the Russian Orthodox a distinctive minority group. Missionary activity has divided up much of the native countryside by faith.

In the state as a whole the largest denomination is Catholic, closely followed by the Southern Baptists (the highest percentage outside of the South and Interior Southwest). Other significant groups are Mormons, Presbyterians, Methodists, Episcopalians, and Lutherans."[81]

CALIFORNIA

The California returns present a mixed picture. Kennedy fell just 35,000 votes short (out of 6.5 million votes cast) of toppling Nixon in his home state. But his overall gain (5.3 percent) over Stevenson was lower than his national eight point gain. And anti–Catholic literature seems to have been heavily distributed, and even originated in some cases, in Southern California.

The Central Valley counties, where many residents came from Oklahoma and Kansas, actually trended against Kennedy. He lost Bakersfield (Kern County), a Democratic stronghold where he ran even with Stevenson, and dropped one point in Fresno though he still carried it. His vote dropped in Stanislaus County, which he barely held by 89 votes.

In some other Southern California counties — Ventura, for example, in the Simi Valley — his vote was unchanged from that of Stevenson. His gain in Sacramento was less than two points. He gained significantly in Los Angeles and the San Francisco Bay area, foreshadowing much greater Democratic gains in coming years. But the Golden State was not nearly as multicultural as it is a half century later, and white Protestant areas resisted Kennedy's election.

Los Angeles, which has just about every group or subgroup of voter, went comfortably for JFK. A study found an amazing 95 percent for Kennedy and 93 percent for Stevenson in Jewish precincts in Beverly-Fairfax. The senator also received 82 percent in a predominantly black assembly district and 75 percent in a Hispanic district, both modest gains over Stevenson's vote.[82]

A *California Poll* pre–election survey showed sharp religious differences: Kennedy had the support of 91 percent of Jewish voters, 73 percent of Catholics and 38 percent of Protestants. He attracted 31 percent of Catholic Republicans and Nixon won the support of 23 percent of Protestant Democrats, according to polling data. Since Protestant Democrats outnumbered Catholic Republicans by nearly five to one, the loss for Kennedy was significant and may have cost him the state in an election so close (Nixon 50.3 percent, Kennedy 49.7 percent). Protestant defectors to Nixon were disproportionably middle income and women. Catholic Republicans who opted for Kennedy were young.

Religious intensity increased as the campaign progressed. Two California political scientists concluded that "during the period between March and November, a 10 percent shift to Nixon occurred among Protestant Republicans and a comparable shift to Kennedy among Catholic Republicans. When relative size of religious groups, their pre–existing party balance, the level of religious group and party cohesion are all taken into consideration, the net effect seems to be a very slight advantage for Nixon."[83]

Though Californians had refused to withdraw tax exemption for religious schools by a three-to-one margin in 1958, anti–Catholicism plagued Kennedy's campaign from the start. While most suspicion came from fundamentalists in the Central Valley agricultural areas, some reluctance came from liberals, in Beverly Hills and other elite areas, who wanted a third nomination for Adlai Stevenson. Even Governor Pat Brown, the state's first Catholic governor, favored Stevenson. Some have suggested that Brown hoped to be Stevenson's running mate. Others said Brown feared that anti–Catholicism would sink the Democratic ticket. When Brown finally endorsed Kennedy, anti–Catholic zealots blamed a conspiracy directed from the Vatican. During the campaign several newspapers reported that "Republican headquarters in San Diego was openly issuing anti–Catholic literature" (see, for example, the *Cedar Rapids Gazette*, October 24, 1960).

Historian Thomas J. Carty concluded that "anti–Catholicism contributed to Kennedy's failure to win California." He noted that Democratic registration was 60 percent of the total, which in a non–southern state should have assured a Democratic presidential win. Pollster Louis Harris reported that 10 percent of California Democrats would probably vote against Kennedy because "Catholicism is easily the most frequent and most serious negative expressed about Senator Kennedy."[84]

Hawaii

Catholics and Buddhists are the largest religious groups in the Aloha State but Congregationist missionaries were influential during territorial days and founded most private schools, meaning that cultural power was shared. Since the state was participating in its first presidential election, there was little context in which to compare. Kennedy did eke out a narrow win, though the state had elected Republicans to state and congressional offices.

OREGON

Oregon was rather a weak state for Kennedy. Its increasing liberalism made it a Democratic target but Kennedy fell short, winning 47.4 percent compared to Stevenson's 44.8 percent, a slim 2.6 percent gain, one of his lowest gains.

In some respects that was not surprising, since anti–Catholicism was rampant a few decades before. Historian Kenneth Jackson noted that the state's largest city, Portland, had the second highest Klan membership of any city per population in the nation in the 1920s (Indianapolis being first.). Jackson challenged conventional wisdom that Klan anti–Catholicism was solely a rural phenomenon. He discovered considerable prejudicial sentiments in several large cities, including Denver and Dallas.[85] Oregon voters not only elected pro–Klan state officials in 1924 but also approved a measure abolishing all private and parochial schools in 1922. The U.S. Supreme Court unanimously invalidated that referendum in 1925 in *Pierce v. Society of Sisters*.

Despite the state's secular character, having the highest or near highest percentage of religiously nonaffiliated voters, it also had many evangelicals and fundamentalists. Apparently, some voters in both categories remained suspicious of Kennedy, causing his defeat. Portland (Multnomah County) went for Nixon by one point, the last time a Republican carried it for president. Anti–Catholicism may have played a role in that vote.

John Swarthout of Portland State College attributes Kennedy's defeat to "Catholicism, Harvard and the New Deal." Religious and political conservatives disliked Kennedy's liberal stands and feared his religion. He writes: "The 1960 campaign was marked from the start by the religious issue that swirled about Mr. Kennedy, and before election day a series of smears of other sorts appeared, largely in pamphlet form and principally directed at 'New Deal-type liberals.'" Swarthout concluded that Kennedy "lost between 2 and 4 per cent of the total vote cast, and he may have lost more by reason of the non–Fundamentalist Protestants, with whom the religious issue tipped the scales." Swarthout was convinced that "the major influence of religious conviction on the Oregon results is certain and Mr. Kennedy lost more votes than he gained from it."

Swarthout further says that "Fundamentalist Protestant churches are especially thick throughout the middle and upper Willamette Valley" and constituted 38 percent of the Protestant population, even though many Oregonians were not affiliated with any religion. Oregon's tiny Catholic population responded in kind. In Mt. Angel, where there is a monastery and seminary, Kennedy received 67 percent and Stevenson 34 percent. But that result was swamped by Protestant defections. The University of Oregon's Political Research Bureau found that 53 percent of Catholic Republicans were for Kennedy, while 65 percent of Fundamentalist Protestant Democrats went for Nixon. This was tribalism at its worst.[86]

Kennedy ran behind Stevenson in three mostly rural counties, Columbia, Union and Wheeler. That is not a strong enough sample to elicit religious data, but the state's overall result was certainly a Democratic disappointment.

WASHINGTON

Washington had a very mixed political heritage. Progressivism and liberal Republicanism were strong at one time. Teddy Roosevelt carried the state as a Progressive in 1912 and Robert LaFollette ran a strong second in 1924. Socialist Eugene Debs took nearly a fifth of the presidential vote in 1920. But strains of populism, nativism and anti–Catholicism were also strong and had caused Al Smith to lose every county and poll by less than a third of the 1928 vote.

These contradictory elements seemed to have coalesced behind the New Deal, giving FDR and Truman five straight victories. Eisenhower won twice but by a modest 54 percent in 1956. A Democratic trend should have led to a Democratic victory in 1960, according to most analysts, but Kennedy's Catholicism probably cost him the state, which he lost 51 percent to 49 percent. Scandinavian dislike of Catholicism stretched from Wisconsin and Minnesota westward to Washington. Kennedy ran behind Stevenson in six counties and he lost three (Cowlitz in the southwest and Douglas and Grant in the east) that had gone for Adlai.

Hugh Bone of the University of Washington reported: "Local candidates ringing doorbells reported that numerous voters inquired about their church affiliation. A large volume of both identified and anonymous literature was widely circulated among all classes and groups.... [T]he writer found near unanimity that Kennedy's religious faith was of no assistance to him and that it was probably a handicap which neutralized certain assets noted earlier."[87]

Washington has many secular voters but also a good number of evangelicals, Republican governor Arthur B. Langlie the most prominent in the postwar era. In the anti–Kennedy counties Protestants outnumbered Catholics three to one, but there was quite a denominational mix. Kennedy lost ground in Adams County, where many Russian-German farmers lived. Liberal Seattle (King County) was not quite born yet, as Nixon carried it by four percentage points. Kennedy ran into trouble in Walla Walla County, where there are many Seventh-day Adventists and in the Dutch precincts in Whatcom County.

The Pacific Coast states almost mirrored the nation in their extremely close popular vote — Nixon by 50.6 percent to 49.4 percent and a margin of just 100,000 out of 8.7 million. But since Nixon eked out victories in all except Hawaii he received 50 electoral votes to Kennedy's three — an example of how the electoral vote differs from the popular vote. (Nixon received 94.3 percent of the region's electoral votes.) As a result, none of the states appeared on either candidate's top ten. Nixon was, of course, the quintessential Southern California man, and this was to all intents and purposes his home area — as New England was to Cape Cod-loving JFK.

The Rocky Mountain West

The Rocky Mountain West (or Interior West, as it is increasingly called) combines numerous cultural strains, including Old Hispanic — more Spain than Mexico — Mormon and the Old West's cowboys and ranchers. It was the region most sympathetic to William Jennings Bryan's brand of Democratic politics in 1896 but it moved toward the Teddy Roosevelt brand of Republican politics a few years later.

The Rocky Mountains were Republican in the 1920s and Democratic in the 1930s and 1940s, pretty much following the national trend. Truman's outspokenness and popularity in small town America helped him carry the region easily in 1948, but in 1952 Eisenhower swept the area, which was ripe for change and increasingly unsympathetic to the federal government.

The only real cities in the Rocky Mountain region were Denver, Salt Lake City, and Phoenix. Las Vegas was still a village, and Tucson and Albuquerque were beginning to blossom. Nixon was the favorite in 1960, partly because of his California upbringing.

The Rocky Mountains were about evenly divided into Catholics, Mormons and Protestants of different hues and varieties. Catholics had a strong following in New Mexico, Arizona and Montana, Mormons in Utah and Idaho, Baptists in Arizona and New Mexico, and Lutherans in Montana. Many voters were unaffiliated with any religion, being far West individualists and libertarians. Despite the Republican edge in the 1950s, there were a number of small town Democrats who remained loyal to the memory of FDR, Truman and Wilson.

Arizona

Historically Democratic Arizona was growing increasingly Republican because of the GOP leanings of many new residents. Senator Barry Goldwater was immensely popular, having been reelected in 1958 by a larger margin over the same opponent he beat in 1952.

Kennedy could attract only 44 percent of the vote, up five points from Stevenson's total, a lower gain than nationally. Most of Kennedy's loss came in Phoenix (Maricopa County), which contributed 40,000 of Nixon's 44,000 vote edge. Religion seems not to have been as important a factor in the outcome as in other states, though JFK was still considerably weaker than Truman or FDR. Still, for the first time since statehood in 1912, Arizona voted for the losing presidential candidate. It also was Nixon's strongest state in the West. Emmet McLoughlin, an ex-priest and a nationally known anti–Catholic zealot and author of such books as *People's Padre* and *Crime and Immorality in the Catholic Church*, lived in Phoenix and was active in the anti–Kennedy campaign. While the state had a significant Hispanic population in Tucson (Pima County) and San Juan County, it was not enough to offset the growing Republican-friendly suburbs of Phoenix.

Colorado

Kennedy ran ahead of Stevenson in Colorado, thanks to Denver, Pueblo and the rural Hispanic counties, but his 45 percent vote was only a five point improvement and fell far short of the vote for Truman and Roosevelt. He lost Boulder, which like most academic counties had no large student vote before 1972. His vote declined in five eastern Colorado rural counties (Bent, Cheyenne, Prowers, Washington and Yuma). Methodists were the largest religious group, with 29 percent of church members, followed by Baptists (10 percent) and Lutherans (9 percent). Methodists were particularly stronger here than statewide.

Anti–Catholicism had a long history in Colorado, and the Ku Klux Klan was a strong force in the 1920s. A colorful leader of the anti–Catholic forces was the so-called Cowboy Evangelist, the Rev. Harvey Springer, who rode his horse and warned of papal intrigues in the eastern Colorado hinterlands for decades.[88] Springer promised, "Five days before the election, I'm releasing 1,500,000 volunteer workers to call on voters and give them our literature on Kennedy."[89] That was undoubtedly an exaggeration, but Kennedy's vote did decline in the targeted area.

University of Colorado professor Curtis Martin thought the religious issue may have caused Kennedy's defeat in the state. He wrote as follows:

> Among the factors influencing the outcome of the election, there appears to be little doubt that the religious issue was uppermost in the minds of many voters. Denver County Democratic Chairman Robert Appel put it this way: "Religion was an undercurrent in the whole campaign. We didn't always feel it, but it went very deep." Congressman Wayne Aspinall stated that he believed that what he called "inter-church" friction of the type that made Colorado one of the last non–Southern Ku Klux Klan states was a strong factor in the election. "We had one of the last Klan governors north of the Mason-Dixon Line," Aspinall remarked, "and there's still a decided hangover."

Morton Margolin, a reporter for the *Rocky Mountain News,* found that objection to Kennedy on religious grounds developed rapidly and strongly during the last ten days of the campaign. Margolin stated that nearly 25 percent of the people he interviewed during the last week before election day were against Kennedy because of his religion, more than double the number he had found a month earlier. Anti–Catholic feelings were fanned by the activities of several religious groups and leaders in Colorado. Methodist Bishop Glenn R. Phillips, of Denver, by letter informed some 20,000 members of his church in a four-state area that he would not "mark my ballot for a Roman Catholic candidate for the presidency." On October 27, five hundred Conservative Baptists, meeting in a regional convention in Denver, unanimously adopted a strongly worded resolution warning of "the danger of voting for a candidate who is committed to a system which jeopardizes both our priceless religious freedom and the absolute separation of church and state."

The most bitter attack against Catholicism was led by Harvey H. Springer, pastor of the First Baptist Church of Englewood, Colorado, who conducted a national as well as a local campaign "to keep any Roman Catholic from being elected president of the United States." This campaign was well organized, well financed and had the support of many volunteer workers.[90]

Springer kept up a frenetic pace during the campaign's closing days. His *Western Voice* newspaper pounded Kennedy mercilessly. In a last-minute appeal for funds from supporters, entitled "Kennedy Cannot and Must Not Win," Springer charged, "The controlled Press says religion does not matter, but children in high schools have been hired to promote discussions on the religious question to carry back home to their parents." There was, of course, no proof to these allegations. Claiming to have made 270 addresses in 27 states, Springer appealed for funds to finish the work and promised to send contributors a new anti–Catholic book, *And So Help Us, God*, written by Art Wilson, president of the Baptist Bible Fellowship. "Time is short," he warned.[91]

Idaho

Mormons dominate southeast Idaho, with majorities approaching the Utah level in some counties, but Protestants of various stripes and Catholics are strong in other parts of the state. There were no counties where Kennedy ran behind Stevenson, and his 46 percent of the vote was a good showing for the West. But the state had backed FDR and Truman in all five elections in the New Deal-Fair Deal era, and Democrats routinely won local and congressional offices. He carried the Catholic counties in the northern panhandle but lost almost all Protestant and Mormon counties, so the religious balance of power probably cost him the state. Idaho also had a large secular and nonreligious vote that seems to have split about evenly in this race.

One political scientist concluded that "a number of precincts where either Latter-day Saints or Methodists are strong gave Kennedy smaller totals than is usual for Democratic candidates."[92]

Montana

Only a half dozen counties gave Kennedy lower support than Stevenson, and five were in eastern Montana. Lutherans ranked first in them, particularly in the most anti–Kennedy county, Sheridan, with 68 percent of church members. But Catholics were a third of the population, a rather high figure for counties where Kennedy did poorly. Many Montanans belong to no church, a common feature of the western landscape.

The Dutch antipathy to a Catholic candidate, noted in Iowa, Michigan, South Dakota, and Wisconsin, also showed up in Montana. In the mostly Dutch town of New Amsterdam, Nixon whipped Kennedy 260–40, even though voters had given a Democratic congressional candidate nearly 90 percent support two years before.[93]

Kennedy did fairly well in Big Sky country, winning almost 49 percent compared to Stevenson's 43 percent, but he fared well below the Truman-Roosevelt level. He carried two of the three Native American majority counties with 53 percent of the total vote, though that community had not yet become politically energized as it did five decades later when it gave a landslide majority to Barack Obama.

Nevada

Nevada was a very different state in 1960, long before huge population gains changed its character. Kennedy won 51 percent, and achieved an above average gain of nine points. The state had been moving in a Democratic direction, giving Stevenson a three point higher share in 1956 than in 1952. One of the few counties to switch from Ike to Adlai was Clark (Las Vegas), though it was a relatively small town at that time. The usual patterns prevailed, with Kennedy taking Las Vegas and Nixon winning Reno (Washoe County). The rural areas were split right down the line.

Nevada had many Catholics, including those of Basque ancestry around Reno — one of whom, Paul Laxalt, became a Republican governor and U.S. senator, Mormons and Episcopalians — who were stronger in Nevada in 1926 proportionally than in any other state. But many were secular non-churchgoers. Kennedy gained in every county.

Don Driggs, of the University of Nevada, wrote: "Although some anti–Catholic literature was circulated, religion did not seem to be the dominant issue in the presidential election.... Any Catholic bloc voting may have been offset by a big vote for Nixon on the part of normally Democratic Mormons,"[94] who had not yet shifted en masse to the Republicans.

New Mexico

New Mexico experienced stark differences and significant changes in 1956–1960 voting between six Baptist "Little Dixie" strongholds in eastern

New Mexico bordering Texas and a similar number of northern New Mexico counties where voters called themselves "Hispanic" rather than "Mexican" because they traced their ancestors to Spain.

Pro–Catholic and anti–Catholic voting just about canceled each other, with JFK squeaking to victory with 50.4 percent, a gain matching his national improvement of eight points. His vote was still six points below Truman's 1948 vote.

Anti–Catholic voting was enormous in Roosevelt County, where Kennedy could draw only 30 percent support compared to Stevenson's 45 percent, one of the biggest anti–trends in the nation. This heavily Baptist rural area gave 76 percent of its 1948 vote to fellow Baptist Harry Truman. Two counties, Eddy and Lea, resembled the South, since they narrowly backed Kennedy with smaller margins than Stevenson; but the other four anti–Kennedy-trending counties went for Nixon. These half-dozen counties were 47 percent Southern Baptist, more than double the state average of 21 percent. Just under a quarter of residents were Catholic, far below the state average of 56.5 percent, and 15 percent were Methodists, above the state average of 9 percent.

The *Deming Headlight*, a newspaper in Luna County, kept a close eye on religious-based propaganda. In its October 13, 1960, issue, it reported the following: "The mail service has been loaded with anti–Catholic literature circulating throughout eastern New Mexico." The newspaper noted that "much of the material is nonsense, quoting Catholic magazines that did not exist." A week later, on October 20, it added that the anti–Kennedy zealots "seem to know next to nothing about the Catholic Church."

Kennedy gained in the Hispanic counties, which had historically leaned Republican since territorial days, though FDR carried most of them. Santa Fe, today a liberal stronghold, voted for Dewey twice and Eisenhower twice, switching to Kennedy with 58 percent. Kennedy made 15 point gains in Taos, Valencia and Rio Arriba Counties — Old Spanish New Mexico — and also carried scientific/high tech Los Alamos and Native American McKinley County, though Nixon carried Albuquerque (Bernalillo County).

Utah

Mormon Utah, which backed FDR and Truman five straight times, embraced the GOP in the 1950s and stayed with Nixon 55 percent to 45 percent. The Mormon Church leadership openly backed Nixon, but many Mormons must have felt kinship with the attacks on Kennedy because of his religion. As a result, Kennedy's 10-point gain in Utah exceeded the nation's, and his vote share increased in every county. His vote was up from 33 percent to 46 percent in Utah County, where Brigham Young University is located, in Provo. Many future Democratic candidates would rarely crack 20 percent in this county, as Mormons drifted rightward. The non–Mormon counties backed Kennedy, giving him 67 percent in Carbon County.

Kennedy spoke at the Mormon Tabernacle in Salt Lake City on September 23, where he praised the Mormons for "their successful battle to make religious liberty a living reality and for having proven to the world that different faiths of different views could flourish harmoniously in our midst."[95] But the church's president endorsed Nixon before the election. This endorsement may have had an impact in several states. Totton Anderson writes: "The Nixon endorsement by President David O. McKay was believed to have greatly influenced members of that faith throughout the West."[96]

In 1960 Utah and its "Mormon Region," which extends into southeastern Idaho, were distinctive and politically competitive, though moving in a Republican direction. Cultural historian Raymond Gastil wrote: "Politically the region has a balanced two-party system. Yet the church hierarchy has always been conservative and generally Republican."[97] Gastil also called Utah "a state with superior social statistics"[98] that made it "a participant and stable society."[99]

WYOMING

Wyoming was a swing state in 1960. It had not yet become the Republican stronghold that it is today. After three Roosevelt victories, the state jumped to Dewey in 1944 and back to Truman in 1948. Eisenhower won two landslides and Nixon won 55 percent.

The state is more Protestant and secular than Catholic, but it is not really dominated by any religious culture. Kennedy's biggest victory (68 percent) came in ethnic–Catholic Sweetwater County, where Stevenson had won twice, and JFK won Laramie County, the state's largest. But his vote stayed only even with Stevenson's in Crook, Goshen and Niobrara counties. Nixon ran strongest in the rural "cowboy" counties in the eastern part of the state. Kennedy did best in the west.

The Rocky Mountain States gave Nixon 25 electoral votes to Kennedy's seven. It was the least populated region. Only 2.6 million of the nation's 68.3 million votes (less than 4 percent) were cast in this region. Nixon defeated Kennedy 53.6 percent to 46.4 percent. Arizona and Wyoming appeared on Nixon's top ten states list, while Nevada was tied for tenth on Kennedy's top ten.

Kennedy's vote gain over Stevenson exceeded his national average in Utah, which still went for Nixon, and in Nevada and New Mexico, which backed JFK.

Regional Summary

The regional vote breakdown shows that this was truly a close election everywhere. In no region did Kennedy or Nixon receive 55 percent of the vote. Kennedy carried only the Northeast and the South with under 53 percent, while Nixon led elsewhere by relatively slim margins (his best regions were the Midwest and the Rocky Mountains).

The popular vote reveals an interesting fact: Slightly over half of the total national vote was recorded in just the 13 states of the Northeast and Great Lakes, where Kennedy won by 700,000 popular votes and dominated the electoral votes 168–50. The urban and multicultural areas outvoted the rest of the nation.

Electoral votes do not always reflect the popular votes. Kennedy actually lost narrowly in popular votes in the Border States and the Great Lakes but won 80 electoral votes to Nixon's 55 in the two regions. But Nixon swept the electoral votes 50–3 in the Pacific Coast region after barely winning the popular votes there by one percentage point.

The Vote by Regions

Region	Electoral Votes Kennedy	Electoral Votes Nixon	Popular Votes Kennedy	Popular Votes Nixon	Popular Vote % Kennedy	Popular Vote % Nixon	Popular Votes Majority
Northeast	121	12	10,562,160	9,436,492	52.8	47.2	1,125,668 (D)
South	81	33*	5,185,115	4,723,753	52.3	47.7	461,362 (D)
Border	33	17**	2,971,351	3,079,773	49.1	50.9	108,422 (R)
Great Lakes	47	38	6,961,721	7,382,147	48.5	51.5	420,426 (R)
Midwest	11	44	3,009,091	3,650,225	45.2	54.8	641,134 (R)

5. The Election by Region

Region	Electoral Votes Kennedy	Electoral Votes Nixon	Popular Votes Kennedy	Popular Votes Nixon	Popular Vote % Kennedy	Popular Vote % Nixon	Popular Votes Majority
Rocky Mountain	7	25	1,224,277	1,415,464	46.4	53.6	191,187 (R)
Pacific Coast	3	50	4,313,016	4,420,303	49.4	50.6	107,287 (R)
Totals	**303**	**219**	**34,226,731**	**34,108,157**	**50.1**	**49.9**	**118,574 (D)**

*Fourteen electors in Mississippi and Alabama voted for Harry Byrd.
**One elector from Oklahoma voted for Harry Byrd.

Anti-Kennedy Voting in Fourteen Metropolitan Areas

State	County	Town	% Anti-Kennedy
Alabama	Jefferson	Birmingham	4.2
California	Fresno	Fresno	1.1
	Stanislaus	Modesto	1.1
	Tulare	Visalia	1.5
Florida	Polk	Lakeland	1.3
Georgia	Fulton	Atlanta	5.2
Missouri	Greene	Springfield	4.7
North Carolina	Buncombe	Asheville	0.3
Oklahoma	Oklahoma	Oklahoma City	1.6
Pennsylvania	Cumberland	Carlyle	0.8
	York	York	3.4
Tennessee	Davidson	Nashville	7.1
	Hamilton	Chattanooga	1.7
	Knox	Knoxville	0.6

Number of Counties in Fourteen States Where Kennedy Ran Weaker Than Stevenson by 10 percent or More

State	Counties
Alabama	1
Arkansas	6
Florida	4
Georgia	25
Kentucky	10
Louisiana	5
Mississippi	52
Missouri	8
New Mexico	1
Oklahoma	17
South Carolina	28
South Dakota	1
Tennessee	16
Texas	13
Total	**187 Counties**

Top Ten Most Anti–Kennedy Counties

	% Anti–Kennedy
1. Barnwell, SC	36.7
2. Calhoun, SC	31.4
3. Clarendon, SC	30.7
4. Montgomery, MS	28.7
5. Sunflower, MS	28.6
6. Noxubee, MS	28.2
7. Williamsburg, SC	28.0
8. Lowndes, MS	27.5
9. Lee, SC	26.6
10. Grenada, MS	26.3

Most Anti–Kennedy Counties

State	County	% Anti–Kennedy
Alabama	Barbour	10.2
Arkansas	Fulton	16.1
	Clay	15.2
	Jackson	14.7
	Greene	13.4
	Randolph	12.2
	Sharp	12.0
	Craighead	11.1
	Poinsett	10.6
Florida	Lafayette	12.1
	Gilchrist	12.0
	Suwanee	10.6
	Taylor	10.3
Georgia	Warren	25.9
	Jeff Davis	19.8
	Bacon	19.2
	Lee	19.2
	Bleckley	18.5
	Johnson	17.3
	Jefferson	16.2
	De Kalb	15.4
	Columbia	14.5
	Fayette	13.6
	Washington	13.1
	Toombs	12.9
	Tattnall	12.3
	Brooks	12.2
	Pulaski	11.7
	Glascock	11.7

5. *The Election by Region*   183

State	County	% Anti–Kennedy
	Catoosa	11.3
	Burke	11.2
	Houston	11.2
	Evans	11.1
	Clayton	11.0
	Screven	11.0
	McDuffie	10.7
	Twiggs	10.1
	Bulloch	10.0
Kentucky	Marshall	17.7
	Calloway	14.6
	Carlisle	12.8
	Graves	11.8
	Logan	11.6
	Gallatin	11.5
	Grant	11.0
	Livingston	10.9
	Owen	10.5
	Boone	10.3
Louisiana	Morehouse	15.2
	Tensas	14.8
	Webster	12.9
	East Carroll	12.0
	Madison	10.2
Missouri	Reynolds	15.7
	Dunklin	14.3
	Oregon	13.8
	Shannon	11.7
	Ripley	11.6
	Stoddard	11.4
	Carter	11.4
	Texas	10.2
New Mexico	Roosevelt	14.9
Oklahoma	Roger Mills	20.4
	Harmon	15.0
	Tillman	14.5
	Garvin	14.3
	McIntosh	14.2
	Beckham	13.7
	Jackson	12.7
	Washita	12.7
	Bryan	12.6
	Kiowa	12.5
	Greer	12.0

State	County	% Anti-Kennedy
	Pushmataha	11.8
	Hughes	11.1
	Pontotoc	11.0
	McClain	10.8
	Atoka	10.1
	Johnston	10.1
South Dakota	Douglas	10.9
Tennessee	Fayette	24.7
	Haywood	20.0
	Gibson	16.6
	Hardeman	16.5
	Crockett	16.2
	Obion	16.0
	Tipton	15.3
	Dyer	14.2
	Warren	13.5
	Rutherford	11.9
	Sumner	11.9
	Lake	11.8
	Cannon	11.1
	Wilson	10.8
	Benton	10.2
	Humphreys	10.2
Texas	Collingsworth	21.2
	Parmer	17.6
	Moore	16.3
	Sherman	13.5
	Briscoe	12.8
	Hall	12.5
	Bailey	12.0
	Lamb	11.6
	Hemphill	11.1
	Hutchinson	11.1
	Childress	11.1
	Armstrong	10.3
	Wheeler	10.0

Intense Anti–Kennedy Voting (10 percent +) in Mississippi and South Carolina

Mississippi

County	% Anti-Kennedy	County	% Anti-Kennedy
Amite	21.5	Marshall	17.8
Attada	12.8	Monroe	26.1

5. The Election by Region

County	% Anti–Kennedy	County	% Anti–Kennedy
Benton	11.5	Montgomery	28.7
Calhow	18.8	Newton	22.6
Carroll	15.0	Noxubee	28.2
Chickasaw	20.4	Oktibbeha	16.4
Claiborne	10.8	Panola	20.3
Clay	16.8	Pike	12.4
Copiah	22.5	Prentiss	12.9
De Soto	16.6	Quitman	11.5
Grenada	26.3	Rankin	22.4
Hinds	15.9	Scott	17.7
Holmes	22.2	Sharkey	13.6
Humphreys	15.4	Simpson	19.1
Jasper	11.2	Stone	16.7
Jeff Davis	17.7	Sunflower	28.6
Lafayette	12.4	Tallahatchie	14.6
Lamar	14.6	Tate	15.2
Laurence	14.4	Tippah	10.0
Leake	14.9	Tunica	20.9
Lee	10.5	Uneon	10.3
Leflore	18.7	Wayne	20.9
Linwen	15.9	Webster	23.3
Lowndes	27.5	Winston	13.2
Madison	13.6	Yalobusha	16.8
Marion	13.3	Yazoo	23.2

South Carolina

County	% Anti–Kennedy	County	% Anti–Kennedy
Abbeville	11.4	Hampton	23.7
Allendale	19.6	Horry	20.2
Bamberg	21.4	Laurens	15.0
Barnwell	36.7	Lee	26.6
Calhoun	31.4	Lexington	24.8
Clarendon	30.7	McCormick	16.6
Colleton	25.9	Marion	17.6
Dillon	20.9	Marlboro	11.0
Dorchester	23.0	Newberry	19.1
Edgefield	13.5	Orangeburg	20.5
Fairfield	13.6	Pickens	13.7
Florence	13.9	Richard	11.6
Greenville	14.2	Saluda	24.4
Greenwood	15.7	Williamsburg	28.0

Number of Counties Where Kennedy Was Weaker Than Stevenson

State	Number of Counties	State	Number of Counties
Alabama	41	Nebraska	28
Arkansas	33	New Mexico	6
California	5	North Carolina	43
Colorado	5	North Dakota	4
Florida	28	Ohio	4
Georgia	106	Oklahoma	70
Illinois	12	Oregon	3
Indiana	21	Pennsylvania	16
Iowa	26	South Carolina	41
Kansas	3	South Dakota	37
Kentucky	85	Tennessee	73
Louisiana	18	Texas	57
Michigan	2	Virginia	6
Minnesota	16	Washington	6
Mississippi	74	West Virginia	1
Missouri	92	Wisconsin	5
Montana	6	**Total**	**973**

CHAPTER 6

Pennsylvania and Wisconsin Case Studies

In Pennsylvania many towns and villages reflected the religious polarization of the 1960 vote. A kind of religious war, fought on the political turf and ending at the polls, was noticeable, particularly in counties where there were large and visible Catholic and Protestant communities. Around Gettysburg in Adams County, Kennedy drew 79 percent support in Catholic McSherrytown but only 13 percent in Lutheran Menallen. Both were rural and German, but religious differences shaped the vote in communities only a few miles apart. Kennedy's in-the-pits support in Menallen remains the lowest vote share for a Democrat between 1928 and 2008. In fact, if we want to fast-forward a bit and look at the Democratic vote percentage over a half century from 1956 to 2008, we find that there are 226 towns in Pennsylvania where Kennedy's vote was the lowest recorded — lower than such losing candidates as Stevenson, McGovern or Mondale, who received a much lower vote nationally and statewide. These towns were almost all rural, Protestant and German ancestry areas, with a few in the Appalachian Mountain counties. A few college towns were here (Lewisburg, Kutztown and Selinsgrove) before the Democratic vote exploded in the Kerry and Obama elections.

The Catholic-Protestant divisions were pronounced in these "traditional" counties, where there is little migration in or out and where residential patterns have remained fixed. In Schuylkill County, for example, 95 percent of residents in the 2000 census were born in Pennsylvania. In this old coal mining region Kennedy's vote was about 80 percent in Catholic towns where many residents trace their ancestry to Lithuania, Ireland and the Ukraine. In German Protestant towns in the southern part of the county, Kennedy's vote plummeted to 20 percent — a 16 percent decline from Stevenson's support. In neighboring Northumberland County, Catholic villages went 81 percent for JFK but in Protestant towns he was the choice of only 17 percent, compared to 38 percent for Stevenson. These Catholic-Protestant divisions in the countryside also appeared in some larger towns. Here are some examples:

- In Berwick Borough in Columbia County, Kennedy received a scant 23 percent in the Protestant Ward 1, though nearly half of voters were registered Democrats and 26 percent had supported Stevenson. In Precinct 3, where 59 percent were Democrats, Kennedy drew less than 26 percent. In that precinct Nixon picked up 137 votes over Eisenhower while Kennedy's vote declined by five. But in Catholic Precinct 2 in Ward 3, Kennedy was supported by 85 percent of voters, up from Stevenson's 69 percent.
- Near Pittsburgh, the town of Shaler in Allegheny County recorded 75 percent for Kennedy in a Catholic area and 20 percent in a nearby Protestant jurisdiction.
- In Allegheny Township in Blair County, near Altoona, the figures were 76 percent for Kennedy in a Catholic precinct and 23 percent in a Protestant one.
- In the working-class community of Sayre, in Bradford County near the New York state line, Kennedy was the choice of 91 percent in a tiny Italian-American community and 38 percent in a Protestant blue-collar jurisdiction.
- In Columbia County's Conyngham Township, a mining town sharply delineated by ethno-religious differences, a Catholic precinct was 89 percent for Kennedy while a Protestant precinct rewarded him with only 17 percent.

Historical memories played a large role in the 1960 Pennsylvania vote:

- In a hundred towns where Al Smith could muster only 5 percent of the 1928 vote, Kennedy inched up only to 12 percent.
- In a half dozen towns where an anti–Catholic minor party, the so-called American Party, took a large chunk of the 1924 presidential vote, Kennedy lost 83 percent to 17 percent.
- In a dozen towns where the Prohibition Party either won or came

in second in the 1916 and 1920 presidential races, Kennedy lost 84 percent to 16 percent.

Anti–Kennedy voting took different forms. In Protestant Republican strongholds there was a huge turnout for Nixon, exceeding Eisenhower's vote, while the Democratic vote was unchanged. In Menallen Nixon won 639–93, while Eisenhower won 562–98. Nixon gained 77 votes and Kennedy lost 5.

In the Amish country of Lancaster County, Nixon gained 221 votes in Akron to Kennedy's 26. In West Donegal, Nixon's vote soared by 323 while Kennedy added 24. In a subdivision called New Manor, Nixon piled up a 724–69 (91.3 percent) landslide, adding 268 votes to the Republican column while Kennedy gained just 16 votes. This was essentially the pattern throughout the Mennonite-Amish-Brethren areas of central and southeastern Pennsylvania.

But in Protestant Democratic areas, Kennedy's vote declined and Nixon's increased, suggesting a crossover vote of Protestant Democrats for Nixon. In Monroe Township in Juniata County, Kennedy lost 396–170 while Stevenson lost only 257–250. Nixon gained 139 votes while Kennedy lost 80 votes in a jurisdiction where 62 percent of voters were registered Democrats. Kennedy's 30 percent was less than half of the Democratic registration. In the tiny village of Centerport in Berks County, where 82 percent of voters were Democrats, Kennedy lost 76–42 while Stevenson had won 63–55. In Eldred, in Monroe County in the Pocono Mountains, Kennedy won the endorsement of only 96 voters while 170 supported Nixon, despite an 83 percent Democratic registration. Stevenson had easily carried the town 186–128.

The intensity factor seems to have favored Nixon in small towns. Nixon's vote topped 80 percent in 409 towns compared to that level of support for Kennedy in 22 towns. Nixon ran slightly ahead of Eisenhower and 4 percent ahead of Republican registration. There were towns supporting Nixon by 80 percent or more in 51 of the state's 67 counties. However, the towns where Kennedy's vote exceeded 80 percent, while fewer in number, cast 207,000 votes compared to 161,000 in the Nixon strongholds. Kennedy also ran 4 percent ahead of Democratic registration and 15 percent ahead of Stevenson in his most enthusiastic bailiwicks.

Kennedy ran into a degree of lukewarmness, for want of a better term, in many working-class Protestant Democratic towns. There were 13 towns in the western part of the state which appeared on Stevenson's list of top 40 towns in both 1952 and 1956 but which fell off the Kennedy top 40. Though JFK carried all of these towns, there were actual losses in percentage of vote support in Georges and Washington in Fayette County, in Dunkard in Greene County, Stockdale in Washington County and Export in Westmoreland County. He gained slightly but did not match his statewide gain in the Cambria County towns of Vintondale and Portage Township, in the Fayette County towns of Luzerne and Brownsville townships, in Washington County's Centerville and West Pike Run, in Morgan in Greene County and in Arnold in Westmoreland County. The senator also faced resistance in some German Protestant blue-collar wards in the Lehigh Valley towns of Bethlehem, Allentown and Reading, where he could only muster 44 percent in wards where 59 percent were registered Democrats, though he did run a bit ahead of Stevenson.

Anti–Kennedy voting was widespread in Pennsylvania. While it caused Kennedy to run behind Stevenson in 16 counties, there were incidences of anti–Kennedy voting in 65 counties (all except McKean and Philadelphia). These 16 counties fall into a pattern described by political analyst Kevin Phillips: "Anti–Catholic voting was particularly strong in southern and central Pennsylvania because of the deep-seated anti–Catholicism of the Scotch-Irish Presbyterians, the Lutherans, and the Reformed and German Protestants. Both the Germans and the Scotch-Irish had immigrated to America at a time when and from places where religious feeling ran high on each side."[1]

There are several ways to look at the extent of religion-based voting. One is that 71 towns supported Stevenson in 1956 but switched allegiance to Nixon in 1960. These towns were scattered throughout the state, with the largest concentration in the central and southeast regions, particularly in York County. They were almost all rural or small towns, heavily Protestant, and strongly German in ethnic ancestry. They were mostly low-income and had very low levels of education.

The Stevenson-Nixon towns were overwhelmingly rural, white and Protestant, with Lutherans and Methodists the dominant churches, plus a smattering of Presbyterians, Evangelical United Brethren and United Church of Christ members. German ancestry was also predominant. All of these factors were positively correlated with a strong anti–Kennedy vote in Pennsylvania.

Other demographic factors are important. Most of these towns had low levels of income. Of the 71 towns, only eight had above the state average in income, while 63 were below average and 40 towns were even below $20,000. More important was the extremely low level of education. Only one town had an above average percentage of college graduates, while in 36 towns fewer that 10 percent were college graduates. Even more significant, perhaps, was the unusually high percentage of adults who lacked even a high school diploma. In 44 towns more than 20 percent of adults had failed to complete high school. The percentage was nearly 45 percent in Hopewell Borough in Bedford County, and 64 percent in Grugan in Clinton County. In 59 of the 71 towns more adults had not completed high school than had graduated from college.

A considerable body of social science literature has concluded that low levels of education are a major factor or determinant in prejudiced attitudes toward religious, racial and ethnic minorities, and this may be as significant a factor as active Protestant church membership in interpreting the anti–Kennedy vote in 1960.

The Disparity Level

Examination of the statistics of the time are revealing. If a town has $20,000 per capita income compared to $25,000 statewide, it is 20 percent below average. If 10 percent of its residents are college graduates compared to 25 percent of all state residents, it is 60 percent below average. Therefore, its educational deficiency is greater, relatively speaking, than its economic deprivation. The same is true for affluent towns that exceed state averages in both income and education. College towns represent a major departure, since they usually have an above average percentage of university graduates and a lower income level. These anti–Kennedy towns had higher educational disparities than income disparities. In 67of the 71 towns that were carried by Adlai Stevenson in 1956 and by Richard Nixon in 1960, the percentage of college graduates was relatively lower than would be expected when compared to the average income.

The average per capita income in the 71 voting jurisdictions is 20,133, about 20 percent below the state average. Only 11.4 percent are college graduates, about 54 percent below state average — a significant gap.

And 21.9 percent lack a high school degree, which is above the state average.

Kennedy received a lower percentage of the presidential vote than Stevenson in 1,027 towns, almost 40 percent of all towns in the state. Not only were these in counties where Kennedy's vote slipped, but also in counties where Kennedy made slight gains, often disguising the true extent of the religious backlash. A majority of towns in 25 counties were anti–Kennedy, and half of townships were anti–Kennedy in two counties.

There was such a massive anti–Kennedy vote that six towns cast their first-ever Republican majority vote for Nixon. Most of these towns existed in the days of Andrew Jackson, and their residents loyally supported the party of Jefferson and Jackson, including Al Smith in 1928, but they refused to support Kennedy. Three were in Berks County (Jefferson, Strausstown, Tulpehocken). One, Penn Township, is in Centre County, while another, Franklin Township, is located in Greene County in the state's southwest corner. Finally, Eldred, a town in the Pocono Mountains of Monroe County, gave Kennedy only 36 percent after supporting Stevenson with 59 percent. In the past, it had routinely given Democratic candidates near unanimous support.

In many counties where Kennedy made slight gains, a majority of towns moved against him, revealing unusual animosity in the hinterlands. This was true in Berks County, where Kennedy ran behind Stevenson in 44 of the 75 towns despite running a couple of points ahead in the county, thanks to the small city of Reading, and in Clinton County, where he ran a smidgen ahead of Stevenson but trailed in 21 of the 29 towns. In Columbia County, Kennedy gained 0.3 percent but lost support in 30 of 34 towns.

Anti–Kennedy Towns

The intensity of anti–Kennedy voting can be isolated by breaking down towns and boroughs by percentage. There were 118 towns, scattered throughout 30 counties, where Kennedy ran 10 percent or higher weaker than Stevenson. This is a different measurement from the Stevenson-Nixon towns, though there is some overlap. Most anti–Kennedy towns voted for both Eisenhower and Nixon, and all of them were much stronger for

Nixon. A handful of these towns supported both Democrats, but JFK just squeaked ahead compared to Stevenson. Anti–Kennedy voting increased as income and educational attainment decreased.

Anti–Kennedy Voting, Income and Education

Anti–Kennedy	Per Capita Income	% College Graduates	% No High School Diploma
Over 20 percent	$18,358	9.6	23.1
10–20 percent	$19,994	11.5	22.2
5–10 percent	$20,557	12.0	21.9
Stevenson 1956/ Nixon 1960	$20,164	11.4	21.8

The absence of Catholics in most rural Pennsylvania counties was clearly a factor in the vote. In the 21 counties with the lowest Catholic population, Nixon won by 170,714 votes compared to Eisenhower's 145,371 vote majority.[2]

Political scientist Daryl R. Fair studied the 1960 returns in detail and correlated them with religious affiliation, finding that Kennedy's vote increased when the Catholic percentage of the population reached 20 percent or more, but decreased as Catholics declined and Protestant church membership increased. In the counties where fewer than 10 percent of residents were Catholic, Kennedy's vote declined 5.2 percent. Fair concluded that "religion played a role independent of other factors in determining the voting behavior of Pennsylvanians in 1928 and 1960.[3]

Protestant-Republican Connection

Pennsylvania was a culture characterized by a kind of old-fashioned Republican-Protestant connection, hearkening back even to the Whig and Know Nothing days. In a delicious remembrance of his parents' formative years in rural northern Pennsylvania, W.S. Merwin says of his mother, "She would no more have voted for a Democrat than she would have stolen a wallet or gone to Mass."[4]

On the eve of the Kennedy election, political scientist James Reichley wrote that Pennsylvania "has long been the special stronghold" of evangelical Republicanism: "It is the land of the Masonic Order, the Sunday blue-laws, the YMCA, the prohibition of gambling that keeps horse-racing out of the state."[5]

Four distinct subregions of Pennsylvania contributed disproportionately to anti–Kennedy voting. All were areas of traditional Protestant hegemony that was eventually challenged by the growing Catholic and immigrant communities.

The Presbyterian Valley

Linda K. Pritchard concluded that Presbyterians "controlled approximately 50 percent of Allegheny County's religious establishment between 1850 and 1890," and that "the concentration of Presbyterians in western Pennsylvania qualifies the region for the title 'The Presbyterian Valley.'" She also cited "several studies of farming communities which illustrate the central role of Protestantism in rural areas." In this culture Joseph Baker was elected mayor of Pittsburgh in 1850 while in jail for inciting anti–Catholic demonstrations in Market Square.[6]

Pritchard's study also found that "the Protestant churches continued to exert primary religious authority over Pittsburgh between 1880 and 1920 because their membership included a disproportionate number of the wealthiest and most powerful families in the community. Protestant denominations simply had much greater access to wealth and political power than other groups.... Protestantism also dominated because it promoted the values of the new social order, such as individualism or acquisitiveness, which non–Protestants would eventually adopt and propagate."[7]

The period just prior to Al Smith's campaign saw a move to the suburbs on the part of many Protestants, who felt uncomfortable in a city now two-thirds Catholic, Jewish or Eastern Orthodox. In her study Pritchard observed, "Most Protestant denominations made efforts to convert the immigrants to their own brand of Christianity ... although none was very effective. Suburban flight, not evangelizing or reforming the new immigrants, was the most significant response of the dominant religious culture to the new arrivals." She adds, "Suburban churches provided Protestants with ethnic islands in a sea of diversity in the same way that emerging national parishes did for Catholics and Jews."[8]

Another historian, Nora Faires, also discovered that "many native–

born Protestants used the arm of the state to enforce social norms they believed more fitting. The *Presbyterian Banner* applauded the use of constables in breaking up what it regarded as unruly immigrant wedding celebrations and fought strenuously for the maintenance of Sabbatarian laws and the enactment of Temperance legislation."[9]

Pennsylvania Dutch Country

The religious factor in the Pennsylvania Dutch country's rejection of Kennedy is central. In 1942 historian Ralph Wood made a number of trenchant observations about Pennsylvania German culture. He concluded: "In spite of the competition of Grange events, the automobile and the small-town movie, the church has remained the center of community life in the Pennsylvania German countryside." As for its political impact, Wood suggested, "What the New England town meeting was to the Yankee, the church was to the Pennsylvania German."[10]

This sentiment is echoed by recent observers. Writing in the late 1970s, Noel Bausher Szundy observed, "Today the Lutheran and Reformed churches are still the cornerstone of Pennsylvania Dutch religion.... Ours is a heartwarming and healthy stew of many sects, well balanced and integrated. The Pennsylvania Bible Belt comes honestly by its name ... and not only do we have numerous churches of all flavors, but they are thriving, unlike so many contemporary churches elsewhere.... The 'Dumb Dutchman' has not forgotten his Reformation roots, nor will he ever turn his back on the God who guided his ancestors to these shores."[11]

The Pennsylvania Dutch are also instinctively conservative. Earl Robacher argues that "the strongest single tradition in the Dutch country is what it always has been — maintaining tradition."[12] Historian William T. Parsons maintains that the Pennsylvania Dutch "fit very well into the Isolationist mood of the twenties and early thirties" and "remain committed to a system of private volunteer charities and distrust of impersonal government."[13]

Pocono Mountain Resort Area

Another area characterized by intense anti–Catholic voting was the Pocono Mountain resort area, in Monroe and Pike counties. In a recent study Laurence Squeri concluded, "Monroe County was conservative, wary of new ideas and strongly nativist." Its population was homogeneous, old-stock American. Despite Democratic loyalties that survived the Civil War and after, the county went overwhelmingly for Hoover in 1928 and for Nixon in 1960. The area's most famous national figure was A. Mitchell Palmer, U.S. attorney general under Woodrow Wilson, who promoted the "Red Scare" of 1919 aimed at political dissenters.

Squeri found that the Pocomos were strongholds of temperance sentiment long before Prohibition became national policy: "Xenophobia was not uncommon" and "the Poconos innkeepers invariably had northern European names and were considered morally clean, honest and God-fearing." Local vigilantes enforced the Prohibition laws, and Sunday drinking was prohibited until the 1960s. In 1929 two New York City women were arrested in Stroudsburg for wearing shorts. The local newspaper, the *Daily Record*, "referred routinely to Italians as 'dagoes.'" Local religious groups played a role in maintaining an evangelical subculture: "Christian churches were strong in the Poconos. Social life revolved around their varied activities. Moral control of the resorts was not difficult because the industry was dominated by natives who answered to their small-town neighbors."[14]

Central Pennsylvania

The fourth subregion was Central Pennsylvania. Journalist Paul B. Beers of Harrisburg says that the Protestant bastion of Central Pennsylvania opted for "sameness, stability and rectitude in its public life." Furthermore, he writes:

> An almost steady economic prosperity reduced class antagonisms and helped create a burgeoning middle class ... whose priorities have been common decency within orthodox morality, the sanctity of contract and property and, in general, the doctrines of the Puritan Ethic. Though there is much that is admirable in such principles, the price paid politically has been mediocrity, cronyism, some anti–intellectualism and much anti–culturalism, virtually no innovation, and a steadfast refusal to modernize government to adjust to urban necessities.

This one-party politics has tended toward negativism, reinforced, Beers says, by conservatism, patronage, and fraud. There is also a clear religious element in the picture. Beers continues:

Until recently white Anglo-Saxon Protestantism was a major part of the political situation. No non–WASP candidate for President or U.S. Senator has ever received the Central Pennsylvania vote. Every elected mayor of Harrisburg has been a WASP, and 40 of 42 Dauphin County judges have been WASPs too. Every Congressman for Dauphin County has been a WASP. Cumberland County, in a district with Adams and York counties, has had one Catholic Congressman, James M. Quigley, a lawyer and a capable representative who lasted only three terms until he was swept out as part of the Kennedy ticket.

Republicans even managed to lure a few Catholics into their political boss system. For fifty years, an Irish Catholic Republican, Thomas J. Nelley, kept the multiethnic, blue-collar town of Steelton firmly in the Republican ranks, both in party registration and in presidential voting. Only after his death in 1957 did the Democrats rebound, and Kennedy carried the town.[15]

In another book about the era, Beers wrote the following: "Religious bias was coupled with anti–labor and ethnic opposition. It can be argued that Pennsylvania has been a melting pot, but a slow one. The first Catholic to make high state office was Lieutenant Governor Tom Kennedy in 1934, but the first Catholic governor David L. Lawrence wasn't elected until 1958. No Pole, Slovak or Italian has yet run for governor. There has been only one Pennsylvania U.S. Senator of the Catholic faith, Francis J. Myers of Philadelphia, 1945–1951. And there were only a handful of Catholic mayors of major Pennsylvania cities until after World War II."[16] Beers wrote these observations in 1970, and they were certainly factors in the Kennedy campaign. The state has changed dramatically since 1970, and a number of Catholic and Jewish governors and U.S. senators have been elected.

Bucks County

Even outside the four subregions where religious voting was most virulent, the virus of religious animosity reached to the Philadelphia suburbs. Trouble was gathering in rural Bucks County as conservative German-American Protestants began quietly registering to vote in the fall. In Bedminster the Republicans added 63 new voters and the Democrats seven. In November 73 percent of Bedminster voters chose Nixon, a higher than expected result. In Haycock Township, a heavily German community near Applebachsville, and a traditionally Democratic area, went for Nixon 59 percent to 41 percent despite a 59 percent Democratic registration.

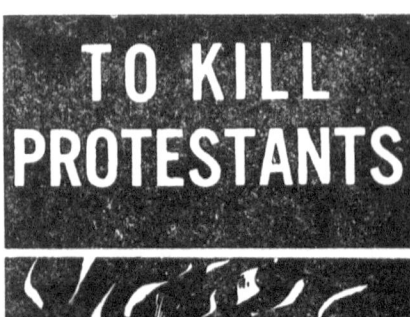

THE WEALTHIEST BODY IN THE WORLD
By a Converted R. C. Priest

AMERICA FACES A GRAVE CRISIS
"How long halt ye between two opinions."
I. Kings, 18:21

There will be a serious question asked in the United States. It will be a question that will shake the continent. And the answer to it may astonish the people who hear it.

There will be no way to dodge this question. It must be asked and it must be answered. It may be just as well to prepare for it now, for, if we are prepared for it when it comes, we may be able the better to answer it.

WHO OWNS THE ROMAN CHURCH?
There is no question but what the Roman Catholic Church, as a corporation, is the wealthiest body in the land. Who owns that Wealth? That is the question that we shall be compelled some day to answer. The property of this corporation is worth billions of dollars, and is increasing at a rapid rate. Somebody is the owner of it. Who is it?

Already the influence of this vast property is felt in city and nation. It dictates the policies of parties and names the candidates for public office. It knows that property rules the nation and its whole aim is to increase its property. By exempting its immense holdings from taxation, the nation is feeding the beast that is waiting to strike it. The property of the Roman Catholic Church, as a corporation, is the most serious menace that threatens the existence of our nation.

Rome's doctrine brings in millions of dollars per year. Her wafer god is more valuable than a gold mine. More than thirty million a year is paid for masses in America. She sells passports to heaven. Sells the intercession of dead saints—indulgences—images— salt— grease— ashes— bones— scapulars— medals—carloads of candles—runs laundries all over

This vile pamphlet that circulated throughout Bucks County, Pennsylvania, particularly offended author James Michener (Fair Campaign Practices Committee Collection, Manuscripts Division, Special Collections, Lauinger Library, Georgetown University).

James Michener, who worked tirelessly for Kennedy in these communities, wrote of the situation: "There are three other districts in northern Bucks County that normally go Democratic, even though they are surrounded by strong Republican areas. This year the combined vote was Nixon 1,358, Kennedy 744."[17] Michener blamed the result on the refusal of voters to support a Catholic candidate: "Ministers preached from their pulpits that a vote for Kennedy was a vote against the basic religion of the area, and parishioners either stayed home or voted Republican."[18]

As Michener surveyed his county's vote, he observed, "In central and northern Bucks County, Kennedy's Catholicism cost him not less than 4,500 votes, represented by Democrats who switched to Nixon and by

Republicans who might otherwise have been won over to the Kennedy banner. This resulted in a swing of 9,000 votes.... If these figures are correct, then had there been no religious issue involved, Nixon would have carried Bucks County by about 1,000 votes instead of the 10,000 by which he did carry it. Thus Kennedy's Catholicism cost him a 9,000-vote differential in Bucks County."[19]

During the campaign Michener angrily confronted "a perfectly normal, college-educated clergyman" who warned parishioners that Protestants would be "crucified" in public squares. Despite Michener's pleadings that this was unsupportable nonsense, "this minister continued preaching in his weekly sermons that if John Kennedy were elected, there would be public crucifixions throughout Bucks County."[20] Michener found the campaign dominated by this issue, rather than by serious discussions of domestic and foreign policy:

> I kept careful record of the impact of religion on the election in my county, and ... the religious issue permeated every meeting I conducted. It influenced Republicans and Democrats alike. Ministers preached politics publicly and churches distributed the most vicious electioneering materials. Practically no one I met escaped the pressure of this overriding problem and, in my county at least, both parties were ultimately forced to make their major calculations with the religious question a foremost consideration. From what I could see, no man among us was clever enough to have judged accurately at the beginning what the ultimate effect of the religious question was going to be.[21]
>
> If John Kennedy had not been a Catholic, he would probably have won Pennsylvania by a substantially bigger margin than he actually did. On balance, the religious issue hurt the Democrats grievously.[22]

An additional way of measuring how much Kennedy lost due to religion is to compare his vote with Democratic registration by county and by precinct. The picture is clear: Kennedy ran behind Democratic registration in 49 of the 67 counties. His vote fell 20 percent or more behind in Monroe and Greene counties and it declined 10 percent to 20 percent in 17 other counties. At the precinct level voters defected from their enrolled parties at a significant rate. In 65 of the state's counties, there was at least one precinct which supported the presidential candidate of the party that enrolled a minority of voters. There were 978 precincts with a Democratic registration majority that supported Nixon compared to 613 precincts with a Republican registration majority that backed Kennedy.

Some rural Democratic precincts showed a massive rejection of their party's presidential candidate. In 163 Democratic majority precincts Kennedy did not even receive half of the registered Democrats. Many were in Berks County outside of Reading. Others were in the German countryside of York, Adams and Northampton counties. Even within the same county, the defection rate among Democrats was much higher in rural homogeneous precincts than in cities. In Reading, for example, 76 percent of Democratic precincts were carried by Kennedy but only 16 percent of Democratic rural areas in the rest of Berks County supported Kennedy. In York City Kennedy carried 47 percent of the Democratic majority precincts but only 10 percent of the rural Democratic precincts.

In suburban Montgomery County Kennedy carried only half of the townships that had a Democratic registration majority. They were the more urbanized areas near Philadelphia, with many Catholic and Jewish voters. The other half (9 of 18), in the rural "Dutch" parts of the county, were for Nixon, including Red Hill, the only town in the Philadelphia suburbs to back Stevenson and Nixon.

In summary, there were 318 precincts where fewer than half of the registered Democrats voted for Kennedy. This translated into 27 percent for Kennedy and 41 percent for Stevenson in these backlash hamlets — a considerable loss that seemed to have escaped notice from political commentators a half century ago.

The German Ancestry Factor

German ancestry was clearly related to anti–Kennedy voting. Of the 343 towns above 2,500 in population that had a German majority, Kennedy's vote declined in 169, went up in 156 and remained about the same as Stevenson's in 18. JFK's vote declined in 49.3 percent of German-majority towns and remained the same in 5.2 percent, while increasing in only 45.5 percent. Size and location also mattered. In small towns between 2,500 and 10,000 in population, Kennedy's vote declined in 51.2 percent, while in the fewer towns above 10,000, his vote dropped in 36.4 percent of them. If we eliminate the 11 predominantly German Catholic small towns (out of 299), which went for Kennedy, the percentage is higher. His vote plummeted in 53 percent of the German Protestant majority towns.

The percentage of German ancestry is also a significant factor. In the 23 Protestant towns where more than 70 percent of residents claim German ancestry, Kennedy's vote declined in 20 of them, or 87 percent. His average decline was 6.5 percent, representing a major anti–trend, as voters moved in the opposite direction from the nation. This was a good deal higher than in the 50 percent–70 percent German majority towns. In other words, the higher the German Protestant population the greater the likelihood there was of anti–Kennedy voting. This is also confirmed by looking at the data in a slightly different way. In the towns where Kennedy's vote declined 10 percentage points or more, 62.6 percent of the population claimed German ancestry, more than double the state average of 30 percent.

German Ancestry and Anti–Kennedy Voting

% German	Town	County	1960 Anti–Kennedy
80.4	Halifax Township	Dauphin	-4
79.3	Hegins	Schuylkill	-5
75.1	Manheim Borough	Lancaster	(+0.5)
74.9	Millcreek	Lebanon	-9
74.2	Heidelberg	York	-8
74.2	Millersburg	Dauphin	-6
73.5	Heidelberg	Lebanon	-3
72.1	West York	York	-5
71.8	East Donegal	Lancaster	(+1)
71.4	Bethel	Berks	-10
71.2	West Cocalico	Lancaster	-4
71.1	Mount Joy Borough	Lancaster	(+2)
70.9	Jackson	York	-8
70.7	Roscombmanor	Berks	-9
70.6	Richmond	Berks	-10
70.5	Paradise	York	-11
70.4	North Codorus	York	-15
70.2	Myerstown	Lebanon	-4
70.1	Bethel	Lebanon	-2
70.0	Akron	Lancaster	-1
70.0	Centre	Berks	-7
70.0	Upper Paxton	Dauphin	-7
70.0	Hanover	York	-1

Top Twenty Anti–Kennedy Towns

Rank/Town	County	% Stevenson	% Kennedy	% Decline
1 East Keating	Clinton	50.0	13.6	36.4
2 Grugan	Clinton	42.9	11.1	31.8
3 Franklin	Columbia	48.1	24.6	23.5

Rank/Town	County	% Stevenson	% Kennedy	% Decline
4 Eldred	Monroe	59.2	36.1	23.1
5 Clay	Huntingdon	51.6	28.6	23.0
6 Hunker	Westmoreland	51.3	28.5	22.8
7 Logan	Huntingdon	43.2	20.9	22.3
8 Upper Mahanoy	Northumberland	37.6	15.4	22.2
9 Railroad	York	67.0	45.0	22.0
10 Curtin	Centre	53.6	32.6	21.0
11 Washington	Northumberland	38.2	18.1	20.1
12 Monroe	Juniata	49.3	30.0	19.3
13 McEwensville	Northumberland	48.4	29.7	18.7
14. Dublin	Huntingdon	35.9	17.2	18.7
15 Lenhartsville	Berks	34.3	15.9	18.4
16 Beech Creek	Clinton	59.8	41.6	18.2
17 Centerport	Berks	53.4	35.6	17.8
18 Cromwell	Huntingdon	50.9	33.2	17.7
19 Manheim	York	58.9	41.3	17.6
20 Arona	Westmoreland	67.8	50.2	17.6

Anti–Catholic Intensity Factor

County	Percent	County	Percent	County	Percent
Adams	6.4	Elk	4.6	Montour	4.3
Allegheny	1.6	Erie	0.5	Northampton	7.7
Armstrong	7.0	Fayette	10.6	Northumberland	17.3
Beaver	4.8	Forest	0.4	Perry	10.3
Bedford	10.1	Franklin	8.0	Philadelphia	0
Berks	15.4	Fulton	9.3	Pike	1.5
Blair	9.0	Greene	6.0	Potter	9.0
Bradford	4.9	Huntington	18.8	Schuylkill	10.4
Bucks	3.5	Indiana	4.8	Snyder	8.8
Butler	9.0	Jefferson	7.5	Somerset	7.3
Cambria	3.4	Juniata	10.4	Sullivan	0.9
Cameron	1.9	Lackawanna	0.3	Susquehanna	2.2
Carbon	7.3	Lancaster	6.1	Tioga	6.3
Centre	15.8	Lawrence	2.7	Union	4.2
Chester	7.0	Lebanon	7.1	Venango	4.9
Clarion	9.7	Lehigh	4.2	Warren	0.8
Clearfield	14.1	Luzerne	3.5	Washington	6.3
Clinton	17.9	Lycoming	11.0	Wayne	0.9
Columbia	15.6	McKean	0	Westmoreland	15.8
Crawford	5.7	Mercer	7.1	Wyoming	5.0
Cumberland	13.4	Mifflin	12.2	York	10.4
Dauphin	12.1	Monroe	9.0		
Delaware	1.0	Montgomery	5.7		

Wisconsin Case Study

Wisconsin was the scene of the first primary of 1960, where Kennedy defeated Hubert Humphrey decisively 56 percent to 44 percent. But commentators noted that Kennedy won the heaviest Catholic districts and Humphrey the most solidly Protestant ones, thereby diminishing the importance of the Kennedy triumph. (Defeating a neighboring state's senator should have been seen as impressive.)

It is true that religious affiliation proved a good predictor of the primary vote, more so, as it turned out, than the November general election. In the primary Kennedy's top county was Brown, where he won 78 percent. Brown includes Green Bay and 61 percent of the population was Catholic. Humphrey secured his best vote, 79 percent, in Lutheran Vernon County, a rural farm area. The religious implications were obvious. Kennedy's top ten counties were 61.7 percent Catholic. His worst ten counties were only 25.4 percent Catholic. The Kennedy strongholds also outpolled the Humphrey strongholds 119,565 to 53,586. The heaviest Catholic counties were 71 percent to 29 percent for Kennedy, while the Lutheran strongholds favored Humphrey 68 percent to 32 percent.[23]

There were black and Jewish voters in Wisconsin as well as non–churchgoers and other Protestants. And there were ethnic as well as religious differences. Kennedy did reasonably well among German Lutherans who voted in the Democratic primary though most voted for Nixon in the Republican primary. The real question was how people would vote in November and whether religion would significantly affect their voting decisions.

The basic facts of the Wisconsin vote show a 52 percent to 48 percent Nixon victory, with a 65,000 vote majority. Kennedy ran 10 points ahead of Stevenson but could not quite put together a winning coalition. Kennedy received 54.7 percent compared to Stevenson's 42.4 percent in the state's urban areas, a 12 point gain that exceeded the state average. He received the support of 46.1 percent of voters in the Milwaukee suburbs, up more than 13 points from Stevenson's 32.7 percent; but rural areas proved to be Kennedy's downfall. As Richard M. Scammon, a nationally known elections expert and onetime director of the Bureau of the Census, observed, "In 1960 some of the most striking examples of religious and ethnic influence could be obtained from the voting behavior of rural areas. The correlation of religious belief with voting patterns in the rural counties of Wisconsin illumines some striking aspects of our political life."[24]

Political scientist Andrew R. Baggaley's detailed study of Wisconsin voting reached this conclusion: "The conclusion which emerges from these figures and other sources of evidence is that the candidacy of Kennedy in 1960 caused the old fires of religious controversy to flare anew in Midwestern rural America.... Religious influences on voting in Wisconsin, although much reduced from 1928, were still considerable enough to have been critical in an election as close as that of 1960."[25]

It is in the rural areas that religious and ethnic voting, which often interact, are most significant in determining the outcome. Wisconsin was always a microcosm of immigrant America, a mosaic of virtually every nationality group that found a welcoming place in this Midwestern state. Fred Holmes celebrated Wisconsin's heritage in his 1944 classic, *Old World Wisconsin*: "Wisconsin is distinctive as a state because a blending of Old World population with the Yankee stock has resulted in founding a successful agriculture; has culminated in diffusing education among the masses, and has flowered in an awakened citizenship that makes the Wisconsin way the touchstone of democracy. The ripening fruit is not from the tree of any one nationality. It is a hybrid."[26]

While ethnic voting is a central factor in Wisconsin, it cannot be separated from religion. LaVern Rippley writes that "religion, much more than ethnic background, was the determining element in Wisconsin politics."[27] In 1960 all of the predominantly Protestant ethnic groups, except the Finns, voted for Nixon, while all the Catholic ethnic groups voted for Kennedy. In most instances, the Protestant groups gave Kennedy a smaller vote than they did Stevenson, while Catholics of all ethnic persuasions supported Kennedy more enthusiastically than they had supported Stevenson.

The differences were dramatic. Kennedy's strongest town (out of 2,000 in the state) was the Polish farm community of Sharon in Portage County, where he won by the incredible margin of 580–7 (99 percent). Stevenson, however, had also carried Sharon 502–84 (86 percent), which showed the Democratic loyalties of Polish Americans in rural Wisconsin.

Nixon's strongest town was Alto, a Dutch Protestant village in Fond du Lac County, where he was supported by 94 percent of the voters. In second place came another Dutch town, Oostburg in Sheboygan County, where the vice president drew 93 percent. Six of Nixon's top ten towns were Dutch—a pattern found throughout the U.S. in 1960. Others included an Icelandic Lutheran town, Washington Island, and Ephraim Village, a town founded by Scandinavian Moravians. The last two are on Wisconsin's "Cape Cod," Door County.

The Stevenson and Kennedy bases were surprisingly different, primarily because of the religious issue in 1960. Kennedy received a lower vote percentage than Stevenson in 19 of Stevenson's top 40 towns, and one town had the same result. Thus, Kennedy ran weaker than Stevenson in about half of Stevenson's strongholds.

Kennedy's top 40 towns generally gave him a much higher level of support than they had given Stevenson four years before, and three of JFK's strongest towns supported Eisenhower in 1956. Only 22 of the staunch Democratic towns appeared on both the Stevenson and Kennedy top 40. In Dane County, all five of Stevenson's strong towns fell off the Kennedy list. All were substantially Norwegian. It was primarily the Polish-American towns that liked Stevenson and JFK.

Adlai Stevenson's strongest towns were Polish, Norwegian, or Finnish far more often than German (53 percent of Wisconsin people claim German ancestry, higher than any other state). In the rural areas the German predominance is even greater. But only a few of Stevenson's top 40 towns were predominantly or significantly German. In 1960 a different pattern prevailed for Kennedy, and some German towns appeared in JFK's top 40. German ancestry predominated in nearly half of Kennedy's top 40. All were heavily Catholic. Much of German Wisconsin is sharply divided by religion. Kennedy's top 40 also included Czech, Polish, Slovak and Austrian ancestry areas.

Eisenhower's top 40 were classically Republican towns (German, Dutch, country club elite). In only two of Ike's top 40 did Nixon run stronger in 1960 (Alto in Fond du Lac County and Friesland Village in Columbia County, both Dutch areas). One of Ike's towns (Lac LaBelle in Waukesha County) even switched to Kennedy. Nixon's top 40 were fuelled by either anti–Catholic sentiment (most likely) or fondness for Nixon (unlikely). Nixon ran ahead of Ike in 16 of his strongest towns.

There were significant shifts between 1956 and 1960 among the largest religious groups—Catholics and Lutherans, who were traditional rivals. As Rippley noted, "Lutherans and Catholics took each other as negative referents."[28] Catholic "swing areas," which often voted Republican, went for Kennedy 63 percent to 37 percent after having supported Eisenhower 68 percent to 32 percent. Catholic Democrats backed both by large margins (93 percent for Kennedy and 78 percent for Stevenson), and Protestant Republicans, including a number of groups other than Lutherans, supported Eisenhower and Nixon by huge margins. Lutheran key precincts gave Stevenson 42.7 percent and Kennedy 36.4 percent. This resulted in a margin for Nixon of 24,000, double Eisenhower's 12,000 margin in a group of representative Lutheran towns. Almost all of these are European ancestry groups. Kennedy also won heavily among the small Jewish, African American and Native American voters.

Anti–Kennedy Voting

The extent of anti–Kennedy voting was obscured by the fact that his vote declined in just five counties (Burnett, Polk, Jackson, Vernon, Green), where a combination of Swedish and Norwegian Lutherans and Swiss Reformed Protestants moved against him. But a further investigation at the township and village level reveals a different picture: There were 79 towns that supported Stevenson but switched to Nixon. They were scattered across 31 counties. Eight were in Scandinavian Dunn County and six were in Scandinavian Polk County.

One of these towns was Clear Lake in Polk County, a 40 percent Norwegian-Swedish town that was the home town of Democratic governor Gaylord Nelson, a liberal who campaigned for Kennedy. Not only did his home switch from Stevenson to Nixon, but it also gave Nelson a lower vote in his reelection campaign than it had given him in 1958. His support for Kennedy had even cost him votes among long-time neighbors and friends. Religious voting had swept from the presidential level down the ticket, leading to a squeaker for Nelson, who won only 51.6 percent of the vote statewide. Nelson's biographer, Bill Christofferson, said the governor was shocked and disappointed; what's more, "For the first time in state history, Wisconsin voters had chosen a governor of one party and given control of both houses of the legislature to the opposition."[29] The GOP had gained ten seats in the state house, mainly in Protestant areas. Nelson, a Norwegian American, went on to three terms as U.S. senator (1963–81), finally losing in the Reagan landslide of 1980.

Anti–Kennedy voting was widespread: 494 of the state's towns gave him a lower vote than Stevenson. In 75 towns Kennedy's vote share dropped 10 percentage points or more. In four towns the anti–Kennedy trend exceeded 20 points. In 52 towns Kennedy dropped 8–10 points. One precinct in heavily German Stettin in Marathon County gave Stevenson 51 percent and Kennedy 24 percent. While German ancestry voters outnumbered Norwegians 44 percent to 27 percent in these towns, there was a tendency for the strongest anti–Kennedy towns to be disproportionately Norwegian.

Kennedy's vote share declined in at least one town in 59 of the 71 counties. The "intensity" of anti–Kennedy voting was greatest in ten counties (see table). The religious configuration in the most intensely anti–Kennedy voting places is somewhat surprising. The largest religious group was the "moderate" American Lutheran Church, which claimed nearly 44 percent of Protestants in these counties, nearly double their statewide share (24 percent) of Protestants. (Catholics are not included in this equation since they are quite weak in these counties.) The moderate Lutheran Church of America was somewhat weaker than statewide. But the conservative evangelical Missouri Synod Lutherans and the fundamentalist Wisconsin Synod Lutherans were very underrepresented in the anti–Kennedy swing precincts (17 percent compared to 33 percent).

It may be that the two more conservative Lutheran bodies were largely Republican in both 1956 and 1960 and so were not prominent in the towns that moved from Democratic to Republican. Methodists were 2 percent overrepresented in these counties, and members of the United Church of Christ were 1 percent more prevalent, a group substantially Swiss in ethnic background.

Lutheran voters were a major factor in Wisconsin, as in Minnesota, Iowa and the Dakotas, owing to their concentration in these Upper Plains states. Lutheran churches and their institutional journals were "intensely concerned about the religious issue and were deeply involved in the public conversation about it," writes John R. Stumme. He added, "Lutheran churches' periodicals gave extensive coverage to developments related to religion and the election."[30]

The American Lutheran Church, which had almost 2.5 million members in 1960, adopted a moderate statement on religion and politics at its convention in April 1960. It said, in part, "The religious faith of a candidate naturally influences his conduct of public office. A vital faith inescapably affects both private and public life. To say otherwise is to deny the relevance of faith to life. Nevertheless, the religious faith of a candidate cannot absolutely determine his conduct of public office. He is subject to pressures, valid and proper, from many sides and sources. In weighing and reconciling them all, he necessarily compromises any absolute rigidities his denominational dogma might impose."[31]

A more critical view was adopted by the predominantly Swedish Augustana Lutheran Church meeting in Rock Island, Illinois, in June. They warned "that the Roman Church, because of its unique institutional claims, poses special problems in relation to the questions of religion and public office," and "that there are grounds for reasonable doubt that a Roman Catholic president would be free of institutional control and from desires to promote in special ways the ends of the Roman Church."[32]

A very hostile essay by a pastor appeared in the Missouri Synod weekly: "I would vote for a Jew or for a Mormon if I thought he was better qualified for the position than his Lutheran opponent. But I would vote against a practicing Catholic because being a Catholic he stands for certain principles which are un–American and because he is subject to certain strong pressures which would endanger our American liberties."[33]

A surprising last-minute endorsement of JFK came from twenty theology professors. The group, which included such distinguished historians as Sidney Ahlstrom and George Lindbeck of Yale and Jaroslav Pelikan of the University of Chicago, issued this ringing declaration:

> It is apparent that the religious issue is still vital to voters in the coming election, in spite of all efforts of the candidates to avoid it. In view of the repeated clear statements of Senator John F. Kennedy, we feel that a vote against him because of his religion would be a breach of our tradition of separation of church and state. Furthermore, because of Senator Kennedy's forceful and imaginative stand on foreign policy, civil rights and social welfare, the undersigned support his candidacy for the Presidency of the United States and thus demonstrate their confidence in his ability to be not a "Catholic" or "Protestant" President but a great American President.[34]

Needless to say, anti–Kennedy Lutherans were furious. While the endorsement probably came too late to do the senator much good, it did reveal the diversity of opinion among Lutherans in this campaign.

Finally, as Table 5 shows, the ethnic/religious pattern in rural Wisconsin shows declines for Kennedy among most Protestant groups, and gains for Kennedy among all Catholic subgroups.

Table 1: Religion and Voting

Winner Primary	*Winner General*	*% Catholic (of church members)*
Kennedy	Kennedy	62.1
Kennedy	Nixon	48.3
Humphrey	Kennedy	47.3
Humphrey	Nixon	34.1
State		50.0

In the Primary:	*% Catholic*
Top Ten Kennedy Counties	61.7
Top Ten Humphrey Counties	25.4

In the General Election:	*% Catholic*
Top Ten Kennedy Counties	61.5
Top Ten Nixon Counties	31.1

Table 2: Top 20 Anti–Kennedy Towns

Number	*Town*	*County*	*% Kennedy Decline*
1	Richwood	Richland	21.4
2*	Christiana	Dane	21.1
3*	Blanchard	Lafayette	20.4
4	Fenwood	Marathon	20.4
5	Monroe	Green	19.7
6*	York	Green	19.2
7	Hewitt	Marathon	19.1
8	Vance Creek	Barron	18.9
9	Tiffany	Dunn	18.8
10*	Rush River	St. Croix	18.7
11	Unity Village	Trempeleau	18.2
12	Homestead	Florence	17.1
13*	Franklin	Jackson	17.0
14*	Grant	Dunn	16.7
15	Sherwood	Clark	16.6
16*	Colfax	Dunn	16.0
17*	Northfield	Jackson	15.9
18	Forest	St. Croix	15.3
19	Akan	Richland	15.1
20	Blue Mounds	Dane	15.0

* Over 25 percent Norwegian ancestry.

Table 3: Intensity of Anti-Kennedy Voting in Selected Precincts

Number	County	% Average Kennedy Decline
1	Dunn	15.8
2	Dane	14.8
3	Marathon	14.6
4	St. Croix	14.2
5	Green	14.1
6	Richland	13.8
7	Vernon	13.4
8	Trempeleau	12.4
9	Jackson	12.2
10	Lafayette	11.4

Table 4: 1956–60 Voting in Rural Dane County, Wisconsin

Identity	% Stevenson	% Kennedy	% Change
Norwegian Lutheran	57.9	51.3	-6.6
German Protestant	57.3	51.8	-5.5
German Catholic	56.2	72.7	+16.5
All	**57.4**	**55.5**	**-1.9**

Note: There are far more Norwegian and German Protestants than German Catholics in rural Dane County, which explains why a 6 percent loss among Protestants offset a 16 percent gain among Catholics, resulting in a 2 percent *net loss* for Kennedy.

Table 5: Ethnic/Religious Voting in Wisconsin 1960

Protestant Groups	% Stevenson 1956	% Kennedy 1960	% Change
Swiss	48.8	40.4	-8.4
Norwegian	44.6	38.2	-6.4
Swedish	42.8	38.8	-4.0
Finnish	68.1	69.2	+1.1
Danish	22.8	25.8	+3.0
English	52.3	51.3	-1.0
Dutch	8.8	8.2	-0.6

Catholic Groups	% Stevenson 1956	% Kennedy 1960	% Change
Polish	70.5	83.6	+13.1
Belgian	34.9	64.4	+29.5
Native American	44.6	76.8	+32.2
French	39.8	59.2	+19.4
Italian	55.7	77.2	+21.5
Slovak	76.2	85.5	+9.3
Czech	59.4	66.4	+7.0
Dutch	34.1	66.3	+32.2

CHAPTER 7

Epilogue and Summing Up

Kennedy and Catholics

Kennedy's election unquestionably raised the spirits of the American Catholic community. The long-closed White House doors were now open, and the stigma of being second-class citizens had been removed. The symbolism also seems to have moved the Catholic community out of its isolation from national life and sparked a new engagement with Americans of other faith traditions in the renewal of public life.

A number of historians concur with this judgment. James Hennesey observed that "John F. Kennedy's election lessened the psychological defensiveness that had historically marked the Catholic American."[1] Charles Morris agreed: "John F. Kennedy's presidential election victory heralded the final breakdown of the separatist American Catholic subculture."[2] So did Phillip Gleason: "John F. Kennedy's election marked a breakthrough and a new stage in the relationship of American Catholics to the life of the nation…. It marked both the culmination of Catholic assimilation into American life and a climactic moment in the Catholic rapprochement with modernity."[3] The always observant John Cogley, writing early in 1964, added this: "Despite his lack of interest in abstract theological matters, John F. Kennedy probably had more influence on the future of the American church than any Catholic, lay or clerical, in the history of the nation…. He showed by his career that American Catholicism as a matter of fact has long since come to terms with religious pluralism."[4]

Villanova professor Rodger Van Allen reiterated this observation: "The election was especially momentous for the self-awareness of American Catholicism. Previous to it, it was easy to find justification for an inward turning, defensive relationship on the part of American Catholics toward

American society and culture. Afterwards, it was not nearly so easy. Further, it was greatly encouraging to the already existing forces within American Catholicism that had been working for years to promote a greater engagement with American society by Catholics."[5]

Kennedy and Civil Religion

We know little about Kennedy's personal Catholicism. His faith was, as was so often said, a private matter. As a public man whose interests were biography, statesmanship, and foreign policy, he wrote and said little about his relationship to the church or about his view of how the church should or could impact political life. Cardinal Richard Cushing, who knew him well, could say modestly, "President Kennedy wore his religion, like his patriotism, lightly, and, again like his patriotism, he felt his religion profoundly."[6]

Close aides and discerning biographers agree that he cared little for theology and was not interested in the internal workings of religion. He did not read lives of the saints but lives of English and American statesmen. He never discussed religion, even with staffers like Ted Sorensen, who knew him well. But he attended church regularly and wanted no fuss or publicity attached to his attendance.

Kennedy had few close relationships with clergy. One exception, though it was not revealed until 2010, was with Archbishop Philip Hannan, who was asked by Jacqueline Kennedy to deliver the eulogy at Kennedy's funeral. In his memoir, the 97-year-old retired cleric remembers: "Though I was immensely privileged to have been his trusted friend and consultant, we didn't always agree on religious matters."[7] Hannan added, "Whenever John Kennedy and I spoke, it was strictly business. Jack was deeply interested in questions of social justice."[8] Kennedy was interested in relationships between church and state and in issues related to charity, justice, liberty and world peace. Hannan writes, "My job, as I saw it, was to help Jack maintain, in any way possible, the proper, if workable, Catholic balance in that often explosive equation of church versus state."[9]

Hannan generally thought JFK's positions were correct, though he admitted, "From my perspective, Kennedy went overboard in emphasizing his independence from the Catholic Church, essentially promising an arms-length manifesto as well as a wall of separation between himself and the Church."[10] This was probably the view of most Catholic bishops at that time, though most Catholic laity thought it was the proper relationship. Hannan himself admits that "John Fitzgerald Kennedy turned out to be the right Catholic at the right time," largely because "in those days, Catholicism was shrouded in the same misunderstanding and mythical fear, as perhaps, Islam is today."[11]

Kennedy consistently denied that he would be subject to ecclesiastical pressure as president, since he had never experienced clerical pressure as a member of Congress. He felt that critics of Catholicism were misinformed about such pressures. He said this in his Houston speech. Even earlier, just before the 1956 Democratic convention when he had made a spirited attempt to win the vice presidential nomination, he answered a reporter's question about where the dictates of his church would conflict with his duties. He said, "In the first place, I can't think of any issue where such a conflict might arise. But suppose it did? Nobody in my church gives me orders. It doesn't work that way. I've been in Congress for ten years and it has never happened. People are afraid that Catholics take orders from a higher organization. They don't. Or at least I don't."[12]

Kennedy was an advocate of religious pluralism in both church and state from his earliest days. Even on the touchy issue of birth control, which was raised during his campaign, Kennedy responded to a questioner in a way which was quite different from the "official" Catholic position in 1959:

> There is considerable difference among Catholics with respect to the application of general principles to specific fact situations. It is for this reason that one finds Catholics who subscribe to the same basic moral principles taking different positions on various issues of public policy. Public issues certainly are not divested of moral implication when they emerge in the political arena, but the responsibility of the office-holder is to make decisions on these questions on the basis of the general welfare *as he sees it*, even if such a decision is not in accord with the prevailing Catholic opinion.[13]

"Kennedy's views on church and state stem from his belief in diversity, in heterogeneity, in pluralism," observed his first biographer, Professor James MacGregor Burns of Williams College. Kennedy told Burns, "I have always been impressed in my study of American history by the fact that this country has been singularly blessed in its ability to take the best of all religions and cultures — not merely tolerating differences but building a new and richer life upon them. I firmly believe that our religious and cultural pluralism has been over the years one of our principal sources of strength."[14]

Did Kennedy's religious worldview reflect or strengthen the privatizing of religion or the secularity of the political realm? And, if so, was this a bad thing? Mark S. Massa, a Jesuit scholar and director of the American Studies Program at Fordham University, takes a nuanced view: "Kennedy's 'secularizing' of the presidency was not aimed at the disappearance or denigration of religion or religious impulses; rather it took the form of the privatization of religion as described by sociologist Peter Berger."[15]

Kennedy's address at the greater Houston Ministerial Association was also a declaration of independence, of sorts, from the ghettoization or separatism that some historians saw as characteristic of American Catholicism in 1960. Massa observes, "Kennedy's Houston speech can be fruitfully seen as a key moment, not only in American Catholicism's 'coming of age,' but also of the articulation of the terms of that rite of passage."[16]

Kennedy did not see himself as High Priest to the American Civil Religion, a role relished by some chief executives. As president he was sparing and judicious in his use of religious rhetoric, or what Eisenhower liked to call God-talk. But he was not a thoroughgoing secularist by any means. He saw religion in a positive light, though tempered by a historical knowledge that knew religion is both noble and profane, depending on how it is being used. He appreciated spiritually insightful and inspirational language and poetry and admired the wisdom of the Bible, which he often quoted, usually in the King James Version, which he thought more literary and more likely to resonate with a broad constituency.

He did not like using religion as a weapon in the Cold War, something the Eisenhower administration seemed all too inclined to employ, especially in the rhetoric of Vice President Richard Nixon and secretary of state John Foster Dulles. Kennedy favored invoking universal values held in common by the world's great faiths, and he was not unwilling to express appreciation for the contributions of those who were not formally involved in religious institutions. Above all he saw peacemaking as a transcendent moral value inherent in many religions and secular traditions.

Kennedy especially mentioned religious liberty as a preeminent source of enlightenment and social peace, and he urged other nations to follow a course of pluralism and tolerance. In an address to the General Assembly of the United Nations on September 20, 1963, the young president reminded members that they must be committed to human rights: "Those rights are not respected when a Buddhist priest is driven from his pagoda, when a synagogue is shut down, when a Protestant church cannot open a mission, when a Cardinal is forced into hiding, or when a crowded church service is bombed. The United States of America is opposed to discrimination and persecution on grounds of race and religion anywhere in the world, including our own Nation. We are working to right the wrongs of our own country."[17]

In a speech during the third week of his presidency, Kennedy reminded a group of religious leaders of the following:

> This country was founded by men and women who were dedicated or came to be dedicated to two propositions: first, a strong religious conviction, and secondly a recognition that this conviction could flourish only under a system of freedom. I think it is appropriate that we pay tribute to this great constitutional principle which is enshrined in the First Amendment of the Constitution: the principle of religious independence, or religious liberty, of religious freedom. But I think it is also important that we pay tribute and acknowledge another great principle, and that is the principle of religious conviction. Religious freedom has no significance unless it is accompanied by conviction. And therefore the Puritans and the Pilgrims of my own section of New England, the Quakers of Pennsylvania, the Catholics of Maryland, the Presbyterians of North Carolina, the Methodists and the Baptists who came later, all shared these two great traditions which, like silver threads, have run through the warp and the woof of American history.[18]

In that address Kennedy saw that religious faith could be preserved and extended only in an atmosphere, and under a regime, of liberty. He suggested that such convictions often evolve as groups new to American soil become convinced of the values of liberty of conscience and of the independence of religion and political institutions.

In his only Christmas address as President (Kennedy was absent from the capital in 1961, visiting his gravely ill father in Palm Beach, and in 1963 he was dead) at the lighting of the National Christmas Tree on December 17, 1962, Kennedy hailed Christmas as "the most sacred and hopeful day in our civilization" and "the universal holiday of all men." But this was not a Christian proclamation for he saw Christmas as "the day when we remind ourselves that man can and must live in peace with his neighbors and that it is the peacemakers who are truly blessed." He added, "It is the day when all of us dedicate our thoughts to others; when all are reminded that mercy and compassion are the enduring virtues; when all show, by small deeds and large and by acts, that it is more blessed to give than to receive."[19] He saw the universality of this beloved holiday and he mentioned that believers in other faith traditions saw the "25th day of December as a celebration of the birthday of the Prince of Peace."

Kennedy rarely referred to his Catholic faith as president, preferring to keep a low profile. But even on two occasions when he did so, he invoked generous and universal principles. In an address at Boston College's centennial ceremonies on April 20, 1963, Kennedy hailed the wisdom and good sense of Pope John XXIII's encyclical *Pacem in Terris*. "As a Catholic I am proud of it; and as an American I have learned from it," he proudly exclaimed. But he mentioned the document's profound analysis of "social welfare, human rights, disarmament and international order and peace" as counsel for "all men and women of good will." He added pointedly that "it closely matches notable expressions of conviction and aspiration from churchmen of other faiths, as in recent documents of the World Council of Churches, and from outstanding world citizens with no ecclesiastical standing." Therefore, the president said, "We are learning to talk the language of progress and peace across the barriers of sect and creed."[20] In a statement on the death of Pope John, Kennedy noted: "He was the chosen leader of world Catholicism, but his concern for the human spirit transcended all boundaries of belief or geography."[21]

Kennedy's "civil religion" made world peace more than just a dream, according to John Cogley: "Just as it was John F. Kennedy rather than John Courtney Murray who dealt the death blow to the notorious Catholic church-state 'thesis' as a factor in American politics, so was it Kennedy more than Reinhold Niebuhr who finally instructed the nation in the responsible use of power." Cogley added that Kennedy's approach to peacemaking rested on "the two foundations of Catholic political thought: an appreciation of power, on the one hand, and recognition of the preeminence of reason, on the other."[22]

Presbyterian minister and philosophy professor James Wolfe wrote that Kennedy succeeded in proving to skeptical Protestants that he had the "symbolic adequacy for carrying out the spiritual functions of the presidency." Wolfe concluded, "Kennedy, as a Catholic, may have better symbolized than his opponent that religious pluralism which, although unrecognized by many Presbyterian clergy, was the actual condition of an

America long loosed from its Protestant moorings; the attainment of the nation's highest office by a Catholic symbolically confirmed the fact that Catholics were now first-class citizens and released among them a greater willingness to cooperate. The symbolic deficiency of a Catholic president was no longer charged."[23]

Historian Robert Alley says that Kennedy reinterpreted civil religion because of "his unwillingness to adapt himself to institutional religion."[24] Kennedy was adamantly opposed to mixing religion and politics: "For him the church was not a legitimate pressure group. He did not succumb to ecclesiastical arm twisting.... He was a secular President who was affiliated with the Catholic Church."[25] Kennedy was a "pragmatist" and a "relativist-realist" who was able to assess problems of his office from a non-ideological frame of reference," says Alley.[26] Kennedy's "moral strength" had "other roots than traditional religion," writes Alley, who places Kennedy in the same tradition as Franklin D. Roosevelt[27]: "His religion did for him what the Episcopal tradition had done for Roosevelt. It made them free men. Religion was personal, so there was no need of conflict between it and political action. It became a personal ethical gauge."[28]

This explains why Kennedy's statement, "I do not regard religion as a weapon in the Cold War,"[29] to the 1961 Prayer Breakfast represents a major break with tradition. It was a repudiation of a cornerstone of the Eisenhower-Dulles foreign policy, and an implicit criticism of Vatican foreign policy under Pope Pius XII.

Alley agreed with Andrew Greeley that Kennedy's candidacy and election "posed a bigger problem for the Church than it could have imagined in 1960, the problem of its own credibility."[30] Kennedy thought churches should emphasize ethical behavior for public officials and encourage prudential judgment in complicated policy matters.

The Kennedy Administration on Church and State

Historian Lawrence H. Fuchs says that JFK "was to do more to blunt the ancient mutual hatred of Catholics and non–Catholics than any other American had ever done."[31] Fuchs took a hopeful view of the outcome of the 1960 election: "Since Protestant-Catholic tensions in America had actually become more complex and deep in many respects in the 1940s and 1950s than they had been in the 1920s, Kennedy's victory was a triumph of reasonableness and fair play."[32]

Illinois senator Paul Simon wrote that Kennedy's policies as president "showed our nation the ridiculousness of anti–Catholicism's claims." He added, "His presidency lifted our vision. He gave us the Peace Corps and pointed the way on civil rights and other issues that his successor would achieve. But he offered more than that. He spoke with an eloquence unmatched by any president since Abraham Lincoln. Words can captivate a nation, bringing out the noble in us."[33]

In retrospect, Kennedy's willingness to confront the religious issue head-on was both courageous and pragmatic. Always a student of history, Kennedy knew that those who wish to shape events must often be bold in confronting obstacles. William D. Smith wrote, "Regarding the religious issue alone, Kennedy made more than fifty public statements, many of which were in direct exchanges with his audiences. He made his position convincingly clear, and the issue was brought under control by daring strategy, vigorous campaigning, and masterful implementation of persuasive techniques."[34]

Kennedy advisor John Cogley added that Kennedy, in dealing with a multitude of religious issues, adopted an honest strategy that was "low-key, more subtle than apparent, more pragmatic than propositional, more indirect than intrusive."[35] Kennedy also, wrote Smith, "reacted calmly but forthrightly, forcing his challengers to substantiate their charges."[36] Smith writes insightfully:

> Both Alfred E. Smith and John F. Kennedy were subjected to unprecedented campaign challenges due to their religion. It can be said to Smith's credit that he faced the issue courageously, if not always adroitly. He frequently withdrew in silence; while Kennedy chose to confront the issue "head-on." Smith tended to resent the intrusion of objections on religious grounds; while Kennedy graciously accepted inquiries and often turned them to his advantage. Out of defiance, Smith resorted to bitterness; while Kennedy was able to maintain his composure and to retort with skill and aplomb. Smith was apt to over–personalize his sentiments; while Kennedy kept the debate on political terms. Smith miscalculated the size and nature of his opposition; while Kennedy exposed the fallacies of his antagonists' position. Smith antagonized his foes; while Kennedy neutralized their effect. Smith was crushed by the "unfairness" of the religious issue; while Kennedy held it in historical perspective.[37]

Kennedy's first church-state crisis was fought over the issue of federal aid to education, a special concern of his. Kennedy proposed the first massive omnibus aid program for the nation's struggling public schools. It did not include faith-based schools, mostly Catholic parochial schools. He felt his program was on solid legal ground. A comprehensive legal brief prepared by both the Departments of Justice and Health, Education, and Welfare defended the Kennedy proposal and warned against any breach in the wall of separation. The brief did conclude, however, that private and church-related colleges might receive some indirect, peripheral public aid because their nature and curricula were structured to prevent some of the constitutional problems. The brief also allowed busing, school lunches, and secular textbooks for parochial schools under the National Defense Education Act's limited aid program.

Kennedy also favored aid to teachers' salaries, classroom construction, expanded library facilities, new vocational-technical centers, federally approved or guaranteed scholarship loans for needy students, literacy programs, aid to retarded and handicapped children, school lunch and library programs, and educational television. The Office of Education called the Kennedy legislative proposals the most far-reaching in a century.

The National Catholic Welfare Conference, the bishops' political arm, opposed the bill unless parochial schools were included. Cardinal Francis Spellman denounced the proposals as "unthinkable" and "discriminatory." Kennedy was outraged at Spellman's role, telling Theodore Sorensen, "He never said a word about any of Eisenhower's bills for public schools only, and he didn't go that far in 1949 either."[38] Kennedy told a press conference that "the Catholic, Protestant, and Jewish clergy are entitled to their views, but they should not change their views merely because of the religion of the occupant of the White House."[39]

Kennedy's bill passed the Senate, but faced tough sledding in the House from conservative Republicans who opposed all federal aid to education and from southern Democrats, who feared federal intervention would lead to school desegregation. One other problem was New York Democrat James J. Delaney, widely seen as Spellman's man. As it turned out, after months of intense backstage maneuvering, Delaney cast the deciding vote against the aid bill in the House Rules Committee in late July 1961. Delaney insisted on an all or nothing approach to the question of including church schools in a national educational program. Two other Catholic Democrats on the Rules Committee, Tip O'Neill of Massachusetts and Ray Madden of Indiana, supported the Kennedy proposal.

Most Protestant, Jewish, secular, and liberal Catholic organizations were disappointed with the decision, which effectively postponed federal aid to education. While angry and disappointed, President Kennedy felt that Catholics were being unfairly singled out for blame. After all, two of the three Catholic Democrats on the Rules Committee voted for his public education bill, while all Protestant-Republicans opposed it. The bill's House sponsor was a Catholic. On one test vote, only six of 166 Republicans voted for it, and virtually all southern segregationists voted against it. "That's who really killed the bill," Kennedy told Sorensen, "just as they've killed it for fifty years, not the Catholics."[40]

However, as John Cooney wrote, "By then Kennedy was sick of the hierarchy. He couldn't believe the bishops and cardinals didn't appreciate his awkward position as the first Catholic President.... The President deeply resented the hierarchy's undermining him."[41] Kennedy had long ago marginalized Cardinal Spellman. John Cooney continued: "When Kennedy won the election, Spellman realized he had gambled and lost. Kennedy's was the first inauguration to which Spellman had not been invited since becoming an archbishop more than twenty years earlier."[42] Andrew Greeley agreed. Writing in 1967 Greeley wondered aloud why *America* magazine and other leaders of Catholic officialdom expected Kennedy "to commit 'political suicide' by supporting legislation of interest only to institutional Catholics or legislation that Kennedy thought to be unacceptable public policy."[43]

Kennedy showed his respect for separation of powers, as well as his desire to support religious tolerance and reason, when the U.S. Supreme Court ruled on June 25, 1962, that school-sponsored or mandated prayers as part of a regularly scheduled devotional exercise in public schools were unconstitutional. U.S. pulpits were set ablaze, as most conservative Protestants and Catholics denounced the ruling in the most unequivocal and even apocalyptic terms. Everyone from Cardinal Spellman to Billy Graham and George Wallace heaped invective on the Court and called for a constitutional amendment to overrule the decision. Into this tempest stepped the young president. At his press conference he called for respect for the rule of law: "I think that it is important ... that we support the Supreme Court decisions even when we may not agree with them. In addition, we have in this case a very easy remedy and that is to pray ourselves.... We can pray a good deal more at home, we can attend our churches with a good deal more fidelity, and we can make the true meaning of prayer much more important in the lives of all of our children. That power is very much open to us."⁴⁴ Wiser and more cautious heads have prevailed over the years, and Congress rejected attempts to repeal the ruling in 1967, 1971 and 1984. Time has proved Kennedy right.

Kennedy maintained cordial but distant relations with the Vatican and the U.S. hierarchy. He did not invite Cardinal Spellman to his inauguration, apparently infuriating the New York prelate, who had attended all the previous ones going back to Roosevelt. He chose not to meet "officially" with the Vatican apostolic delegate, Archbishop Amleto Cicognani, at the White House. The position of apostolic delegate was the Vatican's representative to the American Catholic Church, not to be confused with an apostolic nuncio, the official representative of the Vatican to a government. Kennedy was wary of Vatican intentions and wanted to keep his distance, rather than reawaken the religious tensions that had marked the recently concluded campaign.⁴⁵ As president, Kennedy met the newly elected Pope Paul VI for a brief visit during the president's European tour in the summer of 1963. The president insisted on shaking the pope's hand rather than kissing his ring, which the president saw as outdated medieval protocol.⁴⁶

After Kennedy, religious issues in politics were not seen in strictly sectarian terms. While JFK had opposed public funding of church-related schools (after supporting peripheral, indirect aid in the form of busing and secular textbooks while a young congressman from Boston), it was a southern Protestant, Lyndon Johnson, who insisted on including these schools in his Elementary and Secondary Education Act, which passed Congress in 1965. While Kennedy chose not to establish formal U.S. diplomatic recognition of the Vatican, it was another Protestant, Ronald Reagan, who inaugurated diplomatic relations with the Holy See in 1984. By then the issue was less controversial, and his nominee for the post sailed through the Senate 81–13.

Kennedy also rescinded an Agency for International Development (AID) policy allowing U.S. government foreign aid funds to be distributed through religious organizations abroad. He vetoed a censorship bill aimed at the District of Columbia because he felt it would violate the Bill of Rights. His appointments to high federal positions, the cabinet, and the federal judiciary show a religious mix similar to those of his predecessors Eisenhower, Truman, and Roosevelt. He received the Family of Man award from the Protestant Council of New York and the Brotherhood of Man award from the National Conference of Christians and Jews.

Kennedy's presidential record on church-state relationships elicited praise from many directions. Andrew Greeley wrote, "The Kennedy Administration put to rest forever the fear that Catholicism was an alien religion and that Catholic political leaders would use their position to interfere with American freedoms."[47] The editors of the *Journal of Church and State*, published by Baptist-related Baylor University, concluded: "An examination of President Kennedy's positions and pronouncements on church and state indicates that he embraced the tradition of Washington, Jefferson and Madison.... Not since James Madison has any American President so definitely expressed his own position on church-state relations in the American schema. The prejudiced predictions of many of America's nativists and spokesmen of religious divisiveness seem delusory and far removed from the present reality of American life."[48]

Perhaps even more than his principled and pragmatic campaign, Kennedy's record as president on church-state issues convinced most Americans that he was what he said he was, a free man who made his decisions without reference to religious bias or favoritism. His presidency was a model of fairness, tolerance and moderation in religious matters. Some critics said he was too secular. He would probably have responded that this is what the constitution of a secular democratic nation presupposes. Kennedy esteemed many religions, it appears, and he believed that his administration should pursue policies that brought diverse peoples together rather than separating them unnecessarily for reasons that made little sense. Religious intolerance was anathema to his cool, rational mind.

Closing Thoughts

Religion, as we have seen close-up in this study, affects the political decisions of voters, often intensely and often negatively. Since religion shapes the way individuals see the universe, it impacts social, cultural and political life in various ways. How to insure that religious people have input into the political system without weakening religious pluralism and official neutrality toward religious groups on the part of the government remains an ever-changing and tricky business.

7. Epilogue and Summing Up 223

Clergy clearly have power to shape voting attitudes through their sermons and endorsements and have done so back to the days of Thomas Jefferson and John Adams. All too often, however, they have tended to set one religion against others and to assume that individuals who share their faith are also competent to lead governments and make decisions that impact all citizens. Most Americans, in polls dating to the late 1960s, strongly oppose churches acting as partisan political agents. They do not want their clergy to endorse candidates or to tell them how to vote. Discretion may indeed be the better part of valor.

Decades after the Kennedy-Nixon race, questions are raised about religious group involvement in partisan politics. Would direct or indirect endorsements jeopardize the tax exemption status of churches engaging in such activities? The issue became more noticeable after the Religious Right, a political-religious movement founded in evangelical and fundamentalist churches, emerged in the late 1970s. It intensified during the 2004 reelection campaign of George W. Bush. Liberal and pro-separation groups raised the questions with the Internal Revenue Service, which, in turn, has not rendered any definitive rulings. None of these groups challenged the activities waged by militant Protestant groups against Kennedy in 1960 or their covert links with the Nixon campaign.

Some individuals did raise these concerns in 1960. Charles P. Taft, chairman of the Fair Campaign Practices Committee, warned that churches that distribute defamatory anti–Catholic literature in an attempt to influence the election outcome could face a possible loss of their tax exemption.[49] But nothing seems to have come of it, and the distribution of these materials only intensified. In some states action was taken. A preliminary injunction was issued in Finleyville, Pennsylvania, against Reverend W.L. King's Voice of the Nazarene Bible Church for disseminating the bogus "Knights of Columbus Oath."[50]

William Smith wrote: "Legal complications entered the picture as well. The Department of Justice investigated the mailing of a four-page tract which contained anti–Catholic sentiments purportedly made in a sermon by W.A. Criswell, a prominent Baptist clergyman. A spokesman for the F.B.I. said it was in violation of Federal law to mail material that had a tendency to affect the results of any election if the source of the material was not given."[51]

After describing the reams of "obscene" material, and "numerous pamphlets not founded on fact but consisting mostly of ranting, rodomontade and bigotry" that were circulating in Bucks County, James Michener wrote: "What infuriated me personally, as head of a committee trying to elect John Kennedy, was that the dissemination of material in all the above categories, from the factual to the obscene, was paid for by personal contributions which were made for a political purpose and which were tax exempt! ... Religious hatreds ought not be propagated at all, but certainly not on a tax-exempt basis."[52]

The tax exemption question for religious group involvement in politics remains unresolved. Issue advocacy is apparently acceptable and will not result in a loss of tax exemption, but partisanship and endorsement of candidates would appear to trigger a possible revocation. It depends on Congress and the IRS. But a major section of the American electorate remains wary of campaigning in the pulpit and the remembrance of the repugnance of a campaign a half-century ago strengthens that concern.

Kennedy's record on church-state matters, particularly on issues that meant most to his critics, makes it unlikely that anti–Catholicism will significantly affect, or nearly defeat, another Catholic candidate. In 1968's Democratic race the Catholicism of Robert Kennedy and Eugene McCarthy was hardly mentioned as a factor. When John Kerry became the Democratic nominee in 2004, the first Catholic since Kennedy to be nominated, he faced little concern that he would impose Catholic values on all voters. In fact, he was criticized by conservative Catholics and Protestants for not being Catholic enough.

The jury is still out on whether candidates of other minority faiths will face hostility, primarily because none have been nominated. Opinion surveys consistently show that a Mormon, Muslim or atheist candidate would face considerable opposition at the polls, especially from evangelical white Protestants.

Former Massachusetts governor Mitt Romney was the first Mormon to seek the presidency and failed to secure the GOP nomination in 2008. Religion-based opposition may have been a factor in his rejection, especially among white evangelicals, who comprised 43 percent of Republican primary voters. The evangelical vote in the GOP primaries, according to combined exit polls, was 39 percent for Mike Huckabee, a Baptist preacher and former Arkansas governor, 33 percent for Senator John McCain, the eventual nominee, and only 20 percent for Romney.

7. Epilogue and Summing Up

Religious intolerance has clearly declined in America, and two Muslims and three Buddhists now represent districts in the U.S. House of Representatives. But the Presidency remains off-limits, it seems, especially in the Republican Party, whose 78 candidates for president and vice president since 1856 include 77 white Protestants and one white Catholic. The Democrats have nominated seven Catholics, one Jew, and one Greek Orthodox Christian for president or vice president and, of course, one African American, who is now president.

Religious voting seems more issue-focused, rather than fixated on whether voters share the religious affiliation of the candidate. This is not always true, however. Religious voting seems to rest more on the relative conservatism, or traditionalism, or relative liberalism, or modernism, of voters, as well as on frequency of attendance at worship services. Whether this will remain the case is not certain. Even religious lobbies and coalitions seem to be more broadly based and have largely, though not entirely, replaced denominational lobbies.

The Kennedy campaign should not be forgotten. It was the first modern (postwar) election in which organized religious opposition to a candidate was directed by networks of like-minded religious zealots who sincerely believed they were trying to save the Republic. In many respects this foreshadowed the Religious Right activism that began with the Reagan campaign in 1980 and accelerated in the efforts to reelect George W. Bush in 2004. A countermovement activated religious moderates and progressives, and foes of bigotry in 1960, foreshadowing a smaller but significant Religious Left that found its voice again in 2004 and 2008. Beneath the often irrational din of bigotry, there were some intelligent discussions of the proper relationship between church and state, the complexities engendered by calls of conscience and the importance of preserving religious pluralism, freedom and diversity.

It may be significant that not only American Roman Catholics but also Americans of other minority religions and races saw in the Kennedy candidacy a hope for a better future for themselves and a possibility that someone in their community could also aspire to the nation's highest office. It is no surprise that Kennedy was the overwhelming choice of Jewish Americans and African Americans, of Hispanics and Native Americans (90 percent in Maine and 80 percent in Wisconsin, for example) and of Eastern Orthodox Christians from Tarpon Springs, Florida, to Lowell, Massachusetts.

Historians will forever debate the merits of Kennedy's policies, and whether his presidency should be remembered as successful or unsuccessful. But his idealism and his ability to transcend ancient religious animosities will long be remembered and appreciated as bright spots in the history of the American experiment in self-government.

APPENDIX

Two Kennedy Campaign Addresses on the Issue of Religion

Address of Senator John F. Kennedy to the Greater Houston Ministerial Association, Rice Hotel, Houston Texas, on September 12, 1960

Reverend Meza, Reverend Reck, I'm grateful for your generous invitation to speak my views.

While the so-called religious issue is necessarily and properly the chief topic here tonight, I want to emphasize from the outset that we have far more critical issues to face in the 1960 election; the spread of Communist influence, until it now festers 90 miles off the coast of Florida — the humiliating treatment of our President and Vice President by those who no longer respect our power — the hungry children I saw in West Virginia, the old people who cannot pay their doctor bills, the families forced to give up their farms — an America with too many slums, with too few schools, and too late to the moon and outer space.

These are the real issues which should decide this campaign. And they are not religious issues — for war and hunger and ignorance and despair know no religious barriers.

But because I am a Catholic, and no Catholic has ever been elected President, the real issues in this campaign have been obscured — perhaps deliberately, in some quarters less responsible than this. So it is apparently necessary for me to state once again — not what kind of church I believe in, for that should be important only to me — but what kind of America I believe in.

I believe in an America where the separation of church and state is absolute — where no Catholic prelate would tell the President (should he be Catholic) how to act, and no Protestant minister would tell his parishoners for whom to vote — where no church or church school is granted any public funds or political preference — and where no man is denied public office merely because his religion differs from the President who might appoint him or the people who might elect him.

I believe in an America that is officially neither Catholic, Protestant nor Jewish — where no public official either requests or accepts instructions on public policy from the Pope, the National Council of Churches or any other ecclesiastical source — where no religious body seeks to impose its will directly or indirectly upon the general populace or the public acts of its officials — and where religious liberty is so indivisible that an act against one church is treated as an act against all.

For while this year it may be a Catholic against whom the finger of suspicion is pointed, in other years it has been, and may someday be again, a Jew — or a Quaker — or a Unitarian — or a Baptist. It was Virginia's harassment of Baptist preachers, for example, that helped lead to Jefferson's statute of religious freedom. Today I may be the victim — but tomorrow it may be you — until the whole fabric of our harmonious society is ripped at a time of great national peril.

Finally, I believe in an America where religious intolerance will someday end — where all men and all churches are treated as equal — where every man has the same right to attend or not attend the church of his choice — where there is no Catholic vote, no anti-Catholic vote, no bloc voting of any kind — and where Catholics, Protestants and Jews, at both the lay and pastoral level, will refrain from those attitudes of disdain and division which have so often marred their works in the past, and promote instead the American ideal of brotherhood.

That is the kind of America in which I believe. And it represents the kind of Presidency in which I believe — a great office that must neither be humbled by making it the instrument of any one religious group nor tarnished by arbitrarily withholding its occupancy from the members of any one religious group. I believe in a President whose religious views are his own private affair, neither imposed by him upon the nation or imposed by the nation upon him as a condition to holding that office.

I would not look with favor upon a President working to subvert the first amendment's guarantees of religious liberty. Nor would our system of checks and balances permit him to do so — and neither do I look with favor upon those who would work to subvert Article VI of the Constitution by requiring a religious test — even by indirection — for it. If they disagree with that safeguard they should be out openly working to repeal it.

I want a Chief Executive whose public acts are responsible to all groups and obligated to none — who can attend any ceremony, service or dinner his office may appropriately require of him — and whose fulfillment of his Presidential oath is not limited or conditioned by any religious oath, ritual or obligation.

This is the kind of America I believe in — and this is the kind I fought for in the South Pacific, and the kind my brother died for in Europe. No one suggested then that we may have a "divided loyalty," that we did "not believe in liberty," or that we belonged to a disloyal group that threatened the "freedoms for which our forefathers died."

And in fact this is the kind of America for which our forefathers died — when they fled here to escape religious test oaths that denied office to members of less favored churches — when they fought for the Constitution, the Bill of Rights, and the Virginia Statute of Religious Freedom — and when they fought at the shrine I visited today, the Alamo. For side by side with Bowie and Crockett died McCafferty and Bailey and Carey — but no one knows whether they were Catholic or not. For there was no religious test at the Alamo.

I ask you tonight to follow in that tradition — to judge me on the basis of my record of 14 years in Congress — on my declared stands against an Ambassador to the Vatican, against unconstitutional aid to parochial schools, and against any boycott of the public schools (which I have attended myself) — instead of judging me on the basis of these pamphlets and publications we all have seen that carefully select quotations out of context from the statements of Catholic church leaders, usually in other countries, frequently in other centuries, and always omitting, of course, the statement of the American Bishops in 1948 which strongly endorsed church-state separation, and which more nearly reflects the views of almost every American Catholic.

I do not consider these other quotations binding upon my public acts — why should you? But let me say, with respect to other countries, that I am wholly opposed to the state being used by any religious group,

Catholic or Protestant, to compel, prohibit, or persecute the free exercise of any other religion. And I hope that you and I condemn with equal fervor those nations which deny their Presidency to Protestants and those which deny it to Catholics. And rather than cite the misdeeds of those who differ, I would cite the record of the Catholic Church in such nations as Ireland and France — and the independence of such statesmen as Adenauer and De Gaulle.

But let me stress again that these are my views — for contrary to common newspaper usage, I am not the Catholic candidate for President. I am the Democratic Party's candidate for President who happens also to be a Catholic. I do not speak for my church on public matters — and the church does not speak for me.

Whatever issue may come before me as President — on birth control, divorce, censorship, gambling or any other subject — I will make my decision in accordance with these views, in accordance with what my conscience tells me to be the national interest, and without regard to outside religious pressures or dictates. And no power or threat of punishment could cause me to decide otherwise.

But if the time should ever come — and I do not concede any conflict to be even remotely possible — when my office would require me to either violate my conscience or violate the national interest, then I would resign the office; and I hope any conscientious public servant would do the same.

But I do not intend to apologize for these views to my critics of either Catholic or Protestant faith — nor do I intend to disavow either my views or my church in order to win this election.

If I should lose on the real issues, I shall return to my seat in the Senate, satisfied that I had tried my best and was fairly judged. But if this election is decided on the basis that 40 million Americans lost their chance of being President on the day they were baptized, then it is the whole nation that will be the loser, in the eyes of Catholics and non-Catholics around the world, in the eyes of history, and in the eyes of our own people.

But if, on the other hand, I should win the election, then I shall devote every effort of mind and spirit to fulfilling the oath of the Presidency — practically identical, I might add, to the oath I have taken for 14 years in the Congress. For without reservation, I can "solemnly swear that I will faithfully execute the office of President of the United States, and will to the best of my ability preserve, protect, and defend the Constitution ... so help me God."

Remarks of Senator John F. Kennedy at the American Society of Newspaper Editors, Washington, D.C., April 21, 1960 "The Religion Issue in American Politics"

I have decided, in view of current press reports, that it would be appropriate to speak with you today about what has widely been called "the religious issue" in American politics. The phrase covers a multitude of meanings. There is no religious issue in the sense that any of the major candidates differ on the role of religion in our political life. Every Presidential contender, I am certain, is dedicated to the separation of church and state, to the preservation of religious liberty, to an end to religious bigotry, and to the total independence of the officeholder from any form of ecclesiastical dictation.

Nor is there any real issue in the sense that any candidate is exploiting his religious affiliation. No one's candidacy, by itself, raises a religious issue. And I believe it is inaccurate to state that my "candidacy created the issue"—that, because I am replying to the bigots, I am now "running on the religious issue in West Virginia"—or that my statements in response to interrogation are "fanning the controversy." I am not "trying to be the first Catholic President," as some have written. I happen to believe I can serve my nation as President—and I also happen to have been born a Catholic.

Nor am I appealing, as is too often claimed, to a so-called Catholic vote. Even if such a vote exists—which I doubt—I want to make one thing clear again: I want no votes solely on account of my religion. Any voter, Catholic or otherwise, who feels another candidate would be a superior President should support that candidate. I do not want any vote cast for me for such illogical reasons.

Neither do I want anyone to support my candidacy merely to prove that this nation is not bigoted—and that a Catholic can be elected President. I have never suggested that those opposed to me are thereby anti–Catholic. There are ample legitimate grounds for supporting other candidates — (though I will not, of course, detail them here). Nor have I ever suggested that the Democratic party is required to nominate me or face a Catholic revolt in November. I do not believe that to be true — I cannot believe our convention would act on such a premise — and I do believe that a majority of Americans of every faith will support the Democratic nominee, whoever he is.

What, then, is the so-called religious issue in American politics today? It is not, it seems to me, my actual religious convictions — but a misunderstanding of what those convictions actually are. It is not the actual existence of religious voting blocs — but a suspicion that such voting blocs may exist. And when we deal with such public fears and suspicions, the American press has a very grave responsibility.

I know the press did not create this religious issue. My religious affiliation is a fact — religious intolerance is a fact. And the proper role of the press is to report all facts that are a matter of public interest.

But the press has a responsibility, I think you will agree, which goes far beyond a reporting of the facts. It goes beyond lofty editorials deploring intolerance. For my religion is hardly, in this critical year of 1960, the dominant issue of our time. It is hardly the most important criterion — or even a relevant criterion — on which the American people should make their choice for Chief Executive. And the press, while not creating the issue, will largely determine whether or not it does become dominant — whether it is kept in perspective — whether it is considered objectively — whether needless fears and suspicions are stilled instead of aroused.

The members of the press should report the facts as they find them. They should describe the issues as they see them. But they should beware, it seems to me, of either magnifying this issue or oversimplifying it. They should beware of ignoring the vital issues of this campaign, while filling their pages with analyses that cannot be proven, with statements that cannot be documented and with emphasis which cannot be justified.

I spoke in Wisconsin, for example, on farm legislation, foreign policy, defense, civil rights and several dozen other issues. The people of Wisconsin seemed genuinely interested in these addresses. But I rarely found them reported in the press — except when they were occasionally sandwiched in between descriptions of my hand-shaking, my theme-song, family haircut, and inevitably, my religion.

At almost every stop in Wisconsin I invited questions — and the questions came — on price supports, labor unions, disengagement, taxes and inflation. But these sessions were rarely reported in the press except when one topic was discussed: religion. One article, for example, supposedly summing the primary up in advance, mentioned the word Catholic 20 times in 15 paragraphs — not mentioning even once dairy farms, disarmament, labor legislation or any other issue. And on the Sunday before the Primary, the *Milwaukee Journal* featured a map of the state, listing county by county the relative strength of three types of voters — Democrats, Republicans and Catholics.

In West Virginia, it is the same story. As reported in yesterday's *Washington Post*, the great bulk of West Virginians paid very little attention to my religion — until they read repeatedly in the nation's press that this was the decisive issue in West Virginia. There are many serious problems in that state — problems big enough to dominate any campaign — but religion is not one of them.

I do not think that religion is the decisive issue in any state. I do not think it should be. I do not think it should be made to be. And recognizing my own responsibilities in that regard, I am hopeful that you will recognize yours also.

For the past months and years, I have answered almost daily inquiries from the press about the religious issue. I want to take this opportunity to turn the tables — to raise some questions for your thoughtful consideration.

First: Is the religious issue a legitimate issue in this campaign? There is only one legitimate question underlying all the rest: would you, as President of the United States, be responsive in any way to ecclesiastical pressures or obligations of any kind that might in any fashion influence or interfere with your conduct of that office in the national interest? I have answered that question many times. My answer was — and is "NO."

Once that question is answered, there is no legitimate issue of my religion. But there are, I think, legitimate questions of public policy — of concern to religious groups which no one should feel bigoted about raising, and to which I do not object to answering. But I do object to being the only candidate required to answer those questions.

Federal assistance to parochial schools, for example, is a very legitimate issue actually before the Congress. I am opposed to it. I believe it is clearly unconstitutional. I voted against it on the Senate floor this year, when offered by Senator Morse. But interestingly enough, I was the only announced candidate in the Senate who did so. (Nevertheless I have not yet charged my opponents with taking orders from Rome.)

An Ambassador to the Vatican could conceivably become a real issue again. I am opposed to it, and said so long ago. But even though it was last proposed by a Baptist President, I know of no other candidate who has been even asked about this matter.

The prospects of any President ever receiving for his signature a bill providing foreign aid funds for birth control are very remote indeed. It is hardly the major issue some have suggested. Nevertheless I have made it clear that I would neither veto nor sign such a bill on any basis except what I considered to be the public interest, without regard to my private religious views. I have said the same about bills dealing with censorship, divorce, our relations with Spain or any other subject.

These are legitimate inquiries about real questions which the next President may conceivably have to face. But these inquiries ought to be directed equally to all candidates. I have made it clear that I strongly support — out of conviction as well as Constitutional obligation — the guarantees of religious equality provided by the First Amendment — and I ask only that these same guarantees be extended to me.

Secondly: Can we justify analyzing voters as well as candidates strictly in terms of their religion? I think the voters of Wisconsin objected to being categorized simply as either Catholics or Protestants in analyzing their political choices. I think they objected to being accosted by reporters outside of political meetings and asked one question only — their religion — not their occupation or education or philosophy or income — only their religion.

And I think they had a right to object. The flood of post-primary analyses on the so-called "Catholic vote" and "Protestant vote" — carefully shaped to conform with their authors' pre-primary predictions — would never be published in any competent statistical journal.

Only this week, I received a very careful analysis of the Wisconsin results. It conclusively shows two significant patterns of bloc voting: I ran strongest in those areas where the average temperature in January was 20 degrees or higher, and poorest in those areas where it was 14 degrees or lower — and that I ran well in the beech tree and basswood counties and not so well among the hemlock and pine.

Anyone who thinks these trends are merely coincidences of no relevance has never tried to campaign in Wisconsin in January. In any event, this analysis is being rushed to West Virginia, where I am assured that the winter is less severe and the basswood are abundant. It has been suggested, however, that to offset my apparent political handicaps I may have to pick a running-mate from Maine or, preferably, Alaska.

The facts of the matter are that this analysis stands up statistically much better than all the so-called analyses of the religious vote. And so do analyses of each county based on their distance from the Minnesota border, the length of their Democratic tradition and their inclusion in my campaign itinerary. I carried some areas with large proportions of voters who are Catholics — and I lost some. I carried some areas where Protestants predominate — and I lost some.

It is true that I ran well in cities — and large numbers of Catholics live in cities. But so do union members and older voters and veterans and chess fans and basswood lovers. To say my support in the cities is due only to the religion of the voters is incapable of proof and an unfair indictment of their political maturity.

Of those Catholics who voted for me, how many did so on grounds of my religion — how many because they felt my opponent was too radical — how many because they resented the attacks on my record — how many because they were union members — how many for some other reason? I do not know. And the facts are that no one knows.

For voters are more than Catholics, Protestants or Jews. They make up their minds for many diverse reasons, good and bad. To submit the candidates to a religious test is unfair enough — to apply it to the voters themselves is divisive, degrading and wholly unwarranted.

Third and finally: Is there any justification for applying special religious tests to one office only: the Presidency? Little or no attention was paid to my religion when I took the oath as Senator in 1953 — as a Congressman in 1947 — or as a Naval officer in 1941. Members of my faith abound in public office at every level except the White House. What is there about the Presidency that justifies this constant emphasis upon a candidate's religion and that of his supporters?

The Presidency is not, after all, the British Crown, serving a dual capacity in both church and state. The President is not elected to be protector of the faith — or guardian of the public morals. His attendance at church on Sunday should be his business alone, not a showcase for the nation.

On the other hand, we are in no danger of a one-man Constitutional upheaval. The President, however intent he may be on subverting our institutions, cannot ignore the Congress — or the voters — or the courts. And our highest court, incidentally, has a long history of Catholic Justices, none of whom, as far as I know, was ever challenged on the fairness of his rulings on sensitive church-state issues.

Some may say we treat the Presidency differently because we have had only one previous Catholic candidate for President. But I am growing weary of that term. I am not the Catholic candidate for President. I do not speak for the Catholic Church on issues of public policy — and no one in that Church speaks for me. My record on aid to education, aid to Tito, the Conant nomination and other issues has displeased some prominent Catholic clergymen and organizations; and it has been approved by others. The fact is that the Catholic Church is not a monolith — it is committed in this country to the principles of individual liberty — and it has no claim over my conduct as a public officer sworn to do the public interest.

So I hope we can see the beginning of the end of references to me as "the Catholic candidate" for President. Do not expect me to explain or defend every act or statement of every Pope or priest, in this country or some other, in this century or the last — and that includes the Mayor of Dijon.

* * *

I have tried to examine with you today the press' responsibility in meeting this religious issue. The question remains: what is my responsibility? I am a candidate. The issue is here. Two alternatives have been suggested:

1. The first suggestion is that I withdraw to avoid a "dangerous religious controversy"; and accept the Vice Presidential nomination in order to placate the so-called Catholic vote.

I find that suggestion highly distasteful. It assumes the worst about a country which prides itself on being more tolerant and better educated than it was in 1928. It assumes that Catholics are a pawn on the political chess-board, moved hither and yon, and somehow "bought off" by the party putting in the second-spot a Catholic whom the party barred from the top. And it forgets, finally, that such a performance would have an effect on our image abroad as well as our self-respect here at home.

Are we going to admit to the world that a Jew can be elected Mayor of Dublin, a Protestant can be chosen Foreign Minister of France, a Moslem can serve in the Israeli Parliament — but a Catholic cannot be President of the United States? Are we to tell Chancellor Adenauer, for example, that we want him risking his all on our front-lines; but that — if he were an American — we would never entrust him with our Presidency — nor would we accept our distinguished guest, Gen. DeGaulle? Are we to admit to the world — worse still, are we to admit to ourselves — that one-third of our population is forever barred from the White House?

So I am not impressed by those pleas that I settle for the Vice Presidency in order to avert a religious spectacle. Surely those who believe it dangerous to elect a Catholic as President will not want him to serve as Vice President, a heart-beat away from the office.

2. The alternative is to proceed with the primaries, the convention and the election. If there is bigotry in the country, then so be it — there is bigotry. If that bigotry is too great to permit the fair consideration of a Catholic who has made clear his complete independence and his complete dedication to separation of church and state, then we ought to know it.

But I do not believe that this it the case. I believe the American people are more concerned with a man's views and abilities than with the church to which he belongs. I believe that the founding fathers meant it when they provided in Article VI of the Constitution that there should be no religious test for public office — a provision that brought not one dissenting vote, only the comment of Roger Sherman that it was surely unnecessary — "The prevailing legality being a sufficient security against such tests." And I believe that the American people mean to adhere to those principles today.

But regardless of the political outcome this issue is here to be faced. It is my job to face it frankly and fully. And it is your job to face it fairly, in perspective and in proportion.

I am confident that the press and other media of this country will recognize their responsibilities in this area — to refute falsehood, to inform the ignorant, and to concentrate on the issues, the real issues, in this hour of the nation's peril.

The Supreme Court has written that as public officials "We are neither Jew nor Gentile, neither Catholic nor Agnostic. We owe equal attachment to the Constitution and are equally bound by our obligations whether we derive our citizenship from the earliest or latest immigrants to these shores ... for religion is outside the sphere of political government."

We must all — candidates, press, and voters alike dedicate ourselves to these principles — for they are the key to a free country.

Chapter Notes

Preface

1. Gaston Espinosa, ed., *Religion and the American Presidency* (New York: Columbia University Press, 2009), 35.
2. Richard Norton Smith, *Thomas E. Dewey and His Times* (New York: Simon & Schuster, 1982), 626.
3. James A. Michener, *Report of the County Chairman* (New York: Random House, 1961), 101.
4. Allan J. Lichtman, *White Protestant Nation: The Rise of the American Conservative Movement* (New York: Atlantic Monthly Press, 2008), 231.
5. Michener, *Report,* 108.

Chapter 1

1. Richard Carwardine, "Lincoln's Religion," in *Our Lincoln: New Perspectives on Lincoln and His World,* ed. Eric Foner (New York: W.W. Norton, 2008), 236.
2. Vincent De Santis, "Catholicism and Presidential Elections, 1865–1900," *Mid-America* 42 (April 1960), 67–79.
3. Robert Swierenga, "Ethno-religious Political Behavior in the Mid-Nineteenth Century: Voting, Values, Cultures," in *Religion and American Politics,* ed. Mark A. Noll (New York: Oxford University Press, 1990), 152–153.
4. Washington Gladden, "The Anti-Catholic Crusade," *Century,* March 1894.
5. Humphrey J. Desmond, *The APA Movement* (Washington, D.C.: New Century, 1912), and Donald L. Kinzer, *An Episode in Anti-Catholicism: The American Protective Association* (Seattle: University of Washington Press, 1964).
6. Harry J. Sievers, "The Catholic Indian School Issue and the Presidential Election of 1892," *Catholic Historical Review* 38 (July 1952), 129–155.
7. Ibid., 129–155.
8. De Santis, "Catholicism," 67–79.
9. Thomas E. Wangler, "American Catholics and the Spanish-American War," in *Catholics in America 1776–1976,* ed. Robert Trisco (Washington, D.C.: National Conference of Catholic Bishops, 1976).
10. Frank T. Reuter, *Catholic Influence on American Colonial Policies 1898–1904* (Austin: University of Texas Press, 1967).
11. Berton Dulce and Edward J. Richter, *Religion and the Presidency* (New York: Macmillan, 1962), 73.
12. Edmund A. Moore, *A Catholic Runs for President* (New York: Ronald Press, 1957), 21.
13. John Dewey, "Why I Am for Smith," *New Republic* 56 (November 7, 1928), 320–321.
14. Moore, *A Catholic Runs,* 41.
15. Ibid., 146, 176.
16. Michael Williams, *The Shadow of the Pope* (New York: Whittlesey House, 1932), 318.
17. *Campaign Address of Governor Alfred E. Smith,* 250.
18. Richard Hofstadter, "Could a Protestant Have Beaten Hoover in 1928?" *Reporter,* March 17, 1960.
19. David Burner, *The Politics of*

Provincialism: The Democratic Party in Transition, 1918–1932 (New York: Alfred A. Knopf, 1968), 208–209.

20. Eleanor Roosevelt, *The Autobiography of Eleanor Roosevelt* (New York: Harper & Row, 1961), 148.

21. Allan J. Lichtman, *Prejudice and the Old Politics: The Presidential Election of 1928* (Chapel Hill: University of North Carolina Press, 1979), 231.

22. Ibid., 233, 245.

23. Thomas J. Donaghy, *Keystone Democrat: David Lawrence Remembered* (New York: Vantage, 1986), 84.

24. Bruce L. Felknor, *Dirty Politics* (New York: W.W. Norton, 1966), 266–267.

Chapter 2

1. Patricia Barrett, *Religious Liberty and the American Presidency* (New York: Herder & Herder, 1963), 9.

2. John F. Kennedy, "The Religion Issue in American Politics" (remarks of Senator John F. Kennedy, at American Society of Newspaper Editors, Washington, D.C., April 21, 1960). John F. Kennedy Presidential Library & Museum. See also copy of speech in Appendix.

3. *New York Times*, April 11, 1959, 8.

4. *New York Herald Tribune*, July 5, 1960, 11.

5. Lawrence H. Fuchs, *John F. Kennedy and American Catholicism* (New York: Meredith, 1967), 182.

6. *New York Times*, February 11, 1960, 29.

7. Theodore Sorensen, *Kennedy* (New York: Harper & Row, 1965), 194.

8. Barrett, *Religious Liberty*, 149–152.

9. *New York Times*, September 9, 1960, 14

10. *Newsday*, September 8, 1960, 98.

11. Carol N.R. George, *God's Salesman: Norman Vincent Peale and the Power of Positive Thinking* (New York: Oxford University Press, 1993), 199.

12. Ibid., 208.

13. Barrett, *Religious Liberty*, 160–164.

14. *New York Times*, September 14, 1960, Editorial page.

15. Ted Sorensen, *Counselor: A Life at the Edge of History* (New York: HarperCollins, 2008), 157.

16. Ibid., 162.

17. Shaun A. Casey, *The Making of a Catholic President: Kennedy vs. Nixon 1960* (New York: Oxford University Press, 2009), 149.

18. Ibid., 152–160.

19. Michener, *Report*, 89–108.

20. *New York Times*, August 25, 1960, 20.

21. Barrett, *Religious Liberty*, 13.

22. Ibid., 3, 25.

23. *New York Times*, August 4, 1960, 11.

24. Casey, *Making of a Catholic President*, 177.

25. Fuchs, *John F. Kennedy*, 171.

26. Lindy Boggs, *Washington Through a Purple Veil* (New York: Harcourt, Brace, 1994), 158.

27. Dulce and Richter, *Religion and the Presidency*, 196.

28. Eugene Bianchi, *John XXIII and American Protestants* (Washington, D.C.: Corpus, 1968), 95–112.

29. Ira V. Birdwhistell, "Southern Baptist Perceptions of and Responses to Roman Catholicism, 1917–1972" (Ph. D. diss., Southern Baptist Theological Seminary, 1975), 97–115.

30. Barrett, *Religious Liberty*, 29.

31. "Change in Attitudes Towards a Catholic for President," *Journalism Quarterly* (Winter 1963).

32. Arthur Schlesinger, Jr., *Kennedy or Nixon: Does It Make Any Difference?* (New York: Macmillan, 1960), 33, 34, 51.

33. Casey, *Making of a Catholic President*, 79.

34. Interview by author with E. Mallary Binns, October 19, 1977.

35. Edward Hughes Pruden, *A Window on Washington* (New York: Vantage, 1976), 116–117.

36. Religious News Service, August 24, 1960.
37. E.S. James, "Vote Your Convictions," *Baptist Standard*, November 2, 1960.
38. Beryl F. McClerren, "The Southern Baptist State Newspapers and the Religious Issue During the Presidential Campaigns of 1928 and 1960" (Ph.D. diss., Southern Illinois University, 1963), 18, 343.
39. Casey, *Making of a Catholic President*, 125.
40. Ibid., 126.
41. William Martin, *A Prophet with Honor: The Billy Graham Story* (New York: William Morrow, 1991), 271.
42. Ibid., 272, 278.
43. Ibid., 275.
44. Karl J. Alter, "A Catholic President," *Sign*, July 1960.
45. "On Questioning Catholic Candidates," *America*, March 7, 1959.
46. Fuchs, *John F. Kennedy*, 184.
47. Casey, *Making of a Catholic President*, 164–166.
48. Ibid., 106.
49. Ibid., 104.
50. Ibid., 193, 194.
51. Ibid., 193.
52. John Cooney, *The American Pope: The Life and Times of Francis Cardinal Spellman* (New York: Times Books, 1984), 265.
53. Ibid., xvii, 267, 268.
54. *New York Times*, September 4, 1960, 48.
55. *The Speeches of Senator John F. Kennedy*, 506–507.
56. Ibid., 944.

Chapter 3

1. Robert N. Bellah, "Civil Religion in America," *Daedalus* 96 (Winter 1967), 1.
2. Robert S. Alley, *So Help Me God: Religion and the Presidency, Wilson to Nixon* (Richmond, VA: John Knox, 1972), 17.

3. Ibid., 24.
4. Ibid., 33–35.
5. Ibid., 92.
6. Ibid., 94.
7. Ibid.
8. "The State-by-State Study of Smear: 1960." A report by the Fair Campaign Practices Committee, Inc., New York, February, 1962, 16.
9. Glen Jeansomme, *Gerald L.K. Smith: Minister of Hate* (New Haven: Yale University Press, 1988), 165.
10. *Ironwood (Michigan) Daily Globe*, October 17, 1960.
11. Fair Campaign Practices Committee Collection, Georgetown University Library, is the primary source for most of the materials reviewed in this chapter.
12. Letter and Memorandum, Wine to Sorensen, June 20, 1960, James Wine Personal Papers, John F. Kennedy Library.
13. Casey, *Making of a Catholic President*, 155.
14. Ibid., 127–131.

Chapter 4

1. John Higham, *Strangers in the Land: Patterns in American Nativism* (New Brunswick, NJ: Rutgers University Press, 1955), 181.
2. Justin Nordstrom, *Danger on the Doorstep: Anti-Catholicism and American Print Culture in the Progressive Era* (Notre Dame, IN: University of Notre Dame Press, 2006), 63.
3. Ibid.
4. Ibid., 68.
5. Paul T. David, ed., *The Presidential Election and Transition 1960–61* (Washington, DC: Brookings Institution, 1961), 174–175.
6. Angus Campbell et al., *Elections and the Political Order* (New York: John Wiley and Sons, 1966), 113.
7. Dulce and Richter, *Religion and the Presidency*, 216–217.
8. Lyman A. Kellstedt and Mark A. Noll, "Religion, Voting for President, and Party Identification, 1948–1984," in *Reli-*

gion & American Politics: From the Colonial Period to the 1980s, ed. Mark A. Noll (New York: Oxford University Press, 1990), 375.
9. Ibid., 374.
10. Ibid., 376.
11. Theodore H. White, *The Making of the President, 1960* (New York: Atheneum, 1961), 356.
12. Donald C. Lord, *John F. Kennedy* (Woodbury, NY: Barron, 1977), 94–95.
13. White, *Making of the President*, 353.
14. Ibid., 351.
15. American Institute of Public Opinion, April 12, 1968, cited in *Religions of America*, ed. Leo Rosten (New York: Simon & Schuster, 1975), 324.
16. These are American National Election Studies data. See David Paul Kahn, *The Neglected Voter: White Men and the Democratic Dilemma* (New York: Palgrave Macmillan, 2007).

Chapter 5

1. David B. Walker, "The Presidential Politics of the Franco-Americans," *Canadian Journal of Economics and Political Science* 28 (August 1962): 353–363.
2. Kevin Phillips, *The Emerging Republican Majority* (New Rochelle, NY: Arlington House, 1969), 104.
3. Lucy S. Dawidowicz and Leon J. Goldstein, *Politics in a Pluralist Democracy: Studies of Voting in the 1960 Election* (New York: Institute of Human Relations Press, 1963), 9–15.
4. Gerald F. DeJong, *The Dutch in America, 1609–1974* (Boston: Twayne, 1975), 231.
5. Phillips, *Emerging*, 72, 159–167.
6. Dawidowicz and Goldstein, *Politics*, 16–21.
7. Michael Weber, *Don't Call Me Boss: David L. Lawrence, Pittsburgh's Renaissance Mayor* (Pittsburgh: University of Pittsburgh Press, 1988), 365.
8. Ibid., 36.
9. Dawidowicz and Goldstein, *Politics*, 28–34.

10. White, *Making of the President*, 356.
11. James J. Thompson, Jr., *Fleeing the Whore of Babylon: A Modern Conversion Story* (Westminster, MD: Christian Classics, 1986), 53–54.
12. Ibid., 53.
13. Ibid., 54.
14. Edith L. Blumhofer, *Restoring the Faith: The Assemblies of God, Pentecostalism and American Culture* (Urbana: University of Illinois Press, 1993), 234–235.
15. Ibid., 235.
16. Dan B. Fleming, Jr., *Kennedy vs. Humphrey, West Virginia, 1960: The Pivotal Battle for the Democratic Presidential Nomination* (Jefferson, NC: McFarland, 1992), 135.
17. Ibid., 138.
18. Ibid., 139.
19. Ibid., 139–140.
20. Ibid., 140.
21. Ibid., 139.
22. Ibid., 141.
23. Governor Hulett C. Smith, recorded interview by William L. Young, June 17, 1965, pages 11–12, John F. Kennedy Library Oral History Program.
24. Ibid., 39.
25. Esther Peters, recorded interview by William L. Young, July 14, 1964, page 10, John F. Kennedy Library Oral History Program.
26. J. Raymond De Paulo, recorded interview by William L. Young, February 19, 1965, pages 11 and 12, John F. Kennedy Library Oral History Program.
27. Carl V. Harris, *Political Power in Birmingham, 1871–1921* (Knoxville: University of Tennessee Press, 1977), 86–87. See also Glenn Feldman, *Politics, Society and the Klan in Alabama, 1915–1949* (Tuscaloosa: University of Alabama Press, 1999).
28. See the riveting account in Sharon Davies, *Rising Road: A True Tale of Love, Race and Religion in America* (New York: Oxford University Press, 2010).
29. Virginia V. Hamilton, *Lister Hill: Statesman from the South* (Chapel Hill: University of North Carolina Press, 1987).

30. Harris, *Political Power*, 86–87.
31. Ibid., 197.
32. Ibid., 198.
33. Andrew S. Moore, *The South's Tolerable Alien: Roman Catholics in Alabama and Georgia 1945–1970* (Baton Rouge: Louisiana State University Press, 2007), 11.
34. Ibid., 12–13.
35. Ibid., 19, 25.
36. Ibid., 27.
37. Ibid., 25.
38. Ibid., 35.
39. *New York Times*, September 7, 1960, 32.
40. Quoted in Michael Newton, *The Invisible Empire: The Ku Klux Klan in Florida* (Gainesville: University Press of Florida, 2001), 159.
41. Thomas J. Carty, *A Catholic in the White House?: Religion, Politics, and John F. Kennedy's Presidential Campaign* (New York: Palgrave Macmillan, 2004), 151–156.
42. Bernard Cosman, "Religion and Race in Louisiana Presidential Politics, 1960," *Southwestern Social Science Quarterly* 43 (December 1962): 235–241.
43. Dawidowicz and Goldstein, *Politics*, 41–42.
44. Ibid., 42.
45. Richard Hughes, *Reviving the Ancient Faith: The Story of the Churches of Christ in America* (Grand Rapids, MI: Eerdmans, 1996), 263–266; James Talley, "Evins Mounts Pulpit, Answers Political Sermon," *Nashville Tennessean*, October 11, 1960. Also, see Casey, *Making of a Catholic President*, 181–183.
46. Ann Richards, *Straight from the Heart: My Life in Politics and Other Places* (New York: Simon & Schuster, 1989), 101.
47. Quoted in D.B. Hardeman and Donald C Bacon, *Rayburn: A Biography* (Lanham, MD: Madison, 1987), 434.
48. Ibid.
49. Ibid., 445.
50. *New York Times*, August 24, 1960, 19.
51. *New York Times*, September 1, 1960, 1.

52. Susan Allen Toth, *Blooming: A Small-Town Girlhood* (New York: Ballantine, 1998), 13, 14.
53. Marjorie Hart, *Summer at Tiffany* (New York: William Morrow, 2007), 23.
54. Jesse Ventura, *I Ain't Got Time to Bleed* (New York: Villard, 1999), 45.
55. Noel Iverson, *Germania, U.S.A.: Social Change in New Ulm, Minnesota* (Minneapolis: University of Minnesota Press, 1966), 66.
56. Ibid., 47.
57. Ibid., 132.
58. Ibid., 66.
59. Ibid., 158.
60. Iverson, *Germania*, 134.
61. *WPA Guide to Minnesota* (St. Paul: Minnesota Historical Society Press, 1985), 263. This indispensable volume was originally published in 1938.
62. *Minneapolis Tribune*, December 9, 1977, 2B.
63. Louis M. DeGryse, "The Low Countries," in *They Chose Minnesota: A Survey of the State's Ethnic Groups*, ed. June Drenning Holmquist (St. Paul: Minnesota Historical Society Press, 1981), 197.
64. Timo Riippa, "The Finns and Swede-Finns," in Holmquist, *They Chose*, 306.
65. Sarah Rubinstein, "The British," in Holmquist, *They Chose*, 111–129. See also John G. Rice, "The Old-Stock Americans," in Holmquist, 55–72.
66. Jon Gjerde & Carlton C. Qualey, *Norwegians in Minnesota* (St. Paul: Minnesota Historical Society Press, 2002), 46. See also Lowell J. Soike, *Norwegian Americans and the Politics of Dissent, 1880–1924* (Northfield: St. Olaf College Press, 1991).
67. Dawidowicz and Goldstein, *Politics*, 61–65.
68. Ibid., 44.
69. Ibid., 44, 46.
70. Ibid., 46.
71. Paul Simon, *P.S.: The Autobiography of Paul Simon* (Chicago: Bonus, 1999), 118.
72. Ibid., 246.
73. Ibid.
74. Ibid., 248.

75. Leonard J. Moore, *Citizen Klansmen: The Ku Klux Klan in Indiana, 1921–1928* (Chapel Hill: University of North Carolina Press, 1991).
76. Dawidowicz and Goldstein, *Politics,* 66–70; quote on page 70.
77. William D. Jenkins, *Steel Valley Klan: The Ku Klux Klan in Ohio's Mahoning Valley* (Kent, Ohio: Kent State University Press, 1990).
78. Dawidowicz and Goldstein, *Politics,* 48.
79. Ibid., 22–27.
80. Gastil, *Cultural Regions,* 277.
81. Ibid., 276.
82. Dawidowicz and Goldstein, *Politics,* 35–37.
83. Eugene C. Lee and William Buchanan, "The 1960 Election in California," *Western Political Quarterly* 14 (March, 1961): 309–326.
84. Carty, *A Catholic?,* 131–141.
85. Kenneth L. Jackson, *The Ku Klux Klan in the City, 1915–1930* (Chicago: Ivan R. Dee, 1992).
86. John M. Swarthout, "The 1960 Election in Oregon," *Western Political Quarterly* 14 (March 1961: 356–358.
87. Hugh A. Bone, "The 1960 Election in Washington," *Western Political Quarterly* 14 (March 1961): 376.
88. Robert Alan Goldberg, *Hooded Empire: The Ku Klux Klan in Colorado* (Urbana: University of Illinois Press, 1981), 104.
89. *New York Times,* October 16, 1960, 1.
90. Curtis Martin, "The 1960 Election in Colorado," *Western Political Quarterly* 14 (March 1961): 327–328.
91. Fair Campaign Practices Committee Collection, Georgetown University Library.
92. Boyd A. Martin, "The 1960 Election in Idaho" *Western Political Quarterly* 14 (March 1961): 342.
93. White, *Making of the President,* 356.
94. Don W. Driggs, "The 1960 Election in Nevada" *Western Political Quarterly* 14 (March 1961): 348.
95. *The Speeches of Senator John F. Kennedy,* 346.
96. Totton J. Anderson, "The Political West in 1960," *Western Political Quarterly* 14 (March 1961): 287–299 (quote on page 289).
97. Raymond D. Gastil, *Cultural Regions of the United States* (Seattle: University of Washington Press, 1975), 240.
98. Ibid., 241.
99. Ibid., 242.

Chapter 6

1. Phillips, *Emerging,* 132.
2. William J. McKenna, "The Influence of Religion in the Pennsylvania Elections of 1958 and 1960," *Pennsylvania History* 29 (1962), 407–419.
3. Daryl R. Fair, "The Reaction of Pennsylvania Voters to Catholic Candidates," *Pennsylvania History* 32 (1965), 305–315.
4. W.S. Merwin, "Distances," in Lee Gutkind, ed., *Our Roots Grow Deeper Than We Know* (Pittsburgh: University of Pittsburgh Press, 1985), 270.
5. James Reichley, *The Art of Government: Reform and Organization Politics in Philadelphia* (New York: Fund for the Republic, 1959), 84.
6. Linda K. Pritchard, "Religion in Pittsburgh," in *City at the Point: Essays on the Social History of Pittsburgh,* ed. Samuel Hays (Pittsburgh: University of Pittsburgh Press, 1989), 330, 333, 337.
7. Ibid., 341.
8. Ibid., 341, 343, 344.
9. Nora Faires, "Immigrants and Industry," in Hays, *City at the Point,* 12–13.
10. Ralph Wood, *The Pennsylvania Germans* (Princeton: Princeton University Press, 1942), 14, 87.
11. Noel Bausher Szundy, in the introduction to Mildred Jordan, *The Distelfink Country of the Pennsylvania Dutch* (New York: Crown, 1978), xxiii.
12. Earl Robacher, quoted in Jordan, *The Distelfink Country of the Pennsylvania Dutch* (New York: Crown, 1978), 13.

13. William T. Parsons, *The Pennsylvania Dutch* (Boston: Twayne, 1976), 237, 249.
14. Laurence Squeri, "The Pocono Resort Economy: Economic Growth and Social Conservatism, 1865–1940," *Pennsylvania Magazine of History and Biography* 115 (October 1991), 489–491.
15. Paul B. Beers, *Profiles from the Susquehanna Valley* (Harrisburg, PA: Stackpole, 1973), 59, 126, 129, 130.
16. Paul B. Beers, *The Pennsylvania Sampler* (Harrisburg, PA: Stackpole, 1970), 84.
17. Michener, *Report*, 270.
18. Ibid., 271.
19. Ibid., 267, 268.
20. Ibid., 104, 105.
21. Ibid., 106–107.
22. Ibid., 268.
23. George J. Marlin, *The American Catholic Voter: 200 Years of Political Impact* (South Bend, IN: St. Augustine's, 2004), 251.
24. Foreword to Dawidowicz and Goldstein, *Politics*, xi.
25. Andrew R. Baggaley, "Religious Influence on Wisconsin Voting, 1928–1960," *American Political Science Review* 56 (March, 1962): 66–70.
26. Fred L. Holmes, *Old World Wisconsin* (Eau Claire, WI: E.M. Hale, 1944), 355.
27. LaVern J. Rippley, *The Immigrant Experience in Wisconsin* (Boston: Twayne, 1985), 56.
28. Ibid., 53.
29. Bill Christofferson, *The Man from Clear Lake: Earth Day Founder Senator Gaylord Nelson* (Madison: University of Wisconsin Press, 2004), 136.
30. John R. Stumme, "Lutherans on Religion and the 1960 Presidential Election," *Journal of Lutheran Ethics* 7 (November 2007): 1–24.
31. Ibid., 10.
32. Ibid., 9.
33. (Reverend) H. Earl Miller, *Lutheran Witness*, August 23, 1960.
34. *New York Times*, November 6, 1960.

Chapter 7

1. James Hennesey (S.J.), *American Catholics: A History of the Roman Catholic Community in the United States* (New York: Oxford University Press, 1981), 308–309.
2. Charles R. Morris, *American Catholics: The Saints and Sinners Who Built America's Most Powerful Church* (New York: Times Books, 1997), 319.
3. Philip Gleason, *Keeping the Faith: American Catholicism Past and Present* (Notre Dame, IN: University of Notre Dame, 1987), 187, 32.
4. Quoted in Patrick Jordan and Paul Baumann, eds., *Commonweal Confronts the Century: Liberal Convictions, Catholic Tradition* (New York: Simon & Schuster Touchstone, 1999), 69.
5. Rodger Van Allen, *The Commonweal and American Catholicism: The Magazine, the Movement, the Meaning* (Philadelphia: Fortress, 1974), 140.
6. T.S. Settel, ed., *The Faith of JFK* (New York: E.P. Dutton, 1965), 5.
7. (Archbishop) Philip Hannan, *The Archbishop Wore Combat Boots*, with Nancy Collins and Peter Finney, Jr. (Huntington, IN: Our Sunday Visitor, 2010), 24.
8. Ibid., 202.
9. Ibid., 203.
10. Ibid., 206.
11. Ibid., 202.
12. Burns, *John Kennedy*, 243.
13. Ibid., 249–250.
14. Ibid., 250.
15. Mark S. Massa, "A Catholic for President?: John F. Kennedy and the 'Secular' Theology of the Houston Speech, 1960," *Journal of Church and State* 39 (Spring 1997): 297–317.
16. Ibid., 301.
17. Settel, ed., *Faith of JFK*, 50.
18. Ibid., 108–109.
19. Ibid., 126.
20. Ibid., 114.
21. Ibid.
22. Quoted in Patrick Jordan and Paul Baumann, eds., *Commonweal*, 71.

23. James S. Wolfe, "The Religious Issue Revisited: Presbyterian Responses to Kennedy's Presidential Campaign," *Journal of Presbyterian History* 57 (Spring 1979): 1–18.
24. Alley, *So Help Me*, 95.
25. Ibid., 96.
26. Ibid., 98.
27. Ibid., 101.
28. Ibid., 103.
29. *Public Papers of the President of the Unites States: John F. Kennedy—1961* (Washington: U.S. Government Printing Office, 1962), 77.
30. Alley, *So Help Me God*, 100.
31. Fuchs, *John F. Kennedy*, 31–32.
32. Ibid., 187.
33. Simon, *P.S.: The Autobiography of Paul Simon*, 119, 249.
34. William D. Smith, "Alfred E. Smith and John F. Kennedy: The Religious Issue during the Presidential Campaigns of 1928 and 1960" (Ph. D. diss., University of Southern Illinois, 1964), 295.
35. John Cogley, "Kennedy the Catholic," *Commonweal*, 79 (January 10, 1964), 424.
36. William D. Smith, 297.
37. Ibid., 299.
38. Sorensen, *Kennedy*, 360.
39. *Washington Post*, March 16, 1961.
40. Sorensen, *Kennedy*, 362.
41. Cooney, *American Pope*, 273.
42. Ibid., 272, 273.
43. Andrew Greeley, *The Catholic Experience* (Garden City, NY: Doubleday, 1967), 290.
44. Sorensen, *Kennedy*, 364.
45. Cooney, *American Pope*, 272–273.
46. Massimo Franco, *Parallel Empires: The Vatican and the United States, Two Centuries of Alliance and Conflict* (New York: Doubleday, 2008).
47. Greeley, 284.
48. "The Church-State Legacy of JFK," *Journal of Church and State* 6 (Winter 1964): 1–2.
49. *New York Times*, September 18, 1960, 44.
50. *New York Times*, September 17, 1960, 23.
51. William D. Smith, 181.
52. Michener, *Report*, 91, 94, 95.

Bibliography

Alley, Robert S. *So Help Me God: Religion and the Presidency, Wilson to Nixon.* Richmond: John Knox 1972.

Alter, Karl J. "A Catholic President." *Sign*, July 1960.

Anderson, Charles A. *White Protestant Americans.* Englewood Cliffs, NJ: Prentice Hall, 1970.

Anderson, Totton J. "The Political West in 1960." *Western Political Quarterly* 14 (March 1961), pp. 287–299.

Baggaley, Andrew. "Religious Voting in Wisconsin 1928–1960. *American Political Science Review* 56 (March 1962), pp. 66–70.

Barrett, Patricia. *Religious Liberty and the American Presidency.* New York: Herder & Herder, 1963.

Beers, Paul B. *The Pennsylvania Sampler.* Harrisburg, PA: Stackpole, 1970.

_____. *Profiles from the Susquehanna Valley.* Harrisburg, PA: Stackpole, 1973.

Bellah, Robert N. "Civil Religion in America." *Daedalus* 96 (Winter 1967), p. 1.

Bianchi, Eugene. *John XXIII and American Protestants.* Washington, D.C.: Corpus, 1968.

Billington, Ray Allen, *The Protestant Crusade, 1800–1860.* New York: Macmillan, 1938.

Birdwhistell, Ira V. "Southern Baptist Perceptions of and Responses to Roman Catholicism, 1917–1972." Ph. D. diss., Southern Baptist Theological Seminary, 1975.

Blanshard, Paul, *American Freedom and Catholic Power.* Boston: Beacon, 1949.

_____. *God and Man in Washington* Boston: Beacon, 1960.

_____. *Personal and Controversial: An Autobiography* Boston: Beacon, 1973.

Blumhofer, Edith L. *Restoring the Faith: The Assemblies of God, Pentecostalism and American Culture.* Urbana: University of Illinois Press, 1993.

Bodnar, John E., ed. *The Ethnic Experience in Pennsylvania.* Lewisburg, PA: Bucknell University Press, 1973.

Boggs, Lindy. *Washington through a Purple Veil.* New York: Harcourt, Brace, 1994.

Bone, Hugh A. "The 1960 Election in Washington." *Western Political Quarterly* 14 (March 1961), pp. 373–382.

Brenner, Saul. "Patterns of Jewish-Catholic Democratic Voting and the 1960 Presidential Vote." *Jewish Social Studies* (July 1964), pp. 169–178.

Brown, Robert McAfee. "Types of Anti-Catholicism." *Commonweal* 53 (November 25, 1955), pp. 193–196.

Brown, Thomas Elton. *Bible Belt Catholicism: A History of the Roman Catholic Church in Oklahoma, 1905–1945.* Yonkers: U.S. Catholic Historical Society, 1977.

Burner, David. *The Politics of Provincialism: The Democratic Party in Transition, 1918–1932.* New York: Alfred A. Knopf, 1968.

Burns, James MacGregor. *John Kennedy: A Political Profile.* New York: Harcourt, Brace, 1960.

Campbell, Angus, et al. *Elections and the*

Political Order. New York: John Wiley and Sons, 1966.

Carty, Thomas J. *A Catholic in the White House?: Religion, Politics, and John F. Kennedy's Presidential Campaign*. New York: Palgrave Macmillan, 2004.

Carwardine, Richard. "Lincoln's Religion." In *Our Lincoln: New Perspectives on Lincoln and His World*, edited by Eric Foner. New York: W.W. Norton, 2008.

Casey, Shaun A. *The Making of a Catholic President: Kennedy vs. Nixon 1960*. New York: Oxford University, 2009.

Christofferson, Bill. *The Man from Clear Lake: Earth Day Founder Senator Gaylord Nelson*. Madison: University of Wisconsin, 2004.

Cogley, John. *A Canterbury Tale: Experiences and Reflections, 1916–1976*. New York: Seabury, 1976.

_____. *Catholic America*. New York: Dial, 1973.

_____. "Kennedy the Catholic." *Commonweal* 79 (January 10, 1964).

Converse, Phillip E. *Religion and Politics: The 1960 Election*. Ann Arbor: University of Michigan Survey Research Center, 1961.

_____. "Stability and Change in 1960: A Reinstating Election." *American Political Science Review* 55 (June 1961), pp. 269–280.

Cooney, John. *The American Pope: The Life and Times of Francis Cardinal Spellman*. New York: Times Books, 1984.

Cosman, Bernard. "Presidential Republicanism in the South, 1960." *Journal of Politics* 24 (May 1962), pp. 303–322.

_____. "Religion and Race in Louisiana Presidential Politics, 1960." *Southwestern Social Science Quarterly* 43 (December 1962), p. 235–241.

Curry, Lerond. *Protestant-Catholic Relations in America: World War I through Vatican II*. Lexington: University Press of Kentucky, 1972.

Dallek, Robert. *An Unfinished Life: John F. Kennedy, 1917–1963*. Boston: Little, Brown, 2003.

David, Paul T., ed. *The Presidential Election and Transition 1960–61*. Washington, D.C.: Brookings Institution, 1961.

Davies, Sharon. *Rising Road: A True Tale of Love, Race and Religion in America*. New York: Oxford University Press, 2010.

Dawidowicz, Lucy S., and Leon J. Goldstein. *Politics in a Pluralist Democracy: Studies of Voting in the 1960 Election*. New York: Institute of Human Relations, 1963.

DeJong, Gerald F. *The Dutch in America, 1609–1974*. Boston: Twayne, 1975.

De Santis, Vincent P. "Catholicism and Presidential Elections, 1865–1900." *Mid-America* 42 (April 1960).

Desmond, Humphrey J. *The APA Movement*. Washington, D.C.: New Century, 1912.

Dewey, John. "Why I Am for Smith." *New Republic* 56 (November 7, 1928).

Dolan, Jay P. *The American Catholic Experience*. New York: Doubleday, 1985.

_____. *In Search of an American Catholicism: A History of Religion and Culture in Tension*. New York: Oxford University Press, 2002.

_____. "The Right of a Catholic to Be President." *Notre Dame* (Autumn 2008).

Donaghy, Thomas J. *Keystone Democrat: David Lawrence Remembered*. New York: Vantage, 1986.

Donaldson, Gary A. *The First Modern Campaign: Kennedy, Nixon, and the Election of 1960*. Lanham, MD: Rowman and Littlefield, 2007.

Driggs, Don W. "The 1960 Election in Nevada." *Western Political Quarterly* 14 (March 1961).

Dulce, Berton, and Edward J. Richter. *Religion and the Presidency*. New York: Macmillan, 1962.

Ellis, John Tracy. *American Catholicism*. Chicago: University of Chicago Press, 1955.

Espinosa, Gaston, ed. *Religion and the American Presidency*. New York: Columbia University Press, 2009.

Fair, Daryl R. "The Reaction of Pennsylvania Voters to Catholic Candidates." *Pennsylvania History* 32 (1965), pp. 305–315.

Feldman, Glenn. *Politics, Society and the Klan in Alabama, 1915–1949.* Tuscaloosa: University of Alabama Press, 1999.

Felknor, Bruce L. *Dirty Politics.* New York: W.W. Norton, 1966.

Fenton, John H. *The Catholic Vote.* New Orleans: Hauser, 1960.

———. *Salt of the Earth: An Informal Portrait of Richard Cardinal Cushing.* New York: Coward-McCann, 1966.

Fleming, Dan B., Jr. *Kennedy vs. Humphrey, West Virginia, 1960: The Pivotal Battle for the Democratic Presidential Nomination.* Jefferson, NC: McFarland, 1992.

Franco, Massimo. *Parallel Empires: The Vatican and the United States, Two Centuries of Alliance and Conflict.* New York: Doubleday, 2008.

Fuchs, Lawrence H. *John F. Kennedy and American Catholicism.* New York: Meredith, 1967.

Gastil, Raymond D. *Cultural Regions of the United States.* Seattle: University of Washington Press, 1975.

George, Carol N.R. *God's Salesman: Norman Vincent Peale and the Power of Positive Thinking.* New York: Oxford University Press, 1993.

Gifford, Laura Jane. *The Center Cannot Hold: The 1960 Presidential Election and the Rise of Modern Conservatism.* DeKalb: Northern Illinois University Press, 2009.

Gillis, Chester. *Roman Catholicism in America.* New York: Columbia University Press, 1999.

Gjerde, Jon, and Carlton C. Qualey. *Norwegians in Minnesota.* St. Paul: Minnesota Historical Society, 2002.

Gladden, Washington. "The Anti-Catholic Crusade." *Century,* March 1894.

Gleason, Philip. *Keeping the Faith: American Catholicism Past and Present.* Notre Dame, IN: University of Notre Dame Press, 1987.

Goldberg, Robert Alan, *Hooded Empire: The Ku Klux Klan in Colorado.* Urbana: University of Illinois Press, 1981.

Greeley, Andrew. *The Catholic Experience.* Garden City, NY: Doubleday, 1967.

Hamilton, Virginia V. *Lister Hill: Statesman from the South.* Chapel Hill: University of North Carolina Press, 1987.

Hanna, Mary T. *Catholics and American Politics.* Cambridge, MA: Harvard University Press, 1979.

Hannan, (Archbishop) Philip. *The Archbishop Wore Combat Boots,* with Nancy Collins and Peter Finney, Jr. Huntington, IN: Our Sunday Visitor, 2010.

Hardeman, D.B., and Donald C Bacon. *Rayburn: A Biography.* Lanham, MD: Madison, 1987.

Harris, Carl V. *Political Power in Birmingham, 1871–1921.* Knoxville: University of Tennessee Press, 1977.

Hart, Marjorie. *Summer at Tiffany.* New York: William Morrow, 2007.

Hays, Samuel P., ed. *City at the Point: Essays on the Social History of Pittsburgh.* Pittsburgh: University of Pittsburgh Press, 1989.

Hennesey, James (S.J.). *American Catholics: A History of the Roman Catholic Community in the United States.* New York: Oxford University Press, 1981.

Herberg, Will. *Protestant-Catholic-Jew: An Essay in American Religious Sociology.* Garden City, NY: Doubleday, 1955.

Higham, John. *Strangers in the Land: Patterns in American Nativism.* New Brunswick, NJ: Rutgers University Press, 1955.

Hofstadter, Richard. "Could a Protestant Have Beaten Hoover in 1928?" *Reporter,* March 17, 1960.

Holmes, Fred L. *Old World Wisconsin.* Eau Claire, WI: E.M. Hale, 1944.

Holmquist, June Drenning, ed. *They Chose Minnesota: A Survey of the State's Ethnic Groups.* St. Paul: Minnesota Historical Society, 1981.

Hughes, Richard. *Reviving the Ancient*

Faith: The Story of the Churches of Christ in America. Grand Rapids, MI: Eerdmans, 1996.

Iverson, Noel. *Germania, U.S.A.: Social Change in New Ulm, Minnesota*. Minneapolis: University of Minnesota Press, 1966.

Jackson, Kenneth L. *The Ku Klux Klan in the City, 1915–1930*. Chicago: Ivan R. Dee, 1992.

James, E.S. "Vote Your Convictions." *Baptist Standard*, November 2, 1960.

Jeansomme, Glen. *Gerald L.K. Smith: Minister of Hate*. New Haven: Yale University Press, 1988.

Jenkins, Philip. *Hoods and Shirts: The Extreme Right in Pennsylvania, 1925–1950*. Chapel Hill: University of North Carolina Press, 1997.

Jenkins, William D. *Steel Valley Klan: The Ku Klux Klan in Ohio's Mahoning Valley*. Kent, Ohio: Kent State University Press, 1990.

Jordan, Mildred. *The Distelfink Country of the Pennsylvania Dutch*. New York: Crown, 1978.

Jordan, Patrick, and Paul Baumann, eds. *Commonweal Confronts the Century: Liberal Convictions, Catholic Tradition*. New York: Simon & Schuster Touchstone, 1999.

Kahn, David Paul. *The Neglected Voter: White Men and the Democratic Dilemma*. New York: Palgrave Macmillan, 2007.

Kane, John J. *Catholic-Protestant Conflicts in America*. Chicago: Henry Regnery, 1955.

Kellstedt, Lyman A., and Mark A. Noll. "Religion, Voting for President, and Party Identification, 1948–1984." In *Religion & American Politics: From the Colonial Period to the 1980s*, edited by Mark A. Noll. New York: Oxford University Press, 1990.

Kemper, Deane A. "John F. Kennedy before the Greater Houston Ministerial Association." Ph.D. diss., Michigan State University, 1968.

Kennedy, John F. *The Speeches of Senator John F. Kennedy: Presidential Campaign of 1960*. Washington, D.C.: U.S. Government Printing Office, 1961.

Key, V.O., Jr. *The Responsible Electorate: Rationality in Presidential Voting, 1936–1960*. Cambridge, MA: Belknap Press of Harvard University, 1966.

Kinzer, Donald L. *An Episode in Anti-Catholicism: The American Protective Association*. Seattle: University of Washington Press, 1964.

Lally, Francis J. *The Catholic Church in a Changing America*. Boston: Little, Brown, 1962.

Lee, Eugene C., and William Buchanan. "The 1960 Election in California." *Western Political Quarterly* 14 (March 1961), pp. 309–326.

Lenski, Gerhard, *The Religious Factor*. Garden City, NY: Doubleday, 1961.

Levy, Mark K., and Michael S. Kramer. *The Ethnic Factor: How America's Minorities Decide Elections*. New York: Simon & Schuster, 1972.

Lichtman, Allan J. *Prejudice and the Old Politics: The Presidential Election of 1928*. Chapel Hill: University of North Carolina Press, 1979.

_____. *White Protestant Nation: The Rise of the American Conservative Movement*. New York: Atlantic Monthly Press, 2008.

Lipset, Seymour Martin. *The Politics of Unreason*. New York: Harper & Row, 1970.

Lipsky, Roma. "Electioneering Among the Minorities." *Commentary*, 31 May 1961, pp. 428–432.

Lord, Donald C. *John F. Kennedy*. Woodbury, NY: Barron, 1977.

Lubell, Samuel. *The Future of American Politics*. Garden City, NY: Doubleday, 1956.

Marlin, George J. *The American Catholic Voter: 200 Years of Political Impact*. South Bend, IN: St. Augustine's, 2004.

Martin, Boyd A. "The 1960 Election in Idaho." *Western Political Quarterly* 14 (March 1961), pp. 339–342.

Martin, Curtis. "The 1960 Election in

Colorado." *Western Political Quarterly* 14 (March 1961), pp. 327–330.

Martin, William. *A Prophet with Honor: The Billy Graham Story*. New York: William Morrow, 1991.

Marty, Myron A. *Lutherans and Roman Catholicism: The Changing Conflict: 1917–1963.* Notre Dame, IN: University of Notre Dame Press, 1968.

Massa, Mark S. "A Catholic for President?: John F. Kennedy and the 'Secular' Theology of the Houston Speech, 1960." *Journal of Church and State* 39 (Spring 1997), pp. 297–317.

Matthews, Christopher. *Kennedy and Nixon: The Rivalry That Shaped Postwar America*. New York: Simon & Schuster, 1996.

McClerren, Beryl F. "The Southern Baptist State Newspapers and the Religious Issue during the Presidential Campaigns of 1928 and 1960." Ph. D. diss., Southern Illinois University, 1963.

McKenna, William J. "The Influence of Religion in the Pennsylvania Elections of 1958 and 1960." *Pennsylvania History* 29 (1962), pp. 407–419.

Merwin, W.S. "Distances." In *Our Roots Grow Deeper Than We Know*, edited by Lee Gutkind. Pittsburgh: University of Pittsburgh Press, 1985.

Meyer, Carl S. "Symposium on a Roman Catholic President." *American Lutheran*. 43 (May 1960), pp. 6–15.

Michener, James A. *Report of the County Chairman*. New York: Random House, 1961.

Miller, (Reverend) H. Earl. *Lutheran Witness,* August 23, 1960.

Miller, Robert Moats. *Bishop G. Bromley Oxnam: Paladin of Liberal Protestantism*. Nashville: Abingdon, 1990.

Moore, Andrew S. *The South's Tolerable Alien: Roman Catholics in Alabama and Georgia 1945–1970*. Baton Rouge: Louisiana State University Press, 2007.

Moore, Edmund A. *A Catholic Runs for President*. New York: Ronald, 1957.

Moore, Leonard J. *Citizen Klansmen: The Ku Klux Klan in Indiana, 1921–1928*. Chapel Hill: University of North Carolina Press, 1991.

Morgan, Richard E. *The Politics of Religious Conflict*. New York: Pegasus, 1968.

Morris, Charles R. *American Catholics: The Saints and Sinners Who Built America's Most Powerful Church*. New York: Times Books, 1997.

Murray, John Courtney. *We Hold These Truths: Catholic Reflection on the American Proposition*. New York: Sheed & Ward, 1960.

Newton, Michael. *The Invisible Empire: The Ku Klux Klan in Florida*. Gainesville: University Press of Florida, 2001.

Nordstrom, Justin. *Danger on the Doorstep: Anti-Catholicism and American Print Culture in the Progressive Era*. Notre Dame, IN: University of Notre Dame Press, 2006.

Odegard, Peter H., ed. *Religion and Politics*. Dobbs Ferry, NY: Oceana, 1960.

Parsons, William T. *The Pennsylvania Dutch*. Boston: Twayne, 1976.

Phillips, Kevin. *The Emerging Republican Majority*. New Rochelle, NY: Arlington House, 1969.

Pike, James A. *A Roman Catholic in the White House* Garden City, NY: Doubleday, 1960.

Poling, Daniel Alfred. *Mine Eyes Have Seen*. New York: McGraw-Hill, 1959.

Prendergast, William B. *The Catholic Voter in American Politics*. Washington, D.C.: Georgetown University Press, 1999.

Pritchard, Linda K. "Religion in Pittsburgh." In *City at the Point: Essays on the Social History of Pittsburgh*, edited by Samuel P. Hays. Pittsburgh: University of Pittsburgh Press, 1989.

Pruden, Edward Hughes. *A Window on Washington*. New York: Vantage, 1976.

Public Papers of the President of the Unites States: John F. Kennedy, 1961. Washington: U.S. Government Printing Office, 1962.

Raab, Earl, ed. *Religious Conflict in America*. Garden City, NY: Doubleday, 1960.

Reichley, James. *The Art of Government: Reform and Organization Politics in Philadelphia*. New York: Fund for the Republic, 1959.

Reuter, Frank T. *Catholic Influence on American Colonial Policies 1898–1904*. Austin: University of Texas Press, 1967.

Richards, Ann. *Straight from the Heart: My Life in Politics and Other Places*. New York: Simon & Schuster, 1989.

Rippley, LaVern J. *The Immigrant Experience in Wisconsin*. Boston: Twayne, 1985.

Roosevelt, Eleanor. *The Autobiography of Eleanor Roosevelt*. New York: Harper & Row, 1961.

Rosten, Leo, ed. *Religions of America*. New York: Simon & Schuster, 1975.

Roy, Ralph Lord. *Apostles of Discord: A Study of Organized Bigotry and Disruption on the Fringes of Protestantism*. Boston: Beacon, 1953.

Schlesinger, Arthur, Jr. *Kennedy or Nixon: Does It Make Any Difference?* New York: Macmillan, 1960.

Settel, T.S., ed. *The Faith of JFK*. New York: E.P. Dutton, 1965.

Sievers, Harry J. "The Catholic Indian School Issue and the Presidential Election of 1892." *Catholic Historical Review* 38 (July 1952), pp. 129–155.

Simon, Paul *P.S.: The Autobiography of Paul Simon*. Chicago: Bonus, 1999.

_____. "Roman Catholicism and the 1960 Elections." *Cresset*, 23 (April 1960), pp. 6–9.

Smith, Alfred E. *Campaign Addresses of Governor Alfred E. Smith: Democratic Candidate for President, 1928*. Washington, D.C.: Democratic National Committee, 1929.

Smith, Richard Norton. *Thomas E. Dewey and His Times*. New York: Simon & Schuster, 1982.

Smith, William D. "Alfred E. Smith and John F. Kennedy: The Religious Issue during the Presidential Campaigns of 1928 and 1960." Ph. D. diss., University of Southern Illinois, 1964.

Soike, Lowell J. *Norwegian Americans and the Politics of Dissent, 1880–1924*. Northfield, MN: St. Olaf College Press, 1991.

Sorensen, Theodore. *Counselor: A Life at the Edge of History*. New York: HarperCollins, 2008.

_____. *Kennedy*. New York: Harper & Row, 1965.

Squeri, Laurence. "The Pocono Resort Economy: Economic Growth and Social Conservatism, 1865–1940." *Pennsylvania Magazine of History and Biography* 115 (October 1991), pp. 489–491.

Stedman, Murray S., Jr. *Religion and Politics in America*. New York: Harcourt, Brace & World, 1964.

Stumme, John R. "Lutherans on Religion and the 1960 Presidential Election." *Journal of Lutheran Ethics*, 7 November 2007, pp. 1–24.

Swarthout, John M. "The 1960 Election in Oregon." *Western Political Quarterly* 14 (March 1961), pp. 355–364.

Swierenga, Robert P. "Ethno-religious Political Behavior in the Mid-Nineteenth Century: Voting, Values, Cultures." In *Religion and American Politics*, edited by Mark A. Noll. New York: Oxford University Press, 1990.

Taft, Charles P., and Bruce L. Felknor. *Prejudice and Politics*. New York: Anti-Defamation League of B'nai B'rith, 1960.

Thompson, James J., Jr. *Fleeing the Whore of Babylon: A Modern Conversion Story*. Westminster, MD: Christian Classics, 1986.

Toth, Susan Allen. *Blooming: A Small-Town Girlhood*. New York: Ballantine, 1998.

Van Allen, Roger. *The Commonweal and American Catholicism: The Magazine, the Movement, the Meaning*. Philadelphia: Fortress, 1974.

Ventura, Jesse. *I Ain't Got Time to Bleed*. New York: Villard, 1999.

Wald, Kenneth D. *Religion and Politics in the United States.* New York: St. Martin's, 1987.

Walker, David B. "The Presidential Politics of the Franco-Americans." *Canadian Journal of Economics and Political Science,* 28 (August 1962), pp. 353–363.

Wangler, Thomas E. "American Catholics and the Spanish-American War." In *Catholics in America 1776–1976,* edited by Robert Trisco. Washington, D.C.: National Conference of Catholic Bishops, 1976.

Watson, Richard A. "Religion and Politics in Mid-America: Presidential Voting in Missouri in 1928 and 1960." *Midcontinent American Studies Journal* 5 (Spring 1964).

Weber, Michael P. *Don't Call Me Boss: David L. Lawrence, Pittsburgh's Renaissance Mayor.* Pittsburgh: University of Pittsburgh Press, 1988.

White, Theodore H. *The Making of the President, 1960.* New York: Atheneum, 1961.

Williams, Michael. *The Shadow of the Pope.* New York: Whittlesey, 1932.

Wolfe, James S. "The Religious Issue Revisited: Presbyterian Responses to Kennedy's Presidential Campaign." *Journal of Presbyterian History* 57 (Spring 1979), pp. 1–18.

Wood, Ralph. *The Pennsylvania Germans.* Princeton, NJ: Princeton University Press, 1942.

WPA Guide to Minnesota. (1938) St. Paul: Minnesota Historical Society, 1985.

Additional Bibliographic Information

All election returns are official and certified. County returns for 1956 and 1960 are found in *America Votes 1956–57,* compiled and edited by Richard M. Scammon (New York: Macmillan, 1958) and *America Votes* 4, compiled and edited by Richard M. Scammon (Pittsburgh: University of Pittsburgh Press, 1962).

Detailed precinct returns by township, village and borough were provided by the office of the secretary of state for Connecticut, Massachusetts, Maine, New Hampshire, New Jersey, Rhode Island and Vermont. The Pennsylvania returns are from the *Pennsylvania Manual* 93 (1957–58) and *Pennsylvania Manual* 95 (1961–62), published by the Commonwealth of Pennsylvania in Harrisburg. Wisconsin data are published in the *Wisconsin Blue Books* for 1957–58 and 1961–62, published by the Wisconsin Legislative Reference Bureau in Madison. Iowa returns are from the Iowa *Official Register,* 1957–58 and 1961–62 (vols. 37 and 39), published by the State of Iowa in Des Moines. Minnesota returns are found in the *Legislative Manual,* 1957–1958 and 1961–1962, published by the State of Minnesota at the state capitol in St. Paul.

Religious membership data pertinent to this study include *Churches and Church Membership in the United States 1971* by Douglas W. Johnson, Paul R. Picard, and Bernard Quinn (Washington, DC: Glenmary Research Center, 1974). It was based on material gathered by the National Council of the Churches of Christ in the U.S.A. Earlier, but somewhat less reliable, NCC data from 1952 are found in Wilbur Zelinsky, *Exploring the Beloved Country: Geographic Forays into American Society and Culture* (Iowa City: University of Iowa Press, 1994), pp. 63–131.

Useful comparative data are found in *Religious Bodies 1926* and *Religious Bodies 1936,* published by the Bureau of the Census in 1930 and 1941 respectively. These volumes, often ignored by scholars, include a mountain of religious membership data for each county and major city. Similar studies were compiled by the Census Bureau in 1916, 1906 and 1890.

The personal papers of James Wilson Wine, Jr., are preserved at the John F. Kennedy Presidential Library in Boston.

Series 1 includes approximately 300 items classified as the John F. Kennedy Campaign Files.

The Fair Campaign Practices Committee Collection is housed in the Manuscripts Division, Special Collections, Lauinger Library, at Georgetown University, 3700 O Street, NW, Washington, DC 20057. It covers the life of the committee, from 1954 through 1976, and includes 48 boxes of material. Boxes 2, 3, and 4 include material from the 1960 presidential election.

Index

Numbers in ***bold italics*** indicate pages with photographs.

The Abaree 57
Adams, George W. 66
Advent Christian Church 57
Advent Christian Witness 57
Agency for International Development 221
Ahlstrom, Sidney 208
Alabama 22–24, 49, 53, 68, 122–125
Alaska 168–169
Alley, Robert S. 44–45, 217
Almond, Gov. Lindsay 137
Alter, Archbishop Karl J. 37–38, 70
America 33, 37–38, 68–69, 220
American Ecclesiastical Review 69–70
American Jewish Committee 33
American Jewish Congress 33
American Protective Association 8
American Rationalist Federation 62
American Society of Newspaper Editors 22, 231–238
Anderson, Totton 179
Andrews, Charles R. 70
anti–Catholic literature 5, 30, 32–33, 46–68, 117, 128, 159, 165–166, 170, 178, 198, 224
Anti-Defamation League of B'nai B'rith 33, 71–72, 80
Appel, Robert 175
Archer, Glenn 71
Arizona 68, 174
Arkansas 65, 125–126
Armstrong, O.K. 39–40
Arrien, John 63–64
Article VI, U.S. Constitution 22, 27–28, 31, 42, 44, 71, 237
Aspinall, Rep. Wayne 175
Assemblies of God 32, 61, 117

Atlanta Constitution 129
Atlantic Monthly 13–14, 33
Ave Maria 69

Bacon, Donald C. 136
Baggaley, Andrew R. 204
Bailey, John 77
Baptist Examiner 56
Baptist Joint Committee 35
Baptist Standard 35
Baptists 22–24, 30–35, 39–40, 48–50, 56, 61, 65–66, 84, 87, 89–91, 94–95, 117, 126–127, 129–132, 134, 136, ***161***, 161–162, 175–178, 222
Barrett, Patricia 22, 30, 33, 68
Baxter, Rev. Batsell Barrett 135
Bealty, Rev. Henry C. 50
Bedini, Gaetano 6
Beenken, Rev. Gilbert M. 49
Beers, Paul B. 196–197
Bell, Rev. L. Nelson 24, 49–50
Bellah, Robert N. 44
Benedict XV, Pope 11
Bennett, John C. 25, 70–71, 73
Benson, Ezra Taft 141
Bible reading in publics schools 7, 19, 74
Bible School Press 61
Billington, Ray Allen 5
Binns, Walter Pope 35
Black, Hugo 123
Blaine, James G. 7–8
Blake, Rev. Eugene Carson 73
Blanshard, Paul 73
Blikstad, Vernon 59
Blumhofer, Edith L. 117
Boggs, Lindy 32

255

Index

Bone, Hugh 172–173
Bonnell, John Sutherland 71
Book and Bible House 58
Border States 110–111
Borleis, Harry F. 64
Bosley, Rev. Harold A. 48, 70
Brandeis, Louis 11
Brewer, Rollin 19
Broder, David 31
Brown, Rev. Dennis J. 64
Brown, Gov. Edmund 19, 74, 77, 80, 170
Brown, Rev. Robert McAfee 70
Bryan, William Jennings 10
Buchanan, James 6
Burchard, Rev. Samuel D. 7
Burner, David 16
Burns, James MacGregor 73, 213–214
Bush, George W. 223
Bushnell, George 42
Byrd, Sen. Harry 83, 137

Calderwood, David 68
Caldwell, Willie W. 14–15
California 18–19, 42, 51, 67–68, 80, 169–170
California Poll 169
Callahan, Daniel 70
Campbell, James 5
Carlson, C. Emanuel 35
Carolina Israelite 71
Carroll, Charles 5, 47
Carty, Thomas J. 129, 170
Carwardine, Richard 7
Casey, Shaun A. 31, 34, 36–37, 40, 81
Cater, Douglass 72
Catholic press 9, 37–38, 68–70
Catholic World 37, 69
Catts, Sidney J. 126
Cedar Rapids Gazette 170
Charleston Gazette 119
Chillicothe Constitution-Tribune 117
Christian Advocate 23
Christian Century 25, 49, 65, 70
Christian Herald 24, 70
Christian Heritage 57, 62
Christian Nationalist Crusade 67
Christian Science Monitor 75
Christianity and Crisis 70
Christianity Today 23–24, 70–71
Christmas address by JFK 215
Christofferson, Bill 206
Christ's Mission 57, 62, 64
Church Herald and Holiness Banner 57

Church History 17
Church of Christ 31, 68, 89, 94–95, 124–125, 134–135
Church of God 61
The Church Speaks 57
church-state issues 18, 27–28, 217–222
Cicognani, Archbishop Amleto 221
Citizens for Religious Freedom 24–25, 58–59
Civil religion 44–45, 216–217
Clancy, William 73
Clark, Mark 18, 49
Clay, Henry 5
Cleveland, Grover 9
Cogdill, Roy E. 65
Cogley, John 34, 211, 216, 218
Collins, Carr 40
Colorado 66, 174–176
Colson, Charles 1
Commentary 33, 71
Commonweal 37, 69
Concordia Publishing House 57–58
Conn, Charles W. 61
Connecticut 46, 67, 98–99
Connell, Rev. Francis J. 70
Converse, Philip E. 90
Conversion Center, Inc. 64
The Convert 59
Cooney, John 40–41, 220
Coronet 60, 73
Cosman, Bernard 131
Coughlan, Robert 33, 73
The Cresset 163
Criswell, Rev. W.A. 22–23, **23**, 48, 51
Cronin, Rev. John 40
Cross Currents 70
Cunneen, Joseph 70
Cushing, Cardinal Richard 38, **39**, 212

Daley, C.R. 56
Davidson, Rev. James E. 49
Davis, John W. 13
Dawidowicz, Lucy S. 134, 162, 167
De Gryse, Louis M. 150
DeJong, Gerald F. 104
Delaney, Rep. James J. 219
Delaware 110–111
Delaware County Daily Times 107
Deming Headlight 178
Democratic National Committee 16, 42–43
Democratic National Convention 67–68, 75–80
De Paulo, J. Raymond 120–121

De Santis, Vincent P. 8–10
Dewey, John 13
Dewey, Thomas E. 1
Di Domenica, Rev. Angelo 59
Disciples of Christ 94, 164
District of Columbia 221
Donaghy, Thomas J. 19
Donegan, Bishop Horace 28
Dorchester, Daniel 9
Douglas, Sen. Paul 60, 73
Douglas, Stephen 7
Driggs, Don 177
Duffy, Patrick 13
Dugger, Ronnie 73
Dulce, Berton 32, 90
Dulles, John Foster 214
Dun, Bishop Angus 28
Dunham Publishing Company 74–75
Dunlap, Alexander O. 64
Dutch Reformed Church 65, 85, 87, 94, 104, 139–140, 150, 157, 165, 173, 177, 204–205

Eau Claire Daily Telegraph 144
Eisenhower, Dwight D. 45, 62, 98, 214
Eisenhower, Julie Nixon 1
Emrich, Bishop Richard 42
England, Archbishop John 47
Episcopalians 6, 13, 16, 19, 28, 42, 73
Espinosa, Gaston 1
Evangelicals 31, 35–37, 50, 60, 62, 166, 171–173, 193
Evins, Joe 135

Fair, Daryl R. 193
Fair Campaign Practices Committee (FCPC) 20, 29, 31–33, 46, **54**, **55**, **63**, **78**, **161**, **198**, 223
Faires, Nora 194–195
Faith, Prayer and Tract League 65
farm states 92, 138
Faubus, Gov. Orval 40, 127, 131
Felknor, Bruce L. 20, 29, **30**, 74
Feuer, Lewis S. 72
Fey, Harold E. 25, 65
Fillmore, Millard 5–6
Fitzsimmons, Daniel 5
Fleming, Dan B. 119–120
Florida 49, 56, 126–128
Ford, George L. 60
Freethinkers of America 67
Fremont, John C. 5
Fuchs, Lawrence H. 23, 69, 217–218

Full Salvation Tract Society 65
Fulton, Justin Dewey 64

Gallup Poll 2, 82, 92
Garver, Rev. Stuart P. 62, 64
Gastil, Raymond D. 168–169, 179
Gaston, Rev. Marcus 51
Gates, Rev. Robert P. 50
George, Carol 25–26
Georgetown University Lauinger Library 46, 254
Georgia 55–56, 61, 128–129
Gettysburg Times 106
Geyelin, Philip L. 73
Gibbons, Cardinal James 47
Gilbert, Rabbi Arthur 80
Gilbert, Dan 67, 79
Gilpin, John R. 56
Gjerde, Jon 151
Gleason, Phillip 211
Golden, Harry 71
Goldstein, Leon J. 134, 162, 167
Gospel Advocate 52
Gospel Defender 53
Gospel Hour News 53
Graham, Rev. Billy 35–37, **36**, 220
Grant, Ulysses S. 7
Great Lakes States 159–160, 167
Greeley, Rev. Andrew 217, 220
Gunther, John 121

Ham, Rev. Mordecai Fowler 49
Hampel, Harry 51, **54**, 56
Hancock, Winfield 7
Hannan, Archbishop Philip 212–213
Hansen, Rev. Thomas 49
Hardeman, D.B. 136
Hardon, Rev. John 69
Harper's 33
Harper's Weekly 7
Harris, Carl 123
Harris, Louis 170
Harrison, Benjamin 9
Harrison, Eugene 66
Hart, Marjorie 141
Hawaii 170–171
Heflin, Tom 14
Hennesey, James 211
Herald Press 165–166
Hermann, Albert 40
Hertzberg, Arthur 71
Higgins, Monsignor George 81
Higham, John 86

Index

Hill, Lister 123
Hillis, Don W. **52–53**, 74–75
Hobbs, Rev. Herschel H. 49
Hofstadter, Richard 16
Holdridge, General Herbert G. 57
Holmes, Fred L. 204
Homiletic and Pastoral Review 69
Hoover, Herbert 15
Howard, V.E. 135
Hoyt, Robert 69
Humphrey, Hubert 22, 143, 203

Idaho 176
Illinois 37, 48, 50–51, 60, 66, 73, 160, 162–163
Indian schools 8–9
Indiana 163–164
Iowa 138–142
Ireland, Archbishop John 10
Iverson, Noel 145

Jackson, Andrew 8, 31
Jackson, D.N. 66
Jackson, Kenneth L. 171
James, E.S. 35
Jeansomme, Glen 67
Jefferson, Thomas 5, 8, 222
Jewish Forum 72
Jewish Frontier 72
Jewish Ledger 72
Jews 16, 42, 71–72, 165, 169
John XXIII, Pope 55, 141, 216
Johnson, James Harvey 67
Journal of Church and State 222
Journalism Quarterly 33
Jubilee 69
Judaism 72
Judd, Walter 144
Junior, Rev. Fred 58

Kamp, Jos. P. 67
Kansas 46, 57, 142–143
Keating, Sen. Kenneth 70
Kefauver, Estes 18
Kellstedt, Lyman A. 91
Kennedy, Robert F. 1, 42, 80, 224
Kentucky 42, 56, 61, 110, 112–113
Kerry, Sen. John 224
Kerwin, Jerome 70
Key, V.O. 90
Kieda, Francis J. 57
King, Rev. W.L. 58, 223
Knebel, Fletcher 33, 73

"Knights of Columbus Oath" 119, 223
Know Nothing Party 6–7
Knowland, William 19
Ku Klux Klan 11–13, 103, 123, 126–127, 163–164, 168, 171, 175

LaFollette, Robert 13, 73
Lambert, O.C. 68, **125**
Langlie, Gov. Arthur B. 173
Larson, Martin A. 61–62
Lawrence, Gov. David L. 19–20, 80, 105
Lehmann, Leo H. 62
Leo XIII, Pope 8
Leonard, Bishop Adna W. 12
Lewis, Joseph 67
The Liberal: Bulletin of Friendship 61
Liberal League 61
Lichtenberger, Right Rev. Arthur C. 28
Lichtman, Allan J. 2, 17–18
Life 33, 73
Lincoln, Abraham 6–7
Lindbeck, George 208
Lindsay, Gordon 51
Lindsey, Rev. Harold E. 50
Lipset, Seymour Martin 33
Long, Huey 130
Look 21, 33, 73
Lord, Donald C. 91–92
Louisiana 130–131
Lowell, Rev. C. Stanley 71
Lutherans 19, 32, 57–58, 84–85, 87, 94–95, 129, 141, 143, 150–152, 156–158, 162–163, 176, 203, 205–208

Mackay, Rev. John 72
Madden, Rep. Ray 219
Madison, Pres. James 222
Maine 99–101
Margolin, Morton 175
Marin, Munoz 32
Marney, Carlyle 28
Marshall, Charles C. 13
Martin, Curtis 175
Martin, Luther W. 61
Martin, William 35–37
Maryland 6, 15, 110, 113–116
Masonic Home Journal 61
Masons 42, 50, 54, 60–62, 193
Massa, Mark S. 214
Massachusetts 46, 50, 66, 101–102
McAdoo, William G. 13
McCarthy, Sen. Eugene 70, 224
McClerren, Beryl F. 35

Index

McGlothlen, Rev. Gaye L. 50
McGonigle, Arthur T. 19
McIlnay, Philip 65
McKay, David 40, 179
McKinley, William 10–11
McLoughlin, Emmett 59, 68, 174
Meadows, Ethel 64
Mennonites 42, 142, 166
Merwin, W.S. 193
Methodist Challenge 54
Methodists 15, 23–24, 48, 50, 54, 71, 73, 85, 87, 89, 94–95, 103–104, 175–176
Meyer, Carl S. 57–58
Michener, James A. 1–2, 4, 29, 198–199, 224
Michigan 65, 164–166
Midwest/Plains States 138
Miller, William Lee 71
Ministerial Association of Greater Houston 26–27, 227–231
Minnesota 49, 51, 59, 65, 143–156
Mississippi 131–132
Missouri 31–32, 56, 110, 116–117
Montana 176–177
Montano, Walter 62
Montas, Jacques 57
Moore, Andrew 124–125
Moore, Edmund A. 14
Morgan, Thomas J. 9
Mormons 40, 88, 176–179
Morris, Charles 211
Morse, Samuel F.P. 5
Murphy, J.F. 66
Murray, John Courtney 69, 216

Nation 33
National Association of Evangelicals 22–23, 31, 60
National Catholic Welfare Conference 81, 219
National Conference of Christians and Jews 33, 222
National Council of Churches 33–34, 80
Nebraska 50, 67, 156
Nelley, Thomas J. 197
Nelson, Gov. Gaylord 206
Neusner, Rabbi Jacob 72
Nevada 177
New Age 54
New England 50, 97, 108–109
New Hampshire 42, 102–103
New Jersey 103–104
New Leader 33, 72–73

New Mexico 177–178
New Republic 13, 33, 72
New York 67, 104–105
New York Times 27
Newsweek 33, 72
Niebuhr, Reinhold 25, 72, 216
Nixon, Richard, and the religious issues 39–41, 137
Noll, Mark A. 91
Nordstrom, Justin 86
North Carolina 49–50, 56, 132–133
North Dakota 156–157
Northeast 97–98

O'Brien, Rev. John 73
Ockenga, Rev. Harold J. 24, 50
Odom, Jack 65–66
Ohio 15, 25, 53, 65, 74–75, 166–167
Oklahoma 15, 46, 49, 57, 79, 110–111, 118–119
O'Neill, Rep. Tip 219
Oregon 50, 57, 61, 171–172
Oshkosh Daily Northwestern 159
Osterhus Publishing Company 59
Oxnam, Bishop G. Bromley 28, 73

Pacific Coast States 167–168
Palmer, Gordon 56
Parochial school aid 7, 12, 18, 25, 49, 52, 219–220, 233–234
Parsons, William T. 195
Patterson, Gov. John 23
Paul VI, Pope 221
Peale, Norman Vincent 24–26, 71
Pearson, Roy 56
Pelikan, Jaroslav 73, 208
Pennsylvania 19–20, 29, 32, 42, 59, 61, 64–65, 105–107, 187–202, 223
"Pennsylvania Dutch" 195
Pentecostal Evangel 51, 61, 117
Pentecostal Free Will Baptist Messenger 56
Pentecostals 51
Peters, Esther 120
Phillips, Bishop Glenn R. 175
Phillips, Kevin 101, 105
Pierce, Franklin 6
Pike, Bishop James 19, 28, 73
Pius XI, Pope 12
Pius XII, Pope 40
Poling, Rev. Daniel A. 24
Polk, James K. 5
Pollard, Rev. Ramsey 24, *24*
Presbyterian Banner 195

Presbyterian Journal 50
Presbyterian Life 71
Presbyterian Outlook 71
Presbyterians 29, 49–50, 70–71, 73, 80, 140, 194–195, 216–217
Price, Rev. Sterling L. 56
Pritchard, Linda K. 194
Progressive 33, 73
Prohibition 15, 46–47, 79, 97, 102–103, 122, 150, 166, 196
Prophetic Ensign 56
Protestant Action 64
Protestant Council of New York 222
Protestant Journal 56
Protestant press 23, 32, 35, 70–71
Protestants and Other Americans United 81
Pruden, Edward Hughes 35
Puerto Rico 32, 69

Qualey, Carlton C. 151

Ramm, Bernard 57
Raskob, John J. 16
Rayburn, Sam 135–136
Reconstructionist 72
Reed, John Shelton 121
Reformation Sunday 31–32, 74
Reichley, James 193–194
The Reporter 72
Republican National Committee 15, 17–18, 31
Rhode Island 107
Richards, Ann 136
Richter, Edward J. 32, 90
Riddle, Oscar 62
Riippa, Timo 151
Rippley, LaVern J. 204–205
Robacher, Earl 195
Rocky Mountain News 175
Rocky Mountain West 173–174, 180
Roosevelt, Eleanor 17
Roosevelt, Pres. Franklin Delano 49, 217
Roosevelt, Pres. Theodore 10
Roper, Elmo 73, 82
Ross, Bob L. 56
Rowell, J.B 57
"Rum, Romanism and Rebellion" 7
rural vote 85–87, 147–153

The Saints Herald 51
Saturday Review 73
Sayre, Dean Francis B. 28
Scammon, Richard M. 91, 203–204

Scharper, Philip 69
Schlesinger, Arthur, Jr. 34, 73
Scott, Leslie M. 61
Scott, Winfield 6
Scottish Rite Torch 61
Seventh-day Adventists 19, 113–115, 173
Sheboygan Journal 159
Sheerin, John B. 69
Shepherd, Margaret 58
Sherrill, Bishop Henry Knox 28
Shuler, Rev. Robert P. 54
Shuster, George N. 72
Sievers, Harry J. 9
The Sign 37–38
Simon, Paul 162–163, 218
small town vote 96, 145–147, 153–156
Smith, Alfred E. 12–18, 49, 54, 84, 89, 136, 162
Smith, Gerald L.K. 67
Smith, Gov. Hulett C. 120
Smith, Luther A. 54, 62
Smith, W.R. 40
Smith, Wallace 51
Smith, William D. 218, 223
Smylie, James H. 17
Social Order 69
Social Progress 71
Soike, Lowell J. 151
Sorensen, Theodore 27–28, 80, 219–220
the South 121–122
South Carolina 37, 133–134
South Dakota 157
Southerner 55–56
Spanish American War 10
Spellman, Cardinal Francis J. 13–14, 38, 40–41, *41*, 74, 219–221
Springer, Rev. Harvey 78, 175–176
Squeri, Laurence 196
States' Rights Party 83, 85, 87–88, 130–132, 137
Stedman, Murray 71
Sterling, Claire 72
Stevenson, Adlai 18, 25, 34, 69–70
Stumme, John R. 207
suburban vote 92, 98
Sumner, Robert L. 51
Sunday School Times 57
Sunshine News 51
Swarthout, John 171–172
Swierenga, Robert P. 8
Swiss Reformed Protestants 206, 210
The Sword of the Lord 51
Szundy, Noel Bausher 195

Taft, Charles P. 20, 223
Taft, William Howard 11
tax exemption and church political activity 223–224
Taylor, Myron 49
Tennessee 24, 50–52, 61, 134–135
Texas 22, 50–51, 53, 65–66, 135–136
Texas Observer 73
Thompson, James J., Jr. 114–115
Time 33, 72, 126
Tolle, James M. 66
Toth, Susan Allen 140–141
Truman, Harry S. 18, 34–35, 49

Unitarians 11
United Church Herald 56
United Church of Christ 95
University of Michigan 2, 83
urban vote 83
U.S. News and World Report 33, 72
Utah 178–179

Van Allen, Rodger 211–212
Van Dusen, Rev. Henry 70
Vatican 7, 10–13, 18, 49–51, 53, 72, 221, 234
Vaught, Rev. W.O., Jr. 65, 126
Ventura, Jesse 143–144
Vermont 107–108
Virginia 136–137
Virginia Statute of Religious Freedom 27, 229
Voice of Freedom 51
Voice of Healing 51
Vorspan, Albert 72

Walker, David B. 100–101
Wall Street Journal 73
Wallace, Gov. George 220
Wangler, Thomas E. 10
Ward, Dudley 28
Washington Star 31
Washington State 172–173
Watchman-Examiner 56
Watson, Tom 128
Weber, Michael P. 105
Wells, Albert N. 71
Wells, Norman H. 65
West, Earl 65
West Virginia 22, 111, 119–121
Western Recorder 56
Western Voice 176
Wheaton College 37
White, Theodore H. 91–92, 112–113
white women for Nixon 92
Willebrandt, Mabel Walker 15
Wilson, Art 176
Wilson, Pres. Woodrow 11
Wine, James 34, 80–81, **81**
Wisconsin 22, 157–159, 203–210
Wisconsin Rapids Daily Tribune 159
Woelfel, LaSalle 33
Wolfe, James S. 216–217
Wood, Ralph 195
World Outlook 23
Wyoming 179

Youngsma, Syd 65

Zacchello, Joseph 59–60
Zimmerman, Thomas F. 61, 117

www.ingramcontent.com/pod-product-compliance
Lightning Source LLC
Chambersburg PA
CBHW051214300426
44116CB00006B/574